A PRACTICAL INTRODUCTION TO VIRTUAL REALITY

A PRACTICAL INTRODUCTION TO VIRTUAL REALITY

From Concepts to Executables

Lori Rebenitsch
Lisa Rebenitsch
Rohan Loveland

ELSEVIER

ISBN: 978-0-443-14036-5

For Information on all Morgan Kaufmann publications visit our website at https://www.elsevier.com/books-and-journals

Publisher: Peter Linsley
Acquisitions Editor: Stephen Merken
Editorial Project Manager: Ellie Barnett
Production Project Manager: Gayathri S
Cover Designer: Greg Harris

Typeset by MPS Limited, Chennai, India

Printed in the United States of America

Last digit is the print number: 9 8 7 6 5 4 3 2 1

Working together to grow libraries in developing countries

www.elsevier.com • www.bookaid.org

Contents

Helpful ancillaries have been prepared to aid learning and teaching.

Please visit the student companion site for more details: https://www.elsevier.com/books-and-journals/book-companion/9780443140365

For qualified professors, additional, instructor-only teaching materials can be requested here: https://educate.elsevier.com/book/details/9780443140365

Acknowledgments

We are grateful for the assistance of Dr. Charles Owen for sharing his expertise and images, and getting Lisa started in virtual reality in the first place. We would also like to thank the following students: Karissa Schipke for providing early precourse testing and checking additional virtual reality headsets and Christian Olson and Patrick McBride for further adding to the textbook and tutorial materials, especially the virtual reality environments. Lastly, we greatly appreciate all the South Dakota Mines virtual reality students for willingly taking this experimental class as alpha testers and smashing the proficiency requirements with their awesome final projects.

Introduction

The purpose of this book is to introduce coders to virtual reality (VR) development. The concepts are kept general so that Unity, Unreal, or other modern game engines may be used. While game engines are heavily referenced, the focus is on the broad-spectrum needs of virtual reality development, not game design or storyline development. Some graphics topics are included due to needing code support in larger multiteam projects and to enable a coder to know what to ask for from the graphics team! This text is meant for those who want to develop the underlying code of a virtual reality application.

This book began as a need for a virtual reality course. In reviewing potential books, the top contenders did not have a single line of code or pseudocode in their 600+ pages! The course materials also needed to meet a broad range of skills. The course in question had sophomore to master students in both computer science and computer engineering. As an added challenge, this was in a school that taught objects late. There was no skipping the fundamentals of object-orientated programming here! The course needed a book where the code logic was explained, and *worked*, rather than trying the top solutions on a code help board online until finding the one that somewhat worked three solutions down. Code needed to be shown and not described in a video that then couldn't be found again. Topics had to be built up and focused without requiring searching through dozens of projects that *may, or may not*, have the code logic for a particular problem buried in it and *may, or may not*, work in the current version of the engine because the code was so focused on the *current version*. This was further accentuated by the software deprecating, which broke the author's code, and seemingly at random, and then froze the project while waiting for updates. This resulted in a stronger object-oriented approach to cope. The frustration was strong.

Who cares if the code is deprecated in a month from now? The person trying to use it, that's who! However, if the developer knows what the deprecated line is supposed to do, then the developer can still continue by either writing their own version or knowing how to search for the correct version in the new documentation.

In other words, the text needed to start with concepts and fundamentals and then build on them. This is why the book largely uses pseudocode but then expands upon that with 1.5- to 2.5-hour written tutorials in a given framework. The text was meant to build *from concepts to executables.*

This text was written in tandem of a first run of a virtual reality course. The resulting feedback was prompt and integrated into the book. If something broke, it was fixed. If a question was asked, it was added to the book. For example, anything about shaders is not intrinsically VR, but after more than six questions on the shader code that the students found on their own, a section on shaders was added. The class was eager and found items originally not intended to be included in this text. The timing was tested with students.

This book was written for real students without much, if any, graphical experience. The student is expected to have a minimum of 1.5 years' experience coding and is ready for more advanced topics of object-oriented program but is, by and large, new to game engines and virtual reality. Physics 1 and calculus 1 prerequisites are also assumed. While some of these topics are used in several chapters, a relevant review is also provided in the appendix. Prior graphical experience is not expected but will help. Knowledge of inheritance is expected, but advanced skills in object-oriented patterns are not.

Virtual Reality vs 3D

A couple of questions received in the course were, "What is the difference between 3D and virtual reality? Why is this a virtual reality text, and not 3D?"

Both virtual reality and three-dimensional applications present 3D information. The difference is in the interaction.

The oldest method to interact with 3D information is to use 2D methods: a screen and mouse! As an example, the reader has likely seen a 3D graph at some point that could be spun around and zoomed in. The data is 3D, but it is presented on a 2D screen, and the 2D interaction is mapped to a 3D space. At most, a game console controller is used, but the buttons are still laid out in a 2D fashion on the controller. These systems have the most established methods in interaction and more built-in support in code.

The next step is the stereoscopic screen. This is what 3D movies use: one image per eye each frame of the movie. Now the data is presented as 3D, but interaction is still 2D. Not much changed in the coder's perspective. Maybe there are a few extra settings to get the two images for the stereoscopic imagery, but not much else.

Virtual reality presents in 3D and *interaction is in 3D*. Turns out, this changes things, sometimes fundamentally. The text will do callouts to 3D with 2D interactions as the original for some interaction methods where applicable due to their familiarity. Moreover, coding for *both* 3D and virtual reality is done where possible to support *both* selling to a wider audience and easier debugging available in 3D. In addition, since VR has a head and 1+ hands to track, the old methods can start to break down. Which one of those new interactions activates an event when a threshold is crossed? Another possibility is that the 3D option can turn annoying in virtual reality. Who wants to use a virtual reality controller's trackpad and then a button to throw something when the user can just grab it naturally?!

This text places emphasis on elements that change with virtual reality from 3D. This is not to say that prior 3D programming is expected. This is to note that 3D programming methods used blindly in virtual reality can fail.

Suggested Order

The order of the text was based on this question: "How often is this topic used in an application?" The more often the item, the earlier in the book it is placed. It is hard to get anywhere in virtual reality programming without the object-oriented structure of the entity-component structure of Unity and Unreal. Some topics are placed toward the back, since these topics may either require a base from earlier chapters or may occur less frequently in development. Not all applications are going to need inverse kinematics after all!

The suggested chapter for no graphics background is to start at the beginning. However, if objected-oriented programming experience is limited, the object-oriented programming appendix is suggested before anything else. Then continue, in order, to Chapter 6, Menus and Heads-Up Displays. Chapters 7 to 10 can be mixed somewhat. Walking needs larger spaces, which means understanding larger models, terrains, and textures. A large plane with a few blocks will do if in a rush. This is also why the walking tutorial is somewhat mixed with terrains.

The suggested chapters differ for those with a prior graphics background, including scene trees and 3D model composition, yet are new to virtual reality. The suggested starting point for this student is Chapter 1 to learn the virtual reality components, and then move on to Chapter 3 or 4. Chapter 3 introduces basic physics, which tends to be more important in virtual reality due to the grabbing. If there is some game experience, then Chapter 4 is more likely the better starting point, which introduces how to handle different hardware in one application. Coding just for Oculus can result in the application losing the Vive population, not to mention the nightmare of updating when Oculus makes a new headset, which is sure to happen! The next chapter likely to be needed is either Chapter 5 or 6, both of which focus on the challenges of virtual reality interaction. Chapters 7 to 9 can likely be skipped as these are heavily focused on graphics. Chapter 10 introduces navigation techniques that are common in virtual reality but may not be present in 3D systems. Chapters 11 to 17 are on more specialized topics and can be used as needed.

Chapter 18 is publishing, and it is suggested before starting to develop your first demo. The language appendix can be used at any time for a pseudocode to C++, C#/Java, or Python translation.

Object-Oriented Programming in Virtual Reality

This chapter covers the object-oriented programming (OOP) structures and the entity-component structure commonly used in virtual reality (VR). It is assumed that the reader has prior knowledge of the basics of OOP, the SOLID principles as first described by Martin [1] (acronym for single responsibility principle, open-closed principle, Liskov substitution principle, interface segregation principle, and dependency inversion principle), and the structure of an OOP pattern. (If the reader is unfamiliar, please refer to the Appendix for a review.) The focus is on OOP elements in VR that differ from console and basic graphical user interface (GUI) contexts or may be somewhat unique to VR.

Overview

VR, and most three-dimensional (3D) games, to a large degree, use OOP. GUIs also tend to have a higher level of OOP and typically require some OOP to make and place widgets. However, more of the remaining code can be placed in a single class. This is not true in VR, and it is nearly impossible to code in Unity or Unreal without it! One source of the difference is that VR tends to use a game engine rather than a system typical for a standard GUI.

One of the most fundamental structures for a game engine and graphical system is a tree structure to store the content in a hierarchy of objects of the same type. A very common example of this is the scene tree, which is covered in detail in Chapter 3. More formally, this is the composite pattern. Unity and Unreal engines go a step further and use what is called an entity-component structure. The change causes some unexpected effects on the code, such as making a standard singleton structure very likely to be buggy. It also results in some fundamental differences in how different objects gain references to each other.

Most game engines use a few common OOP structures in their frameworks beyond that of standard graphical or console systems.

A Practical Introduction to Virtual Reality. https://doi.org/10.1016/B978-0-443-14036-5.00024-8

For those with primarily console or backend experience, having one or more parent classes from which everything is derived for most of the framework may be jarring. For those with GUI experience, the different initialization sequence may be surprising.

OOP in Game Engines

When a project is first made, one of the most obvious changes from a console or standard GUI is the missing entry point. There is no "main" function or "initialize window" function to be seen. This is a highlight of many modern game frameworks. That startup is handled entirely by the engine. Unity goes a step further; there is not even a *constructor* function allowed in many cases. Unreal permits a *default, empty* constructor, only. Clearly, some coding techniques that are not typical in console or standard GUIs will be needed in development.

Game engines avoid having an explicit entry point by using a **game loop**. Game loops rely on the composite pattern and messaging rather than allowing the user to make the calls themselves. The developer instead makes a derived class from a special parent class that has a set of functions that the framework calls during known events. Essentially, the engine will call these functions on each game framework class, in a loop with the application running. More details on this loop are given in the later discussion of game engines, including the figures with game loops.

This initially feels like the classes are made out of nowhere, and in fact, there is not always a guarantee in creation order. Therefore, game engines use a high degree of multistage initialization. Take the lack of nondefault constructors as an example. In a standard system, if we make a point class with x and y, the code may look as follows:

```
class Point
  x = 0
  y = 0

  constructor( x1, y1 )
    x = x1
    y = y1
```

This is not legal in Unreal or Unity. At best, the x and y can be exposed to the developer in the game development suite by a special means that will autofill some member variables at object creation time. If that is not possible, and the variable needs to be set mid-run, the class must be derived from a special class and then override an initialization function the game engine will call later during its setup phase. Both Unity and Unreal call this special object a **game object**. This changes in code to the following style:

```
class Point inherits GameObject
  x = 0
  y = 0

  // set is called after Point has been made by the engine
  function Set( x1, y1 )
    x = x1
    y = y1
```

Expect this technique to be used regularly.

The next element that differs due to the lack of entry point and nondefault construction is making connections between classes. Classes that do not use the game framework can set the references as normal. However, because the game engine will be making all the game framework objects for the developer, at no point does one game framework class have all that it needs to reference other instances. This is solved by adding a means to search all the objects currently active. GUIs often provide a look-up function for their various widgets for dynamics interface updates. Game engines work similarly. For those with a primarily console/backend experience, this may seem inefficient, and wasteful—*it is*. Many readers will likely be familiar with the annoyance of long loading periods for new levels that is partially a result of this. These functions normally come with a warning that they are slow, and as such, there are alternative functions that can search in narrower scopes. But, in the worst case, a global search is required. As an example, consider trying to make a list of nodes of a game object in a specific order. These nodes can be anywhere, and their names are known. In this case, the format is typically as follows:

```
class NodeList inherits GameObject
  list = []

  // this is overridden GameObject function that is
  // called after all objects are made
  function LateInitialization()
    node = Find( "Node" + 0 )
    i = 1

    // while nodes are still found
    while( node != null )
      list.append( node )

      node = Find( "Node" + i )
```

The last element that will initially not feel very different from the composite but later have notable effects is that both Unreal and Unity use an entity-component structure. Entities are composed into trees with the components being the leaves. Entities are the game objects in the application such as a cube, room, hammer, gong, etc. Components are their individual behaviors such as what sound a gong would make if tapped. The benefit of this structure is consistency in the objects and a standardized way for the objects to communicate. This has been seen in the above examples with the loss of the entry points. More details are given in the Entity-Component section along with some behaviors that arise with this structure.

From Console to GUI to Game Engine

One of the big changes in game engine coding is that communication between classes is message or event focused. The developer loses some control concerning when a function is called but not as much as it may initially feel. To demonstrate this, consider trying to make a basic menu.

In console programming, programming structure often assumes a general menu loop within the program and a function is run for each menu item as demonstrated in the code below and visually in Fig. 0.1.

```
while !done
  printMenu()

  input = GetInput()
  if input == 1
    Func1()
  if input == 2
    Funct2()
  if input == 3
    done = true

function Func1()
  print "A"

function Func2()
  print "B"
```

GUIs add a layer between the function prompt and running the function by being fundamentally event-based OOP. Here the operating system watches for an event and then forwards to the associated event function. The menu loop is essentially controlled by the operating system, which changes the structure to the demonstration in code on the next page and visually in Fig. 0.2.

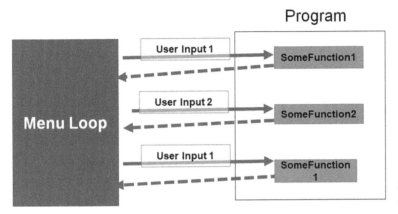

Fig. 0.1 Graphic representation of a menu loop.

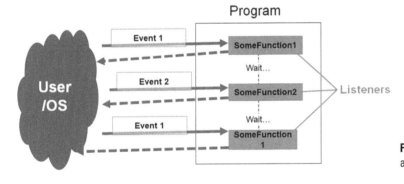

Fig. 0.2 Graphic representation of an event loop.

```
RegisterCallback( event1, Func1 )
RegisterCallback( event2, Funct2 )

function Func1()
  print "A"

function Func2()
  print "B"
```

In game engines, such as Unity or Unreal, the operating system forwards to a class and then calls the functions all the way down the associated scene tree. This is formally called a game loop. This is demonstrated in code on the next page and visually in Fig. 0.3. Registration of events can occur at any time, and is excluded from the code example for this reason.

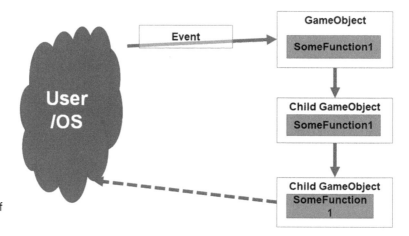

Fig. 0.3 Graphic representation of a game loop.

```
class MainGameLoop
  RegisteredObject registeredObjects = []

  function RunLoop()
    while !done
      // Process any input
      // Advance
      // Render
      // Play sounds
      // Message pump

  function MessageAll()
    for obj in registerObjects
      if event1 occured
        obj.Func1()
      if event2 occured
        obj.Func2()
      if event3 occured
        exit()

class MyResponse inherits RegisteredObject
  function Func1()
    print "A"

  function Func2()
    print "B"
```

Fig. 0.3 uses a class-based implementation. Many modern systems use an event-based system with a specialized data type that acts almost as shorthand.

After reaching a game object, the associated children's components are called as needed. To register an event, we simply override the method desired. This is a variation of the template pattern and is described in more detail later in this chapter.

The key takeaway is that the "menu" loop does not go away. We focus only on the code that is run during tasks and leave the rest of the loop management to the engine.

Design Patterns in VR

As seen already, there are a few OOP patterns commonly used in VR coding. Patterns that VR uses, often within minutes of making a project, are entity-component, template, and factory. The Model-View-Controller (MVC) pattern [2], while not immediate, becomes critical in any larger project or unit testing and needs to be used early in a project to be most effective. An overview of these key patterns in a VR context provides context to allow for better understanding of how the code flows. More foundational patterns to GUI in general, such as the composite pattern and observer, are provided in the Appendix. If more details are desired, Source Making (https://sourcemaking.com/) has an excellent introduction with examples in code of many of the patterns.

Before continuing, one caveat is that patterns are only that, patterns. While the exact format may have changed, the ideas and purposes of these patterns are still very pertinent today. Patterns must adapt to the problem or they may fail. As an example, the original format of the singleton pattern, which is common in many facets of coding, will fail spectacularly in the entity-component structure (Fig. 0.4).

Fig. 0.4 Example of a misapplied method or pattern. (Epic Fail by Epsilon60198 is licensed under CC BY-ND 2.0.)

Another example is undo/redo, which is a critical pattern in developing a work tool rather than games. However, it is based on adjusting the command and memento patterns rather than using them exactly as they are! It is also extremely difficult to add in later, so understanding the problem's long-term need and implementing the pattern early cost some upfront time but gain back the time quickly in flexibility and maintainability.

About Models, Views, and Controllers

MVC is a very common pattern that occurs in almost every GUI (Fig. 0.5). This pattern has other names such as document/view, model/view, model-view/view/model, ·observer, etc. Essentially, MVC requires a degree of separation between models, controllers, and views, because

- data files do not care who opens them (model),
- browsers can handle mouse/keyboard/touch often inter-changeably (controller), and
- the appearance does not change the meaning of a button (view).

The original reason for MVC was for team task separation, but it has since become an important pattern on its own. In entity-component structures like game engines, some of the details of the pattern may be altered, but at a high-level structure is still pertinent to long-term maintenance.

Despite its variation in names, the core idea holds—try to maintain the open-closed principle from SOLID by allowing the model, view, and controller to be separated and swappable. The idea is that there is something being modeled. It might be an image being edited, a Word document, a spreadsheet, or a graphical object. This is the "model." Here, it is also commonly called the "document." To view the model in any way on the screen involves one or more views of the

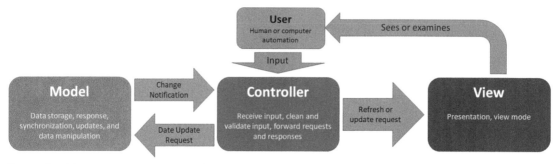

Fig. 0.5 Graphic representation of the MVC pattern.

model. The advantage of this method is that multiple views can exist at the same time for the same document, allowing multiple windows into the document or split windows.

You will have to make decisions as to where data are stored and where commands will be processed in your application. Suppose we have an image and a program that allows for editing that image. The image clearly goes into the model class, but what is in the view class? Well, we might be able to create selection rectangles in the image (selecting a region to cut or paste, for example). The location and dimensions of this rectangle would be in the view class if it is only to appear on one window on the screen.

It is common that multiple windows will provide multiple views of the same object. You might have one window at full scale and another where you have blown the image up much larger so you can edit the pixels. This "scale factor" would be part of the view.

The controller is what processes user input. It will have a reference to the model and views, but it should not change their internal state. Consider a key press. That is an event. It is not how something looks or how many items a class has. It may eventually affect those things, but changes from an A key to a B key should not change the model or view code.

Worst confusion on the MVC is …

What is the controller's main job?

The controller's job is mostly to send the information to the correct spot. Think of it like a translator or "traffic cop" (Fig. 0.6).

At its simplest, this just means forwarding the event to the correct function, like a traffic cop does. If you want a different type of guidance, swap out the traffic cop! The view can stay the same, as can the model. The controller tends to get much more involved in a game engine to keep it flexible. Chapter 5 is dedicated to handling the interaction framework so we can support 3D applications and VR applications simultaneously!

Fig. 0.6 An example of the controller. Here, the traffic cop acts as the controller. (Created using clipart from https://openclipart.org/detail/261667/traffic-control; https://openclipart.org/detail/320713/car-repair-silhouette.)

How does the controller do its job?

The first thing to remember is that the controller does not take possession of the model and view. If the controller is setting and getting values after initial setup, it is acting like a ghost taking possession and overriding the model's and view's control. Instead, it *asks* the model or view to do the task. The controller forwards requests and data, and also forwards responses to the appropriate handler as needed. It does not traverse down the model children's classes or view tree to find an element to edit. A check if the controller is properly sectioned off from the model is if the model could still be used in a console application as opposed to the immersive version.

How does the controller get the layout nodes?

- The controller has access to a dictionary or getters in the layout. The layout is a tree so the request can be chained (chain of responsibility pattern).
- Reminder: The controller should have a member variable to layout.

How does the model talk to the view, and vice versa?

The view has a reference to the model, but often, the observer pattern is used for efficiency and to keep things synchronized.

Entity-Component

Most game engines structure their objects in a tree or graph structure called a scene tree or scene graph. Take the pinball board in Fig 0.7 as an example. We can describe the contents by stating we

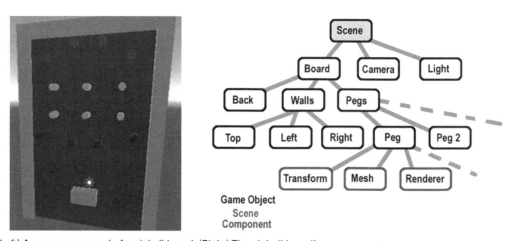

Fig. 0.7 (Left) A scene composed of a pinball board. (Right) The pinball board's scene tree structure.

have a "scene" and that a board contains a backing, walls, and set of pegs. Eventually, we reach a single model that has a placement and orientation (transform), underlying mesh that describes its structure, and how to render the object to the screen.

For the objects themselves, code could be done with a composite pattern, which is the formal name for a generic tree or graph with the purpose of placing and showing objects in a graphical system. However, that describes only what the objects are and their hierarchy. *How* they behave is not currently there. This is where the components come in. Components are the leaves in the tree. Each behavior is its own component.

If the object changes color on a tap? That is a component. If the object moves? That is another component. If the object can be collected? That is yet another component. Moreover, each component is one or more classes.

This means that peg shown in the diagram has a class for the entity and then at least three classes shown as components under it. The idea that behaviors are spread across classes for a single entity may feel wrong at first. After all, does not this violate dependency inversion from SOLID? The key item here is that the component can be *reused* across entities. The peg may need to be changed on tap, but the wall could, too. If that happens without component reuse, there is repeated code, and that's bad! It is still easy to go too far, of course. But used properly, dependency inversion is not broken; it is maintained.

A major caveat to this technique is that some OOP patterns are harder to use as is. Some even go so far as to say the entity-component structure is not OOP. Considering that the above peg had four classes with inheritance to use the game loop, it is OOP, just a different variation of OOP from the classic class-based OOP around which more patterns are designed.

The most obvious effect is on a static variable and the pattern that relies on it, like the singleton pattern. The singleton pattern relies on the fact there is only one instance of the singleton class. What happens if you give two entities a singleton component? You have two instances of a class where there should only be one, and they access the same static variable. As a result, race conditions, overridden variables, sudden null reference exceptions, and more ensue. There are still ways to get a singleton effect, which is important in many cases, but the original structure should not be used.

Another fundamental effect the entity-component structure has on OOP is how the connections between classes are made. In traditional OOP, the parent class (game object) would make its children classes (components) and would set or pass in a reference if another class is needed. Not so in entity-component structures!

The loss of the parameterized constructor forbids this. Instead, this structure uses staged initialization. The first stage is internal setup via a parameter-less constructor or equivalent. The second stage is finding the necessary components or game objects using the search techniques described in the OOP in the Game Engines section.

Template Pattern

A template pattern can be thought of as inheritance with defaults rather than empty methods. For example, consider a template to build something. To prepare, items need to be bought. Then the item needs to be made, and, last, the work area should be cleaned. Any one of those could be the same across many objects. Here is an example template class and then a BuildCheaper child class that only does something a little different at the preparation stage:

```
class Template
  function Prep()
    BuyStuff()
  function Do()
    MakeStuff()
  function CleanUp()
    Clean()

  function Run() // run the three stages in order
    obj.Prep()
    obj.Do()
    obj.CleanUp()

class BuildCheaper inherits Template
  function Prep() // only change the preparation stage
    FindDiscount()
      BuyStuff()

function Main()
  Template original
  BuildCheaper cheaper

  original.Run()
  cheaper.Run()
```

This way, we can have many Templates and BuildCheaper objects already filled with methods to call **Prep**(), **Do**(), and **CleanUp**(), in that order.

This is how many game engines handle the game loop at a conceptual level. Unity has its full order of execution here: https://docs.unity3d.com/Manual/ExecutionOrder.html. An order version for Unreal is here: https://docs.unrealengine.com/4.27/en-US/InteractiveExperiences/Framework/GameFlow/. Unreal allows some edits to their order.

Factory Pattern

Large composition objects are difficult to make from scratch. For example, making a nonplayable character takes many different elements. The factory pattern solution to this is to wrap the objects into another function. Because this commonly involves multiple other objects, the wrapping function gets its own class as shown in the code below

```
class Factory
  function Create()
    // make object 1
    // make object 2
    // link object 1 and 2
    // make object 3

    ...
    return this

class Other
  function Foo()
    f = Factory()
    f.Create()
```

Most game engines have a method to save a set of objects with their code and then build in one go. Essentially, the engine creates all the code to build the full object, and then wraps it so you only need to call this new object.

Unity calls these prefabs, and Unreal calls these blueprints (the exact level of support does vary). In both cases, they focus on making an entity with all of its components and then saving that set, which then can be created using the factory class with just a create function as shown above.

References

[1] Martin R.C. Design principles and design patterns. 2000. objectmentor.com
[2] Reenskaug T. THING-MODEL-VIEW-EDITOR: an example from a planning system, *Xerox PARC*, 1979. https://folk.universitetetioslo.no/trygver/1979/mvc-1/1979-05-MVC.pdf

Basic Virtual Reality Objects and Interactions

This chapter gives a brief overview of the objects and interactions needed for a minimum virtual reality (VR) project. This includes introductions to the following concepts:

- Game objects
- Tracking the head, feet, and hands
- Device input
- Teleportation
- Long-distance selection or rays

Game Objects

VR engines typically use some sort of parent class for their objects. In Unity, these are GameObjects; in Unreal, these are Actors. This text will use game objects, lowercase, to refer to this parent class. These game objects provide a uniform way to affect the environment, trigger events, etc.

In Unity, GameObjects are derived from the template MonoBehaviour. In Unreal, the base class for game objects is UObject.

How much these base objects provide varies with the system. For example, Unity's GameObjects hold

- Name
- Placement and orientation (Transform)
- Tag
- Layer
- Static option

However, Unreal's Actors hold the above and *far more*. In their code level, these base objects start as a placeholder in the scene. From there, meshes, rendering pipelines, events, and more are added. Both Unity and Unreal also have Components, which are smaller classes of code behind the scene that add individual effects. For example, a text component may add text to its object in some fashion but can hold another base object themselves.

A Practical Introduction to Virtual Reality. https://doi.org/10.1016/B978-0-443-14036-5.00001-7

Visible Game Objects

Visible game objects may include simple three-dimensional (3D) objects, such as cubes and spheres and more complicated models. Visible game objects require additional components for defining visibility and potential interactions.

- Mesh—generally, the model of the object, where the shape is described with vertices and triangles.
- Material—the base appearance of the triangles and is mapped over the assigned area ignoring lighting effects. This can vary widely, with the simplest defining a base color plus "shininess" to apply to the mesh.
- Rendering—choice in how to visually present the mesh with its material based on lighting conditions and rendering pipelines.
- Collider—boundaries for collisions; these do not need to match the mesh in shape, and regularly do not.

Additional and important interaction elements are bounding boxes. Bounding boxes are the smallest boxes that can hold all of a set of points. This is commonly used in collision detection to give rough boundaries. This allows more computationally expensive collision calculation on the more detailed mesh or collider if boxes are not overlapping. A two-dimensional (2D) example could look like Fig. 1.1.

Scene Trees

Game objects can be added to other game objects to make a larger game object. For example, an empty game object with three sphere children can be composed into a snowman, as shown in Fig. 1.2.

This tree of game objects chains position, rotation, and scale in useful ways. Using the example in Fig. 1.2, the tree game object allows for movement of the entire snowman in the environment, as opposed to moving each individual sphere. Tree game object structures are called scene trees.

Fig. 1.1 Example of a bounding box.

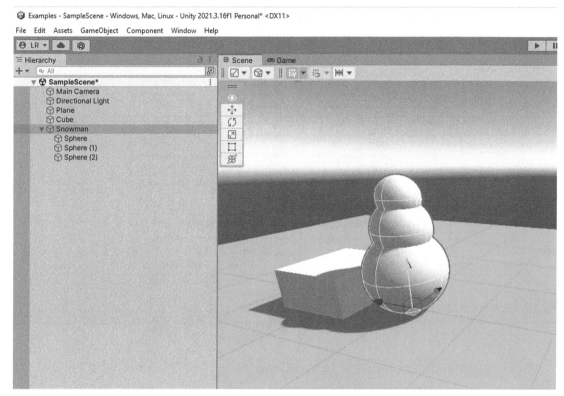

Fig. 1.2 An example of an empty game object, Snowman, with three Sphere children in Unity.

In scene trees, the children's position, rotation, and scale are relative to the parent. Again, components are the "leaves" in the tree, such as in the tree shown in Fig. 1.3.

This is especially useful in VR environments, where VR's tracking rig immediately gives us a nested structure of game objects. A tracking rig here refers to the interface between the VR hardware and the virtual environment. For example, this could include a head-mounted display (HMD) and two hand controllers with inside-out tracking.

We will discuss scene trees in detail in the next chapter, as these can greatly affect the placement interaction of game objects. One of the key aspects of these scene trees is called "parenting." In Fig. 1.4, the right controller is pulled by adding the game object, Stick.

Tracking Basics

Interaction and navigation are the biggest differences between VR and 3D applications. The four elements as opposed to one location for orientation and position can pose a challenge in VR that is not

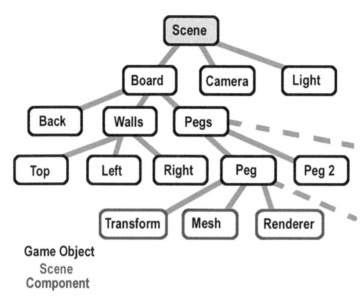

Game Object
Scene
Component

Fig. 1.3 Example of a scene tree structure.

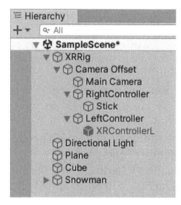

Fig. 1.4 Example of parenting to get a device. Stick is added as a child to RightController. This means that the right controller now controls the position of the Stick object and the Stick can now monitor information from the right controller.

present in 3D applications (Fig. 1.5). In VR, the tracking area is the interactable space for the user in VR and maps to the available movement space in real life. For example, a tracking area the size of the user's living room outlines the interactive range placed in VR. Keep in mind that the interactive space can be moved to another place in the VR world.

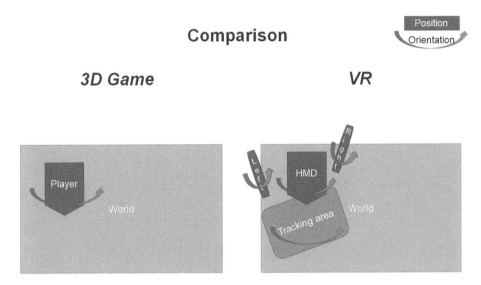

Fig. 1.5 A visual comparison of the orientation/position variables between 3D and VR. VR has more degrees of freedom.

There are two main trouble points of tracking movement:

1. Moving the tracking area moves everything.
2. Collisions are based on the HMD and controllers, but pushing back requires moving the tracking area.

To show this visually, take the VR environment in Fig. 1.6. If the tracking area moves to the right by 3 m, the tracking area can exceed the world area.

Conversely, if the user moves to the right by 3 m but the tracking area does not move, then the user would be moved outside of an effective and safe tracking area as is shown in Fig. 1.7.

We go into detail on how to design for tracking in later chapters. In general, movement takes extra design considerations, but tracking objects comes first.

VR has many tracking options, from fingers to feet. The most common tracking components are

- Tracking area (feet)
- HMD (head)
- Left controller (hand)
- Right controller (hand)

HMDs and controllers normally have six degrees of freedom in tracking: translation along three axes and rotation along three axes. In most systems, the above can be assumed, but some newer systems may include additional trackers to give better body placement recognition. In some older systems, like the Oculus Go, there may be a single controller, with only orientation sensing.

Example: tracking area moves right 3m

Before

After

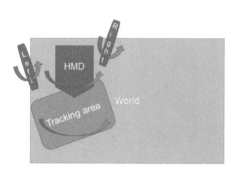

There is nothing stopping the tracking
area from exiting the world area

Fig. 1.6 Example of the tracking area moving off the world area.

Example: person moves right 3m

Before

After

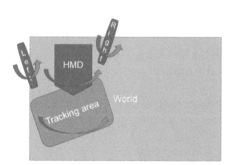

This would be out of bounds of
the tracking area

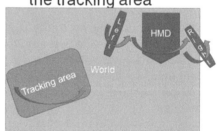

Fig. 1.7 Example of the user moving away from tracking area.

Button Considerations

VR engines have their own input systems to handle the button events, and individual controllers can have different sets of button controls. In general, the minimum supported are

- Trigger,
- Trackpad/joystick,
- Grip,

- Home button, and
- Some other buttons.

Grip may appear new if unfamiliar with VR controllers. This button is placed somewhere on the grip of the controller and is frequently used to grab objects. There are three main input formats from controllers:

- Button: Options are up/down or Boolean.
- Joystick: Options are axial or a 2D vector.
- Triggers: Options are dependent on the degree of pull or a float.

Care must be taken with trigger buttons as only a bool value is guaranteed. The degree of pull is not always supported. Most controllers have more, and the format is slowly being standardized to mirror console game controls with each hand having a trigger, trackpad/joystick, grip, two general buttons, and home button.

Getting a Device to Monitor

Because VR is event based, input from a device, such as a controller, needs to be monitored for events. Doing this takes several steps. First, the list of devices needs to be pulled. A potential catch here is that the devices are usually not available in the first frame or may be lost and regained multiple times during a run. To accommodate this, a flag is typically added to note when the initial setup is completed. Second, the list needs to be filtered to only the required devices. Below is sample pseudocode on how to do this assuming a delayed detection but stable access afterward.

```
Device desiredDevice
bool first = false // flag for the completion

function UpdateFrame()
  if !first
    inputDevices = GetDevices()

    for device in inputDevices
      print( "Device name" + device )
      first = true

      if device.HasFeature( features )
        desiredDevice = device

      else // ready
        CheckForButtons( desiredDevice )
```

After connecting to the device, it is now possible to check the buttons' states. In some engines, only the current button states can be requested. There are no onDown() functions, only isDown() functions. onDown() functions are created uniquely by the coder.

The above pseudocode monitors the button state for the isDown event with a Boolean. From this, the state of the button is pulled. If the button was up on the last frame and down on the current frame, this gives an onDown event. An onUp event is the opposite of onDown. Below is the pseudocode for finding an onDown event.

```
function CheckForButtons(InputDevice device)
  bool state = device.GetState( targetButton )
  if !isPressed // button up on the last frame?
    if state // is the button down on this frame?
      DoButtonDownEvent()

  isPressed = state //update its state
```

Unreal and Unity both provide an input mapping system to aid with this, but there are cases where the built in option may not be sufficient. Chapter 4 will discuss how input mapping systems work and how they are usually better than the raw approach described in this section for anything but the smallest projects.

Teleportation

The simplest movement is to not move the tracking area at all. This works well for tabletop-size play areas and is the safest. However, most applications require longer distances for movement. This is where teleportation comes in as the next simplest movement. It also is less likely to cause cybersickness and, as a result, is a long-distance movement option in the vast majority of VR applications.

However, there is a catch. To illustrate the catch, place a user in the upper left corner of the tracking area and place the tracking area to the left side of the world. Let's say that the user wants to move to the position marked with an "x" Fig. 1.8. If the center of the tracking area is moved to the "x" position, the user is placed at an incorrect offset.

Therein is the catch. To teleport correctly, the user's offset in the tracking area must be used to calculate the correct movement. Fig. 1.9 shows the more correct movement.

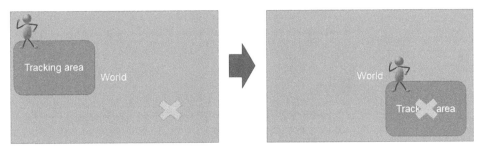

Fig. 1.8 Example of teleporting by only changing the center of the tracking area to the "x" position. After teleporting, the user's position is offset from the correct position.

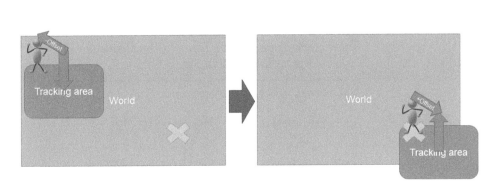

Fig. 1.9 Example of correct teleporting. The user is correctly placed on the "x" position, but now the tracking area is past the world boundaries.

This can be represented with the following pseudocode:

```
TrackingArea feet
TrackerObject head

function TeleportTo( Vector target )
  //offset between play area and head location
  offset = head.position - feet.position

  //ignore changes in y right now,
  //to keep the head at the same height!
  offset.y = 0;

  //final position
  feet.position = target + offset
```

There is still a lingering problem here. In Fig. 1.9, the tracking area is pushed out of the world's bounds. There are some solutions to this, but we will come back to the problem later.

Rays

To teleport long distances, a distance point must be selected. Rays are very common in interactions in VR to express a pointing vector or "pointing in that direction from here." A ray has a starting point and a direction. The variable, t, shows position along the ray. Any location along the ray can be expressed as a kind of 3D parametric equation: $\boldsymbol{p}(t) = \boldsymbol{r}_s + \boldsymbol{r}_d * t$, where $\boldsymbol{p}(t)$ is the position, $\boldsymbol{r}_s$ is the starting position, and $\boldsymbol{r}_d$ is the direction of movement and a vector. Here we are using bolding to indicate 3D vectors. More details regarding rays and vectors are covered in future chapters.

Rays are relatively straightforward, but a common use often checks for collisions along the path of the direction of a controller. In the following pseudocode example, Ray is given to a Raycast and then asked if the ray has hit anything.

```
ray = Ray( starting, direction )
maxDistance = 10
pt = ray.GetPointAtDistance( maxDistance )

// alternatively, use the ray to find a collision point
hit = ray.FindCollision( maxDistance )
if hit!= null
  // check object that was hit
  if hit.HitWhat == "Something"
    DoSomething()
```

Rays are, of course, only useful if seen. There are several ways of doing this, including
- Drawing a line
- Placing a thin cube aligned with the controller
- Placing a reticle at the hit point

Which method you choose will depend on which system is being used as the different systems have their own ray defaults.

Summary

To summarize the minimum requirements for a VR application, all projects require
- Device tracking from the head, feet, and hands
- Device input from controllers and HMDs
- Movement with teleportation being the simplest option
- Long-distance selection using rays

2

Transformations and Scene Trees

This chapter covers geometric transformations and scene trees, including concepts and the associated math. Topics covered include
- Linear algebra connection
  - Translation
  - Scale
  - Skew
  - Rotation
- Matrices
- Homogeneous coordinates
- Quaternions
- Scene trees
- Linear interpolation (LERP)
- Spherical linear interpolation (SLERP)

The Connection to Linear Algebra

First, let's recall a couple of linear algebra terms, such as tuples. Tuples can be represented with different forms of notations. Most commonly, tuple notation uses three-dimensional (3D) Cartesian notation such as
- (x, y, z), or
- $P = (x, y, z)$,

to represent any point in space. For simplicity, "point" will be used instead of "tuple." This information can also be represented in matrix or vector notation:

$$P = \begin{bmatrix} x \\ y \\ z \end{bmatrix} = \begin{bmatrix} x & y & z \end{bmatrix}^T$$

For simplicity's sake, vectors used in pseudocode and other code can be either a vector or a point, depending on the semantics as shown in Fig. 2.1.

A Practical Introduction to Virtual Reality. https://doi.org/10.1016/B978-0-443-14036-5.00002-9

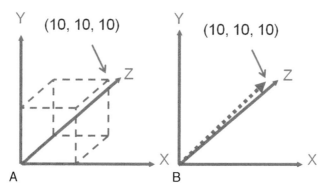

Fig. 2.1 A graphical example of a point in space and a vector. The point in space is to the left, and the vector is to the right. Both representations lead to the same point in space.

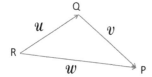

Fig. 2.2 Example of a sum of two vectors, which can be expressed using either vectors or position changes.

With this in mind, there are a handful of math properties to recall before moving into the application.

1. The difference between two points is a vector:

$$V = P - Q$$

2. The sum of a vector and a point is a point:

$$Q + V = P$$

3. The sum of two vectors is a vector:

$$W = U + V = (Q - R) + (P - Q) = (P - R)$$

For comparison, Fig. 2.2 shows an example sum of vectors using the vectors and points outlined earlier.

The rest of this section covers the transformations of objects in VR space. This has a lot of overlap with graphics in general.

Coordinate System

Coordinates initially look like a location in space. In 3D, this is simply x, y and z. Typically x increases to the right, and y increases upward. But wait, what about positive z? We have two options for where to place the z-axis, conventionally called right-handed and left-handed notation. These terms developed based on the direction of the index finger for either the right or left hands, as shown in Fig. 2.3.

Both Unity and Unreal use left-handed coordinate systems. The difference is that Unity has the y-axis up and Unreal has the z-axis up, which is less typical for 3D game engines.

Translation

Translation refers to moving objects in space. Mathematically, this means adding the translation vector to the current position. All that

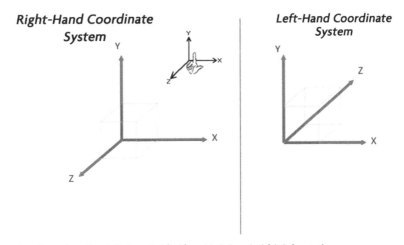

Fig. 2.3 Sample axis orientations for right-handed (left) and left-handed (right) notations.

is required is to add the translation coordinates to the initial starting point. For example,

$$P' = P + V,$$

where P is the object's initial point, P' is the object's position after moving, and V is the translation vector. An example is shown in Fig. 2.4.

Scale

Scale refers to resizing objects in space. Mathematically, this means multiplying coordinates by a scalar. Since expanding or shrinking an object is also a direction, the scaling amount is a vector. In general, every position in a point is multiplied by the scalar,

$$P' = Ps,$$

where P and P' are the initial and final point positions, and s is the scalar. An example is shown in Fig. 2.5.

The equation is scaled about the origin. For example, if the snail was located at $(2,0,0)$ and then was scaled by 2, not only would the snail be twice the size, but its new location would be $(4,0,0)$!

Skew

Skew often refers to distortion relative to the known shape. In graphics, skew usually refers to turning rectangles into parallelograms. Mathematically, this is shown by adding a skew to the original point. For example, a Z relative to Y skew would use a formula, such as

$$Z' = Z + sY, s \in \mathbb{R}^*,$$

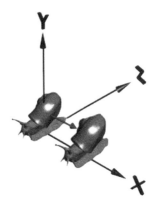

Fig. 2.4 An example of an object being translated or moved along the *x-axis*. (Courtesy of Charles Owen, used with permission.)

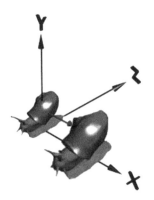

Fig. 2.5 An example of an object being scaled to a large object. (Courtesy of Charles Owen, used with permission.)

Fig. 2.6 An example of an object being skewed to be stretched along the *y*-axis. (Courtesy of Charles Owen, used with permission.)

A tip to remember the direction is to determine if the coordinate system is left- or right-handed: form the axis system as shown in Figure 2.3, with the thumb facing you. The direction of gripping matches the rotation direction.

where Z is the initial point position, Z' is the final skewed position, Y is the skew point, and s is the skew factor and a nonzero number ($\mathbb{R}^*$ means a real nonzero number). In this case, the object is stretched or squished along the *y*-axis. An example is shown in Fig. 2.6.

Other combinations are possible depending on the desired skew. Unity and Unreal do not support skew directly in their geometric transformations for models, although some clever manipulation of the local transforms in the scene tree discussed later in the chapter can result in a skew. Cameras use a different type of matrix that does have some skew-like effects. That will be a later chapter.

Skew, like scale, is also about the origin.

Rotation

Rotation of an object is more involved than the other transformations listed above. Rotation can be applied in different ways, including

- Euler angles
- Vector orientation
- Quaternions

Here, we cover a bit about two-dimensional (2D) rotation and extending to 3D. More involved rotations are covered in their own sections on matrices, Euler angles (or homogeneous coordinates), and quaternions.

For now, let's review 2D rotation.

Rotating points means rotation around the origin and rotating vectors means rotating the vector direction because the vector is relative to the origin. The angle of rotation of a vector is denoted with θ and can be described as the angle of P_1 *rotated to* P_2.

Usually, in math, a positive rotation occurs in the *counterclockwise* direction, which is a characteristic of the right-handed coordinate system. However, both Unity and Unreal use left-handed coordinate systems. This means that a positive rotation occurs in the *clockwise* direction. Left-handed coordinate systems are more common in 3D engines due to being able better set the forward direction as being positive. Because both main VR engines use left-handed coordinate systems, this text also uses the left-handed notation for application consistency. However, the newer Godot game engine, uses a right handed system.

To give an example of how the math changes between right-handed and left-handed coordinate systems, let's take an initial point, $P_1 = (x_1, y_1)$ and rotate it to point $P_2 = (x_2, y_2)$, as shown in Fig. 2.7.

Normally, the θ would either have a negative rotation or would rotate through the other three quadrants counterclockwise for the right-handed system. Using the counterclockwise rotation, this would give

$$(x_2, y_2) = (x_1 \cos\theta - y_1 \sin\theta, \ \mathrm{x}_1\sin\theta + y_2 \cos\theta)$$

for the rotation. In the clockwise rotation, or by using negative θ,

$$(x_2, y_2) = (x_1 \cos\theta + y_1 \sin\theta, -x_1\sin\theta + \cos\theta),$$

which is the left-handed version.

Let's plug in some numbers to verify. Let $P_1 = (4,6.93)$ and $\theta = 30°$ for the left-handed system or $330°$ in the right-handed system. First, let's find the resulting rotated point, P_2, for the right-handed system.

$$P_2 = \left(x_2, y_2\right)$$

$$= (4\cos 330° - 6.93\sin 330°, \ 4\sin 330° + 6.93\cos 330°)$$

$$= (6.93, 4)$$

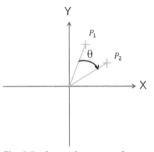

Fig. 2.7. A rotation around the origin using left-handed notation.

Next, let's use the left-handed system.

$$P_2 = \left(x_2, y_2\right)$$

$$= (4\cos 30° + 6.93\sin 30°, \ -4\sin 30° + 6.93\cos 330°)$$

$$= (6.93, 4)$$

The result is the same, regardless of the coordinate system chosen.

Extending rotation to 3D can be done using the same 2D rotation about the z-axis.

$$(x_2, y_2, z_2) = (x_1 \cos\theta + y_1 \sin\theta, -x_1 \sin\theta + y_1 \cos\theta, z_1)$$

Note that z has not changed. Similar 2D rotations can be done on the other axes as well. A single rotation like this or a combination of these rotations can be represented using matrices, which we will cover next.

Matrices

In graphics systems, rotations are not typically done in a system of algebra equations. They are converted to matrices to run on GPUs, which are optimized for linear algebra. Here are some ways of showing a rotation about the z-axis:

- Vector notation (right-handed): $(x_2, y_2, z_2) = (x_1 \cos\theta - y_1 \sin\theta,$ $x_1 \sin\theta + y_1 \cos\theta, z_1)$

- Conventional notation (right-handed): $\begin{bmatrix} x_2 \\ y_2 \\ z_2 \end{bmatrix} = \begin{bmatrix} \cos\theta & -\sin\theta & 0 \\ \sin\theta & \cos\theta & 0 \\ 0 & 0 & 1 \end{bmatrix} \begin{bmatrix} x_1 \\ y_1 \\ z_1 \end{bmatrix}$

A tip to determine if a matrix is in conventional or transposed notation is to look at where the vector is: If the vector is on the left, it is a left-handed system. If the vector is on the right, it is a right-handed system.

- Transposed notation (left-handed):

$$[x_2 \quad y_2 \quad z_2] = [x_1 \quad y_1 \quad z_1] \begin{bmatrix} \cos\theta & \sin\theta & 0 \\ -\sin\theta & \cos\theta & 0 \\ 0 & 0 & 1 \end{bmatrix}$$

Recall that the transpose of a matrix is the matrix flipped along the diagonal: $(AB)^T = B^T A^T$. Since we are using the left-handed coordinate system, the transposed notation will be used here.

A primary benefit to matrices is that matrices can be easily merged into a single 3×3 matrix rather than having to apply the formulas individually one after another. Let's demonstrate this through an example. An object is to be rotated around the x-axis by an angle of ϕ,

$$P \begin{bmatrix} 1 & 0 & 0 \\ 0 & \cos\phi & \sin\phi \\ 0 & -\sin\phi & \cos\phi \end{bmatrix} = P'.$$

and then the object is to be rotated about the y-axis by an angle of θ,

$$P' \begin{bmatrix} \cos\theta & 0 & -\sin\theta \\ 0 & 1 & 0 \\ \sin\theta & 0 & \cos\theta \end{bmatrix} = P''.$$

Models can easily run in the range of thousands of vertices, so performing each rotation can be computationally heavy. Matrices, however, can be combined by being multiplied together. This means that with the combined rotation matrix, only rounds of rotation computation would need to be done, increasing efficiency. Now, matrix multiplication is associative but not commutative, so order matters. The rotation matrices are multiplied in order of the *last* rotation *first* in the list, such as in our example:

$$P \left(\begin{bmatrix} \cos\theta & 0 & -\sin\theta \\ 0 & 1 & 0 \\ \sin\theta & 0 & \cos\theta \end{bmatrix} \begin{bmatrix} 1 & 0 & 0 \\ 0 & \cos\phi & \sin\phi \\ 0 & -\sin\phi & \cos\phi \end{bmatrix} \right) = P''$$

$$P \begin{bmatrix} \cos\theta & \sin\theta\sin\phi & -\sin\theta\cos\phi \\ 0 & \cos\phi & \sin\phi \\ \sin\theta & -\cos\theta\sin\phi & \cos\theta\cos\phi \end{bmatrix} = P''$$

When rendering only the final matrix is sent to the GPU.

All of the other transformations described in Section 1 of this chapter can also be described in matrix notation. The use of matrices for translation, scale, and skew is described next.

Translation in Matrix Form

Translations can be expressed in the following ways:

- $P' = P + T$
- $\begin{pmatrix} x' & y' & z' \end{pmatrix} = (x, y, z) + \left(t_x, t_y, t_z \right)$
- $\begin{bmatrix} x' & y' & z' \end{bmatrix} = \begin{bmatrix} x & y & z \end{bmatrix} + \begin{bmatrix} t_x & t_y & t_z \end{bmatrix} = \begin{bmatrix} x + t_x & y + t_y & z + t_z \end{bmatrix}$

However, how can a translation be expressed as a square matrix, such as

$$\begin{bmatrix} x' & y' & z' \end{bmatrix} = \begin{bmatrix} x & y & z \end{bmatrix} \begin{bmatrix} ? & ? & ? \\ ? & ? & ? \\ ? & ? & ? \end{bmatrix} ?$$

This cannot be expressed using a 3×3 matrix, but it is possible to do something similar using a 4×4 matrix. For a basic 3D translation, the matrix becomes

$$\begin{bmatrix} x + t_x & y + t_y & z + t_z & 1 \end{bmatrix} = \begin{bmatrix} x & y & z & 1 \end{bmatrix} \begin{bmatrix} 1 & 0 & 0 & 0 \\ 0 & 1 & 0 & 0 \\ 0 & 0 & 1 & 0 \\ t_x & t_y & t_z & 1 \end{bmatrix},$$

where t_n are the components of the translation. Notice that the 1 in the bottom right corner is preserved but then ignored. This gives a helpful trick. Whenever a matrix needs to be translated by a vector/point, just add another dimension and an extra 1. The 1 is a *homogeneous* coordinate.

Scale

The matrix for scaling is fairly straightforward. The scaling factor for each component is placed along the diagonal. For the 4×4 example, the scaling factor, S, becomes

$$S(x, y, z) = \begin{bmatrix} S_x & 0 & 0 & 0 \\ 0 & S_y & 0 & 0 \\ 0 & 0 & S_z & 0 \\ 0 & 0 & 0 & 1 \end{bmatrix}$$

Notice the 1 again in the bottom right corner.

Skew

Adding a skew to the matrix just starts with the identity matrix and then adds the skew component off the diagonal. To review, this is the identity matrix:

$$I = \begin{bmatrix} 1 & 0 & 0 & 0 \\ 0 & 1 & 0 & 0 \\ 0 & 0 & 1 & 0 \\ 0 & 0 & 0 & 1 \end{bmatrix}$$

So, for a Z relative to Y skew of $K_{\text{ZrelY}}(k)$,

$$K_{\text{ZrelY}}(k) = \begin{bmatrix} 1 & 0 & 0 & 0 \\ 0 & 1 & 0 & 0 \\ 0 & k & 1 & 0 \\ 0 & 0 & 0 & 1 \end{bmatrix}$$

In Pseudocode

The editors in VR engines provide some matrix options for transforms. More specifically, they usually have a transformation object that allows the user to input the position, scale, and Euler angles, and then converts that to a matrix behind the scenes. An example from Unity and Unreal are shown in Fig. 2.8. However, anything more complex requires developing the needed matrix. Here's an example of creating a transform both in the editor and in pseudocode:

```
// create 4x4 identity matrix
Matrix m

// translate x by 2
m[3,0] = 2

// scale to 0.75
// create 4x4 identity matrix
```

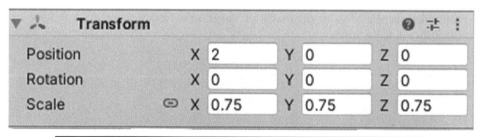

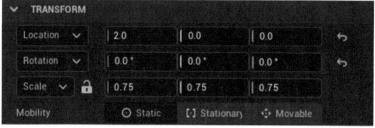

Fig. 2.8 An example transform in Unity (above) and Unreal (below).

```
Matrix s
s[0,0] = 0.75
s[1,1] = 0.75
s[2,2] = 0.75

//multiply both matrices together for final transform
m2 = s * m
```

In general, creating a transform matrix begins with creating an identity matrix of the needed size. The matrix is then converted to the type of transform. Creating a new identity matrix and converting is repeated until the desired transform components are created. Then all of the matrices are multiplied together.

With the built-in transforms that are common in 3D engines, why bother with matrices at all? Matrices are useful for determining axis orientations and directions. Here are some examples of the needed direction, and what part of the identity matrix is affected:

- Forward:

$$\begin{bmatrix} \mathbf{1} & 0 & 0 & 0 \\ \mathbf{0} & 1 & 0 & 0 \\ \mathbf{0} & 0 & 1 & 0 \\ \mathbf{0} & 0 & 0 & 1 \end{bmatrix}$$

- Up:

$$\begin{bmatrix} 1 & \mathbf{0} & 0 & 0 \\ 0 & \mathbf{1} & 0 & 0 \\ 0 & \mathbf{0} & 1 & 0 \\ 0 & 0 & 0 & 1 \end{bmatrix}$$

- Right:

$$\begin{bmatrix} 1 & 0 & \mathbf{0} & 0 \\ 0 & 1 & \mathbf{0} & 0 \\ 0 & 0 & \mathbf{1} & 0 \\ 0 & 0 & 0 & 1 \end{bmatrix}$$

Using these reference points, how would transform be used, for example, to place a sign on the top of a 2-m post, wherever the post was placed in the environment, assuming the post's origin is at its bottom? In pseudocode, first the post's position would be determined from the transform. Then, using the up option gives the information from the correct axis. Post is the post game object and transform is an object that holds the matrix.

```
postPos = post.transform.position
up = post.transform.up
signPos = postPos + up * 2
```

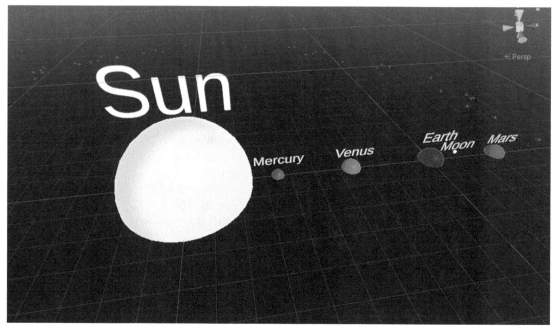

Fig. 2.9 An example VR scene of numerous components.

Scene Tree

Scene trees are simply a structure to describe the contents of a scene. For example, how might the scene in Fig. 2.9 be described in terms of components?

One way would be to start with the solar system, add a sun, and group planetary bodies. This grouping is shown in Fig. 2.10.

The main components of a scene tree are

- Geometry\Models
- Transformations
  - Places geometry
  - Has no model, but moves everything under it
- Groups
  - Group geometry together
  - These are the nested structures like the Asteroids above
- Lights
- Cameras

A scene *graph* is similar to a scene tree but allows some elements to be pointed to twice for efficiency. Unity allows for very few of these and are primarily reused materials rather than models. Unity calls this structure the Hierarchy. Unreal calls this the World Outliner.

One of the more challenging parts of the scene tree is that when items are nested, we "chain" transformations. This means any one

Fig. 2.10 A sample tree structure of the objects in the VR solar system.

object has both local or relative (to its parent) and absolute coordinates (in the world).

Scene Tree Transformations

This biggest part of a scene tree is the chaining of transforms and efficiency in rendering. However, we also need to keep local versus global transforms in mind as this can affect transforms.

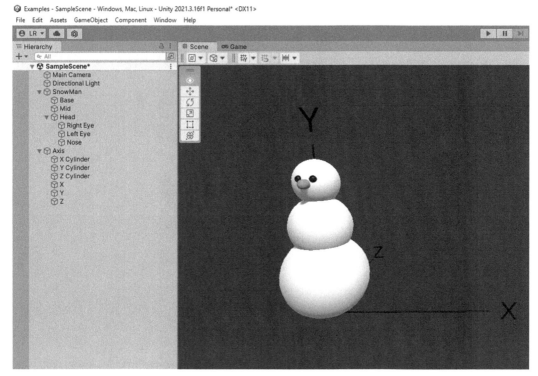

Fig. 2.11 Simple scene tree example. The parent is the Snowman object with three sphere children and the Head Sphere has Eyes and Nose children. Axes are included for reference.

Chaining works in the form of parenting. Parenting occurs when adding a parent to an object's transform. This is very useful if a number of subelements need to be moved together. For an example of this, assume a Snowman object with three Sphere children. The head sphere has Eyes and Nose children, as shown in Fig. 2.11.

Depending on how the different objects nested, the transform of the object changes. The transform may be relative to the parent object or relative to the origin or world space. In a visual example, for Fig. 2.12, selecting and moving the Mid Sphere child moves the just that sphere since it is a child object. Selecting the entire Snowman object and moving it will move the entire snowman. Similarly, if the Mid Sphere is removed from the Snowman scene tree, which means that the Sphere parent was removed, selecting and moving the Mid Sphere only moves that object and not the rest of the Snowman.

Parenting also affects the orientation of computing transforms. In the Snowman example, Fig. 2.13 shows the transform variables for when the Nose is a child of the Head Sphere and for when the Nose is pulled from the Snowman scene tree. Both the position and the scale change, depending on the chaining, even though the Nose has not changed shape at all.

Fig. 2.12 Example of selecting an object and transforming what is parented (left) to the Snowman object and not parented (right).

Local versus global

Local

Relative to its parent

Global

World space. The nose is pulled to a global setting

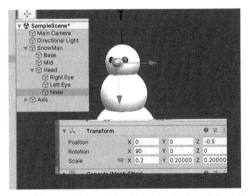 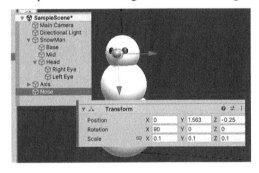

Fig. 2.13 The transform of the Nose is displayed for when the Nose is the child of the Head (left) or when the Nose is pulled from the Snowman scene tree altogether (right).

Chaining effectively works by appending the transforms of a child object to its parent all the way up the scene tree. In pseudocode, finding the chained transform would look a bit like this:

```
function FindGlobalTransform()
  if this.parent == null
    return this.matrix
  else
    return parent.FindGlobalTransform()
              * this.matrix
```

Transforms are typically applied in backwards order in the vast majority of graphics engines. This feels weird and wrong at first. However, there is a very good reason they are in reverse order as it makes building up composite object much easier. Consider a field of corn. It is easier to make a corn objects as a child of a row, and then the rows as a child of the field, and then be able to place multiple fields, by just adjusting the field's position. If the transformation were forward, each corn object would need to be manually updated everytime the field moved!

This means the transformations are applied backward. The transformations are stacked and applied child to parent.

Test Your Understanding 2.1

Let's take the Snowman example again with the full parenting. What would happen if the Snowman shown in Fig. 2.14 is rotated 90° about the x-axis? What would happen if the Nose object is rotated 90° about the x-axis?

To answer both questions, it's helpful to ask if the selected object is a parent to other objects. If the selected object is a parent to another object, then both objects are transformed as a single object. If the selected object is not a parent to another object, then only the selected object is transformed. This is still the case whether the selected object has a parent or not. The selected object's parent is not affected by the selection. Transforms only work in the direction going down the scene tree, not up. With that in mind, let's look at each rotation question.

For the first question, recall that the entire scene tree is parented to the Snowman object. As a result, all of the objects in the scene tree are rotated together as a single, but complex, object. Rotating by 90° around the x-axis rotates the entire snowman to its back, as shown in Fig. 2.15.

For the second question, recall that the Nose object is a leaf in the scene tree. Nose has a parent but is not a parent to another object. All of the other objects are up the tree. As a result, only the Nose is rotated up and the rest of the Snowman is unaffected, as can be seen in Fig. 2.16.

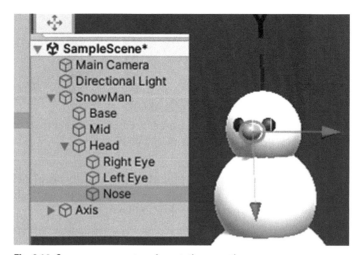

Fig. 2.14 Snowman scene tree for rotation questions.

Continued

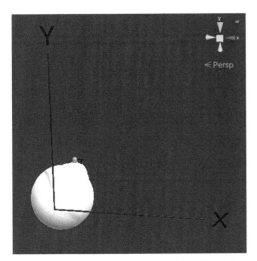

Fig. 2.15 9 Snowman object rotated 90° about the x-axis.

Fig. 2.16 Nose object within the Snowman object rotated by 90°.

In code, there are a few different options for traversing the scene tree. In general, the tree can be climbed with a parent reference and descended with a child reference.

In Unity, this typically means using transform.parent to get the parent reference. In Unreal, this is typically Parent.GetActorTransform().

Quaternions

Matrix Rotation Limitations

As mentioned above, matrices are useful but have some limitations. The matrices used a combination of Euler angles, Cartesian coordinates (x,y,z) or (pitch, yaw, roll). A graphical example of (pitch, yaw, roll) is shown in Fig. 2.17.

However, a rotation problem can occur regardless of the matrix. For simplicity, this problem will be described in 2D.

Let's start with a standing figure like in Fig. 2.18. The figure is to be rotated by a single angle, shown in Fig. 2.19. This angle is readily translated into a rotation. After the rotation, the direction that the figure is facing can be expressed as a single rotation value.

Now, by what angle was the figure rotated? That angle depends on the initial position of the figure. Let's say that the figure's initial direction can be described as $(x,y,z) = (0,0,1)$. (Note: 'y' is up from the feet through the figure's head here.) If the y-axis is taken as up and the

Fig. 2.17 Example demonstrating pitch, roll, and yaw for transformations. (Wiki commons. https://commons.wikimedia.org/wiki/File:Flight_dynamics_with_text.png.)

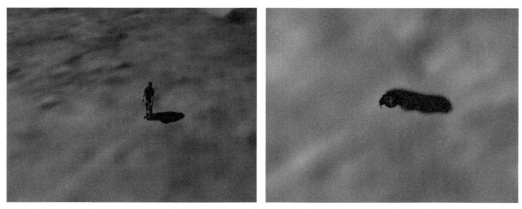

Fig. 2.18 Starting position for the standing figure from a distance (left) and from above (right). (Courtesy of Charles Owen, used with permission.)

Fig. 2.19 Fig. rotated by a single angle. (Courtesy of Charles Owen, used with permission.)

figure is rotated about the y-axis, then the final position of the figure can be described as

$$x' = x \cos \theta - z \sin \theta, \ y' = 0, \ z' = x \sin \theta + z \cos \theta,$$

where (x', y', z') is the figure's final position and θ is the rotation angle. Plugging in the initial position, the final position becomes

$$(x', y', z') = (-\sin \theta, \ 0, \ \cos \theta).$$

This is fairly straightforward. However, the computation becomes trickier for an animated rotation. Let's say that the figure starts out at angle θ_1. An animation requires that the figure rotate to angle θ_2 in t seconds. Each frame update gives a time step of δ. How much of the rotation needs to be completed for each time step? The rotation per step, θ', starts at the initial angle and the time step averaged angle towards the final angle is added. This can be expressed as

$$\theta' = \theta_1 + \frac{\delta}{t}(\theta_2 - \theta_1).$$

While this looks straightforward, the result in the animation is not. Unless the figure starts at the θ_1 orientation, the figure can start at a different orientation, spin the above angular displacement and stop at an orientation that is not θ_2. For example, suppose the figure starts at 36°. The rotation animation is to go from 50° to 320°. Unless the figure's orientation is changed to 50° before the animation begins, the final orientation will be 306° instead of 320°. The animation can also spin more than one complete revolution before reaching the destination orientation as shown in Fig. 2.20.

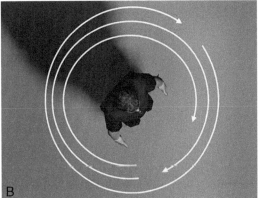

Fig. 2.20 The left side shows the final and initial positions of the figure. The right side shows the different rotation paths that the figure can take for the animation. (Courtesy of Charles Owen, used with permission.)

The problem compounds in 3D. Not only can the problem occur in three directions, but as matrices can be changed by altering the contents directly, a matrix's column magnitudes can be different than 1. Rotation requires that all of the column's magnitude be 1.

To get around this problem, other methods of rotation can be considered, such as quaternions. In this section, we will be covering quaternions at a high level.

Complex Numbers

Quaternions were invented by William Rowan Hamilton in 1843 [1] as a tool to rotation that easily composes and interpolates. The basic idea is that complex numbers can be used for representing 2D rotation, where the imaginary number i is used for the following 2D rotation example.

Recall that $i^2 = -1$. The x-axis represents the real number line and the y-axis represents the imaginary number line. A 2D point is then represented by complex numbers,

$$P = (a, b) = a + bi = \cos\theta + i\sin\theta$$

This is shown graphically in Fig. 2.21. This notation gives the advantage of representing angles without trig functions. In this notation, a normalized complex number represents a rotation. In the example above, the normalized complex number is

$$p = \frac{(a, b)}{\sqrt{a^2 + b^2}}$$

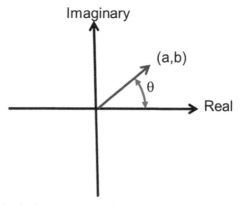

Fig. 2.21 An example of using complex numbers for rotation.

which is just like normalizing a vector. Multiplying two complex numbers together adds the rotation angles. This means that after converting two angles, θ_1 and θ_2, into complex numbers, p_{θ_1} and p_{θ_2}, the angles can be combined by

$$p_{\theta_1} p_{\theta_2} = p_{\theta_1 + \theta_2}$$

Expanding this into 3D requires having three imaginary numbers for the three axes:

$$i^2 = -1$$
$$j^2 = -1$$
$$k^2 = -1$$
$$i \neq j$$
$$i \neq k$$
$$j \neq k$$
$$ijk = -1$$

The imaginary numbers are also called basis vectors or basis elements. The point in space for a 3D quaternion is then

$$q = ix + jy + kz + w$$

and a unit quaternion has the property

$$x^2 + y^2 + z^2 + w^2 = 1$$

One way to view this notation is as four-element vectors. Normalizing into a unit quaternion in 3D is the same as normalizing 3D vectors,

$$q = \frac{(x, y, z, w)}{\sqrt{x^2 + y^2 + z^2 + w^2}}$$

Using Quaternions for Rotations

Imagine an object is already aligned with an axis described by (x, y, z), and then rotate the object around this axis by an angle θ. The quaternion is essentially short-hand for the below rotation in Fig. 2.22.

Since quaternions are comprised of a scalar and a vector, an additional short-hand is often used:

$$q = (q, q_v) = q + iq_x + jq_y + kq_z,$$

where q is the quaternion, q is the scalar component and q_v is the vector component.

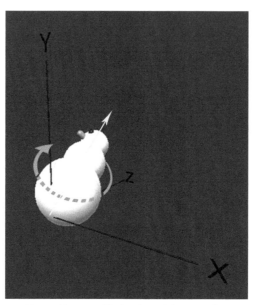

Fig. 2.22 An example of aligning an object with a specified axis and then rotating.

When used for rotations, the quaternion is normalized by $\sin(\theta/2)$ and the scalar is $\cos(\theta/2)$. Therefore, the formula used in graphical contexts follows this form:

$$q = (\theta, \boldsymbol{q}_v) = \sin(\theta/2)(iq_x + jq_y + kq_z) + \cos(\theta/2)$$

With this in mind, a couple of other conventions of using quaternions arise:

- $\boldsymbol{q}_1 * \boldsymbol{q}_2$ represents rotation $\boldsymbol{q}_2$ followed by rotation $\boldsymbol{q}_1$.
- $\boldsymbol{q}$ and $-\boldsymbol{q}$ are the same rotation.
- Inverting the quaternion negates the vector components of the quaternion. If $\boldsymbol{q} = (q, \boldsymbol{q}_v)$, then $\boldsymbol{q}^{-1} = (q, -\boldsymbol{q}_v)$.
- The multiplication rule for quaternions is

$$\boldsymbol{q}_1\boldsymbol{q}_2 = (q_1, \boldsymbol{q}_{1v})(q_2, \boldsymbol{q}_{2v}) = (q_1q_2 - \boldsymbol{q}_{1v} \cdot \boldsymbol{q}_{2v}, q_2\boldsymbol{q}_{1v} + q_1\boldsymbol{q}_{2v} + \boldsymbol{q}_{1v} \times \boldsymbol{q}_{2v})$$

Quaternions are also multiplied like other numbers. Additional multiplication rules on the basis vectors are required. However, this is not necessary for coding. For example, an animated rotation in pseudocode using quaternions can often be only a couple of lines.

```
function Update()
    r = r * spinAmountQuat
    SetRotation( r )
```

LERP and SLERP

Quaternions depend on finding the correct axis for rotation. There is more than one way of computing the rotation axis which affects animation. Here we cover LERP and SLERP, or **l**inear int**erp**olation and **s**pherical **l**inear int**erp**olation [2].

Here interpolation means to move an object from one orientation to another. Interpolation is a valuable tool for rotations. The most basic interpolation is linear or LERP:

$$result = start \times (1 - percent) + end \times percent$$

To give an example, suppose we have an initial vector and we want to move that vector to a new orientation for an animation as shown in Fig. 2.23.

The vector changes according to

$$V' = \frac{V_I + t(V_F - V_I)}{\left| V_I + t(V_F - V_I) \right|}$$

where t is the fraction of the total time,

$$t = \frac{t_{current} - t_{start}}{t_{end} - t_{start}}$$

Using LERP in code is usually only one line similar to

```
object = Lerp( start * ( 1 - progress ) + end * progress start,
end, percent start * ( 1 - progress ) + end * progress )
```

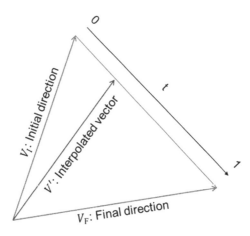

Fig. 2.23 A simple interpolation example.

Fig. 2.24 SLERP example of moving a horizontal ladder (1) to a tilted vertical position (2). (Courtesy of Charles Owen, used with permission.)

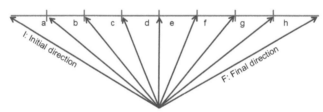

Fig. 2.25 Example of interpolating vectors with numerous steps. Note how the step width widens toward the middle of the interpolation.

Let's look at a more complicated example. In Fig. 2.24 there is a ladder object on the ground (location 1) and we want to move that object upright and against the barn (location 2).

In this case, both the up rotation and the position need to be interpolated. There is also another issue. In Fig. 2.25, note that the steps near the middle of the interpolation are longer, larger angles than the initial and final angles. Steps in a situation like this are not uniform in time. The animation will appear to move faster in the middle of the rotation than near the ends. Look carefully at Fig. 2.25 and notice that a's angle is smaller than d's angle.

SLERP changes the rate of speed so that the angle's steps are constant. The vector changes according to

$$V' = \frac{\sin((1-t)\theta)}{\sin\theta}V_{\mathrm{I}} + \frac{\sin t\theta}{\sin\theta}V_{\mathrm{F}}$$

where V', V_I, and V_F are the interpolating, initial and final vectors, t is the fraction of the total time, and

$$\theta = \cos^{-1}(V_I \bullet V_F)$$

SLERP comes with a few challenges. First, SLERP will always use the shortest path, so it's important to watch for no change situations. Another instance is when $\theta = \pi$. In this case, the direction can be incorrect. Applying SLERP to two vectors is not an exact solution for 'up,' either.

To interpolate the ladder correctly, quaternions are needed again. SLERP with two quaternions will rotate from one orientation to another using a uniform angular velocity and a fixed rotation axis. Both main VR engines have one-line calls for SLERP.

Nonlinear LERP and SLERP

Interpolation is not restricted to only linear interpolation. Exponential decay or stepwise functions can also be used. LERP and SLERP can still be used in a fashion in these cases by adding a mapping function that takes in the percentage and alters the progress speed between the start and ending states.

The original function would be $f(x) = x$, which perfectly maps x to x as shown in Fig. 2.26.

To contrast, consider $f(x) = x^2$ as an example as shown in Fig. 2.27. If the animation is 50% complete, $f(x)$ outputs 0.25, which slows the animation in the early part, and speeds up in the later part.

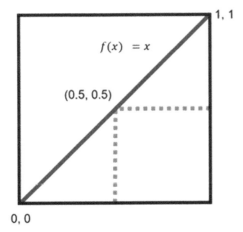

Fig. 2.26 Linear mapping function for LERP.

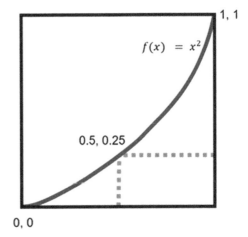

Fig. 2.27 Quadratic mapping function for LERP.

Integrating that into the LERP formula would yield this pseudocode:

```
function ProgressAdjustment( percentage )
  return percentage * percentage

progress = ProgressAdjustment( percent )
result = start * ( 1 - progress ) + end * progress
```

Some care is needed when selecting these adjustment functions. Ideally, the function should output 0 with 0 input, and 1 with 1 input, and between those ranges, never output values outside of the [0, 1] range. For example, any $f(x) = x^n$ or $f(x) = x^{\frac{1}{n}}$ functions would work well. $f(x) = \log(x)$ would not.

References

[1] Hamilton RH. On quaternions; or on a new system of imaginaries in algebra, *Letter to John T. Graves*, 17 October 1843.
[2] Shoemake K. Animating rotation with quaternion curves (pdf), *SIGGRAPH*, 1985.

3

Basic Physics

This chapter covers the basics of physics engines—how to use them, why to use them, and an introduction on where to use them. While game engines typically provide physics engines, there are instances where knowing how a physics engine works is required to get desired effects. VR has increased frequency of these instances due to tunneling described later in the chapter. The topics covered are physics engine components, forces, collision types including tunneling problems, transferring of physics (throwing), physics materials, and calculating paths.

The contents assume that the reader has a background in the following math and physics concepts (the essentials are covered in Chapter 2 and the Appendix): calculus I, calculus-based physics I, and matrices and a little linear algebra.

Some refresher material is included for these items. The contents do NOT assume that the student has a background in undergraduate classical mechanics or computational physics.

What Is a Physics Engine?

Physics engines are the compiled code on how objects move based on approximated physics math rather than us setting the positions and orientation directly. A significant part of physics engines includes different response options for collisions. Computations typically use Euler steps, which will be defined shortly, but how the steps are computed and their computational efficiencies vary.

While physics engines attempt to take care of most of the physics computations, using the engines effectively or changing the physics for special cases (e.g., an application set in low gravity) requires some knowledge of physics and associated math. If you thought that you were never going to need physics and calculus math for coding, this chapter is going to be a surprise! You are going to be using it in this chapter and subsequent chapters.

Physics engines have a few key components:
- Mass—how heavy the object is and how are forces applied
- Acceleration—how the velocity is changing; this can be both linear and rotational
- Velocity—how fast the object is moving; this can be both linear and rotational

A Practical Introduction to Virtual Reality. https://doi.org/10.1016/B978-0-443-14036-5.00003-0

- Friction—type of acceleration that counters current direction of movement; there are several sources here
- Forces—straight from physics with $F = ma$; affect changes in acceleration
- Bounciness—how an item rebounds from a collision
- Shape—affects collisions and movement

The thoroughness of the engine is dependent on the number of affecting elements, supported shapes, and quality of the math.

Source Equations and Euler Steps

The basic source equations are

$$a = \frac{dv}{dt} = \frac{d^2 p}{dt^2} = \text{acceleration}$$

$$v = \frac{dp}{dt} = \text{velocity}$$

$p =$ visible motion, somewhat comparable to displacement

This is run along any dimension. For example, in a two-dimensional (2D) game, this would be along x, y, and perhaps rotation. All motion is based on these three equations.

The catch is that computers do not use continuous motion but instead use discretized motion. Physics engines use the Euler method to discretize the just mentioned parameters. The essential coding concept is that the previous update's physics information and time difference are available to compute the current update's physics. That means that the above equations need to be in a form that uses the previous update's physics information. The conversion to Euler steps is fairly straightforward.

In general, anytime a derivative is found, the function can be discretized by replacing the derivative with Δ. For example,

$$\frac{dv}{dt} = \frac{\Delta v}{\Delta t} = \frac{v_l - v_c}{t_l - t_c} \quad ,$$

where Δ is the difference between the last update and the current update.

This changes the source equations to

$$a = \frac{dv}{dt} = \frac{\Delta v}{\Delta t} = \frac{v_{i+i} - v_i}{\Delta t}$$

$$v = \frac{dp}{dt} = \frac{\Delta p}{\Delta t} = \frac{p_{i+1} - p_i}{\Delta t}$$

$$p = p_{i+1} - p_i$$

To find the physics for the current update, these equations will need to be solved for the current position, velocity, and acceleration. Let's look at velocity first. Assuming no acceleration (i.e., v is constant), the current position can be solved by using

$$v = \frac{p_{i+1} - p_i}{\Delta t}$$

and solving for p_{i+1},

$$p_{i+1} = v\,\Delta t + p_i$$

If constant acceleration is present, then the formula for position changes to the current update's velocity rather than a constant:

$$p_{i+1} = v_{i+1}\,\Delta t + p_i$$

The current velocity can be found by

$$a = \frac{v_{i+i} - v_i}{\Delta t}$$

and solving for v_{i+1},

$$v_{i+1} = a\,\Delta t + v_i$$

Plugging this back into the function for position gives

$$p_{i+1} = (a\,\Delta t + v_i)\Delta t + p_i = a\,\Delta t^2 + v_i\,\Delta t + p_i.$$

If the acceleration is not constant, then the sum of all of the sources of acceleration is used:

$$a = \sum_i a_i$$

If this seems unfamiliar, recall that forces sum:

$$F_{net} = ma = m\sum_i a_i$$

This gives the last of the discretized source equations. The new equations are

$$a = \sum_i a_i$$

$$v_{i+1} = v_i + a\,\Delta t$$

$$p_{i+1} = p_i + v_{i+1}\,\Delta t$$

The smaller the time step, the better the physics but also the more computationally expensive. In virtual reality (VR), these equations apply in three directions and both linear and angular for six degrees of freedom (DOF). As an example, the linear motion can be represented in matrix form:

$$\boldsymbol{v}(t) = \begin{bmatrix} v_x(t) \\ v_y(t) \\ v_z(t) \end{bmatrix} = \begin{bmatrix} \dfrac{dp_x}{dt} \\ \dfrac{dp_y}{dt} \\ \dfrac{dp_z}{dt} \end{bmatrix}.$$

It helps to think of the matrices as multiple equations, one for each dimension. Formally, this is vector calculus.

Basic Collision Steps

The next part of the engine is the collision. This part of the physics engine varies more than the Euler steps. How the engine responds depends on characteristics such as bounciness, amount of overlap, and more. Because this math tends to be rather involved, most engines encourage basic shapes for bounding boxes around objects, "colliders," that are easy to calculate with boxes, spheres, and cylinders. The simple version follows these steps:

1. Calculate/define center of mass (CM) and moment of inertia ($I = \sum_p m_p r_p^{\,2}$, where m_p is the mass and r_p is the vector from the axis of rotation to the CM position of mass, m_p).
2. Set initial position, orientation, linear and angular velocities.
3. Determine all forces on the body.
4. Linear acceleration is the sum of forces divided by mass ($\boldsymbol{a} = \boldsymbol{F}/m$).
5. Angular acceleration is the sum of torques divided by I ($\boldsymbol{\tau} = \boldsymbol{F} \times \boldsymbol{r}$, {left−handed} $\boldsymbol{\alpha} = \boldsymbol{\tau}/I$).
6. Numerically integrate (Euler step) to update position, orientation, and velocities.

Calculating the moment of inertia varies according to the shape of the object. Due to the challenges of discretizing integration, simpler characteristics with known algebraic formulas for the moment of inertia are highly preferred for efficiency in physics engines. Fig. 3.1 has some basic shapes and corresponding formula for calculating I.

Adding Physics to an Object

Physics may or may not be enabled for an object. If enabled, there are a few common elements that are considered:

- Forces
- Mass

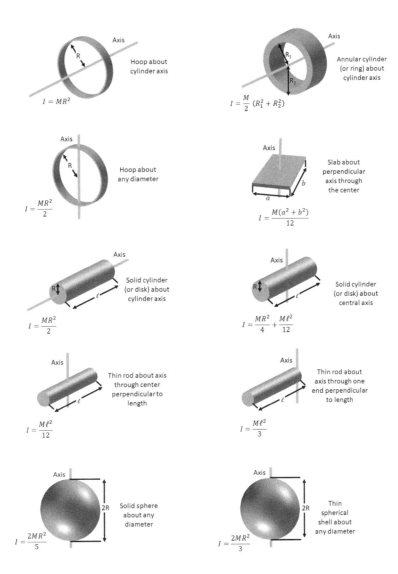

Fig. 3.1 Some basic shapes and their corresponding formula for calculating the shape's moment of inertia. (Recreated from https://s3-us-west-2.amazonaws.com/courses-images/wp-content/uploads/sites/648/2016/11/04025642/Fig._11_03_06-1.jpg.)

- Velocity
- Wind resistance
- Rotational velocity
- Rotational resistance
- Deflective efficiency

The names of these can vary a bit between engines. As an example, Unity calls deflective efficiency "bounciness," while Unreal calls this Restitution.

As the other elements are dependent on forces, we focus on forces for this section.

The number of parameters in an item affects the quality of the physics calculation at the cost of efficiency. As a simple, starting example, suppose an object is traveling at a constant velocity with no rotational forces. Because there is no net force and by extension, no acceleration, mass would not matter. This results in the Euler steps to determine the position:

$$v_{i+1} = v_i$$

$$p_{i+1} = p_i + v_{i+1}\Delta t$$

As a concrete example, assume the velocity is $10\,\text{m/s}$ along the y dimension and 0 otherwise, the current position is $(10, 20, 15)$, and there is a time step of $0.1\,\text{s}$. Because this is in three dimensions, this shifts into the vector calculus form of

$$v_{i+1} = \begin{bmatrix} v_{i_x} \\ v_{i_y} \\ v_{i_z} \end{bmatrix}$$

$$p_{i+1} = \begin{bmatrix} p_{i_x} + v_{(i+1)_x}\Delta t \\ p_{i_y} + v_{(i+1)_y}\Delta t \\ p_{i_z} + v_{(i+1)_z}\Delta t \end{bmatrix}$$

Then, substitute in all the known values:

$$v_{i+1} = \begin{bmatrix} 0 \\ 10 \\ 0 \end{bmatrix}$$

$$p_{i+1} = \begin{bmatrix} 10 + 0.1 \times v_{i+1_x} \\ 20 + 0.1 \times v_{i+1_y} \\ 15 + 0.1 \times v_{i+1_z} \end{bmatrix} = \begin{bmatrix} 10 + 0.1 \times 0 \\ 20 + 0.1 \times 10 \\ 15 + 0.1 \times 0 \end{bmatrix}$$

Therefore, the final position at the next time step would be $(10, 21, 15)$, and the next would be $(10, 22, 15)$.

This is fast to calculate, but is not very realistic. This is equivalent to the object flying through a vacuum with no gravity. To improve realism, the Euler steps add more terms to the formula as needed, as is shown shortly.

Calculating Forces

The forces used in VR are similar to those of an undergraduate first-year physics course. Here is a brief review of the physics forces used in this chapter and the corresponding changes when using forces in VR.

Units in physics typically use a combination of SI (Système International) units and strongly overlap with the metric system. VR engines use their own combination of SI and metric units for physics engines. For example, the SI unit for force is Newton ($N = kg\,m/s^2$) and is used in Unity. Unreal, on the other hand, uses a much smaller force unit: $kg\,cm/s^2 = 0.01N$. For any projects requiring correct physics, it will be necessary to check the physics units. This is very true for angles, because both radians (SI) and degrees (non-SI) are used in VR engines.

The basic equation for force is

$$F = ma = m\frac{dv}{dt},$$

where m is the mass (typically in kg), a is the acceleration (typically in m/s²), v is the velocity (typically in m/s), t is the time (typically in seconds), and F is the force. Usually, the force is discretized into time steps, which often correspond to frame updates in VR.

Discretizing the equation into a single step gives

$$F = m\frac{v_f - v_i}{\Delta t},$$

where v_i and v_f are the initial and final velocities and Δt is the time step.

Test Your Understanding 3.1

A 2-kg cannon ball is launched from rest. The speed of the ball reaches 10 m/s in 0.02 s. What is the force exerted on the ball?

Using the above information, the variables can be assigned the following values:

- $m = 2\,kg$
- $v_i = 0$ m/s (starting at rest means 0 m/s)
- $v_f = 10$ m/s
- $\Delta t = 0.02$ s

For simplicity, the motion is all assumed to be in one direction, which means that the velocity vectors are in one direction. Plugging these values into the discretized formula for force gives

$$F = 2\,kg\frac{(10\,m/s - 0\,m/s)}{0.02\,s} = 1000\,N$$

Test Your Understanding 3.2

For a simulation, a 2-kg cannon ball is fired from a cannon rotated 45° upward. You are aiming for a ground target 6 m away. (a) What is the initial velocity to hit the target, and (b) what is the force on the cannon ball? The time step for firing the cannon is $\Delta t = 0.02$ s. Assume that gravity is 9.8 m/s² and that there is no air resistance.

(a) For the first question, it helps to remember the linear kinematic equations:

1. $v_f = v_i + at$
2. $d = v_i t + \frac{1}{2} at^2$
3. $v_f^2 = v_i^2 + 2ad$
4. $d = \frac{1}{2}(v_f + v_i)t$

where $\boldsymbol{d}$ is the displacement. There are two items to understand together: (1) is that the horizontal speed of the ball does *not* change due to the lack of air resistance and (2) the cannon ball has limited air time due to the force of gravity. In order to determine the horizontal speed necessary to reach the target, the air time needs to be calculated.

First, let's calculate the time the cannon ball is in the air. Because the cannon is aimed up and this simulation includes gravity, the launched cannon ball will fly in an arc before striking the target on the ground. This means that the time the cannon ball spends in the air is limited. Looking at the up direction, and making up +y, we can assign values to some variables for *half* of the arc:

- $\theta = 45°$
- $v_{yi} = v_i \sin\theta$ (v_i is the magnitude of the velocity of the cannon ball leaving the cannon)
- $v_{yf} = 0$ m/s (the ball isn't moving in the y direction at the top of the arc)
- $a_y = -9.8$ m/s² (the ball is accelerating down or in the $-y$ direction)

Because $\boldsymbol{v_i}$, $\boldsymbol{v_f}$, and $\boldsymbol{a}$ are somewhat known in the y direction and we are trying to find t first, the kinematic equation that has all of these variables is 1.

$$v_{yf} = v_{yi} + a_y t_{\frac{1}{2}}$$

$$t_{\frac{1}{2}} = \frac{v_{yf} - v_{yi}}{a_y} = -\frac{v_{yi}}{a_y} = -\frac{v_i \sin\theta}{a_y}$$

However, keep in mind that this only gives half of the air time. Therefore,

$$t = 2t_{\frac{1}{2}} = -2\frac{v_i \sin\theta}{a_y}$$

Now, let's look at what variables can be assigned values in the x direction:

- $\theta = 45°$
- $v_{xi} = v_{xf} = v_i \cos\theta$ (the velocity doesn't change)
- $a_x = 0$ m/s² (no change in velocity also means no acceleration)
- $d_x = 6$ m

Because v_{xi}, v_{xf}, a_x, and d_x are somewhat known and t is also somewhat known, any kinematic equation can be used here. However, we are looking for the initial velocity of the cannon ball at firing, or v_i. Because the cannon ball is to hit a ground target, v_i is dependent on t and d_x. Therefore, the kinematic equation chosen needs to have both of these variables and v_i. Equations 2 and 4 both meet this criteria, as acceleration and final velocity are also known. Let's use equation 4:

$$d_x = \frac{1}{2}\left(v_{fx} + v_{ix}\right)t$$

$$d_x = \frac{1}{2}(2v_i\cos\theta)\left(-\frac{2v_i\sin\theta}{a_y}\right) = -\frac{2v_i^2\cos\theta\sin\theta}{a_y} = -2\frac{v_i^2\left(\frac{1}{2}\sin 2\theta\right)}{a_y}$$

$$v_i^2 = -\frac{d_x a_y}{\sin 2\theta}$$

$$v_i = \sqrt{-\frac{d_x a_y}{\sin 2\theta}} = \sqrt{-\frac{(6\,\text{m})\left(-9.8\,\frac{\text{m}}{\text{s}^2}\right)}{\sin\left(2(45°)\right)}} = 7.668\,\text{m/s}$$

(b) For the second question, just use the discretized formula for force with the velocity found in question (a). Remember that we are looking at the force exerted on the cannon ball by the cannon. That means
- $v_i = 0\,\text{m/s}$ (the cannon ball starts at rest inside the cannon)
- $v_f = 7.668\,\text{m/s}$ (this is the speed of the ball leaving the cannon found in part (a))
- $\Delta t = 0.02$ (this is the time step for the cannon ball to leave the cannon)
- $m = 2\,\text{kg}$

All that's left to do is to plug in the numbers for finding the force

$$\mathbf{F} = m\frac{\mathbf{v_f} - \mathbf{v_i}}{\Delta t} = 2\,\text{kg}\,\frac{7.668\,\text{m/s} - 0\,\text{m/s}}{0.02\,\text{s}} = 766.8\,\text{kg m/s}^2 = 766.8\,\text{N}$$

If you are ever stuck on trying to choose a formula, remember this process:
1. List all the values you know.
2. Place them in the equations.
3. Whichever equation leaves just one variable unfilled is likely the needed equation.
4. Solve for the missing variable if needed.

Adding Force to an Object

In VR, physics may or may not be enabled for an object. Most forces are the "external" acceleration sources. This includes items such as gravity and propulsion. Remember how forces sum as

$$F = ma = m\sum_i a_i,$$

where F is the net force on an object, m is the object's mass, and a is the net acceleration on the object? Most game engines allow for applying forces with and without mass, but the exact set varies widely.

How long the force is assumed to be applied also can vary with the physics engines. Unity offers one physics time step and one second force options, while Unreal has one physics time step and continuous force options.

Where to use which option depends on the movement. Normally, the goal is to launch an object at some velocity. However, the force applied affects the acceleration. Let's choose the force option based on the math.

Test Your Understanding 3.3

An object is to be launched from rest to velocity $v = 2\,\text{m/s}$.

What force and force option is required for this motion if (a) $m = 2\,\text{kg}$ and $\Delta t = 0.02\,\text{s}$ and (b) $m = 10\,\text{kg}$ and $\Delta t = 1\,\text{s}$ in Unity?

First, let's simplify the discretized formula for force a bit:

$$F = m\frac{v_{i+1} - v_i}{\Delta t}$$

Because the object starts from rest ($v_i = 0$ m/s) and the velocity after the force is applied is $v_{i+1} = 2$ m/s in both cases,

$$F = m\,\frac{(2\,\text{m/s} - 0\text{m/s})}{\Delta t} = \frac{(2\,\text{m/s})m}{\Delta t}$$

(a) Plugging in the numbers gives

$$F = \frac{(2\,\text{m/s})m}{\Delta t} = \frac{(2\,\text{m/s})(2\,\text{kg})}{0.02\,\text{s}} = 500\,\text{N}$$

Because the time step is the default minimum time step in Unity, the force is instant. Mass is also given, which means that the case has force instant, includes mass. That means the the force option in this case is the physics time step option with mass.

(b) Plugging in the numbers gives

$$F = \frac{(2\,\text{m/s})v}{\Delta t} = \frac{(2\,\text{m/s})(10\,\text{kg})}{1\,\text{s}} = 20\,\text{N}$$

This force is small, but is exerted over a time longer than the default time step and includes mass. Therefore, the physics option to use here is the one second force option with mass.

Adding Drag to an Object

In the cannon example, we assumed that the cannon ball experiences no air resistance. Objects have options to add an air resistance or drag coefficient. This is available for both angular and linear motion. If the drag coefficient is 0, however, the application is assuming no air. That's right, the cannon was put in a vacuum. To make VR more realistic, frictional forces need to be added and that includes wind resistance or drag. At first thought, it might seem that the drag coefficient somehow goes into the sum of accelerations because drag decelerates, but that is not how a friction force is usually summed.

$$F_{net} = m \sum_i a_i + f_{drag}$$

However, drag is proportional to the velocity:

$$f_{drag} = -kv$$

Acceleration is not present here. The effect of the drag is a force, though, so Newton's Second Law still applies:

$$f_{drag} = -kv = ma$$

This gives a potential discretizing option. First, replace $a = \frac{dv}{dt}$ to bring out a derivative:

$$-kv = m\frac{dv}{dt}$$

Now that the derivative is present, replace the d with Δ and discretize velocity:

$$-kv_i = m\frac{\Delta v}{\Delta t} = m\frac{v_{i+1} - v_i}{\Delta t}$$

$$\frac{\Delta t}{m}(-kv_i) = v_{i+1} - v_i$$

$$v_{i+1} = v_i\left(1 - \frac{k\Delta t}{m}\right)$$

That gives a discretized formula for velocity and that is where the drag goes.

Drag is very important for trajectories. In order to give a visual indicator of the projectile path, the above values would have to be known. The velocity, acceleration, resistance, and so on can be dropped into these equations and used to calculate the path using Euler steps.

Types of Collisions

Physics engines have more involved math for collisions, but there are a few common parameters used to affect how the collision responds:

- Friction
  - Dynamic—amount of force in the opposite direction of movement
  - Static—amount of resistance to start moving
- Deflective efficiency

Friction in VR specifically refers to the friction between two objects. Other forms of friction, such as wind resistance, have their own settings. Deflective efficiency is the amount of rebound that occurs on a collision. 100% rebound means that no energy is lost on collision or an elastic collision (Figs. 3.2 and 3.3).

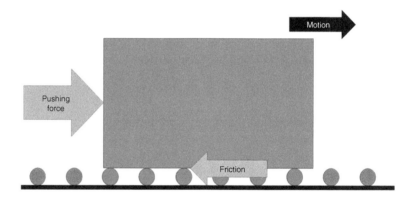

Fig. 3.2 The top image is a visual example of dynamic friction. The bottom image shows the motion difference in sliding blocks with a high friction surface (left) and a low friction surface (right). (From eLimu. https://elimufeynman. s3.amazonaws.com/media/ resources/force_friction_roll-ers_2.JPG.)

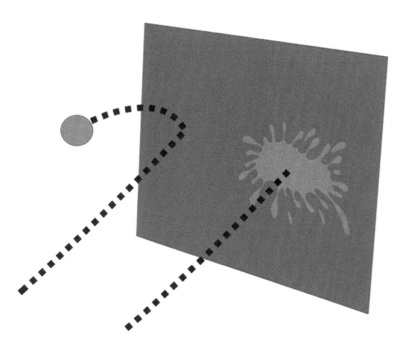

Fig. 3.3 Drawing of a rebounding ball (elastic collision) to the left and a sticking ball (completely inelastic collision) to the right.

Another topic that may come to mind is springs. Springs use another part of physics engines sometimes called joints. Joints are covered in their own chapter (Chapter 16).

Mass also has an effect on collision based on the effect on force. The location to add this can vary, but all modern engines include an option for mass.

Efficiency Considerations

Physics calculations are expensive operations, so most systems do what they can to avoid the calculation if at all possible. These efficiency measures are also where physics engines tend to fail.

Collision detection has some nuances for determining the needed accuracy and precision and for determining the settings needed for speed up and preventing tunneling. Here are some of the speed-ups.

- Ignore physics in some cases.
- Avoid checking certain collision pairs out of range.
- "Static" objects where collisions are permitted but are guaranteed not to move so that half of the collision calculation (for the static object) is skipped.
- Ignore search of some collision pairs.

Certain activities are a good measure of a quality physics engine. This includes elements like a Newton's cradle, where conservation of momentum is critical; a ball pit that strains a system by the number of collisions between balls and the resulting friction is critical; high linear or rotational speed that checks for improper removal of collision pairs; and ropes where constraints based on conservation of momentum and collision responses are critical.

The "Avoid checking certain collision pairs out of range" is the most common source of unexpected responses by the user and is an very common issue in VR. At high speeds, this calculation can skip elements that would have otherwise been caught, as is discussed next.

Tunneling

One issue with discretizing physics is *tunneling*. Tunneling occurs when an item is going so fast that the collider never intersects between updates. In other words, one object *tunnels* through another object. Let's take a car for example. If the simulation updates at 1-second intervals, a car could easily be on one side of a medium before an update and be entirely past the same medium afterward (Fig. 3.4).

To give an example of how easily tunneling can occur, let's calculate the time steps needed to handle a VR golf swing.

A golf swing is a rotational motion with a radius about the length of the club. For simplicity, the movement is approximated as a circle. The circumference of the swing for a club + arm radius of about 4 ft is $2\pi(4\,\text{ft}) = {\sim}25\,\text{ft.}$ (7.7 m). The diameter of the golf ball is 2 inches (5.1 cm), and the swing time is 0.25 seconds.

To prevent tunneling, the circular motion must be checked for a collision at distances smaller than half the diameter of the golf ball. Dividing up the circular motion into half golf ball-sized arc sections gives

$$\frac{\left(\frac{12\,\text{in}}{1\,\text{ft}}\right)25\,\text{ft}}{\left(\frac{1}{2}\right)2\,\text{in}} = 300 \text{ arc sections.}$$

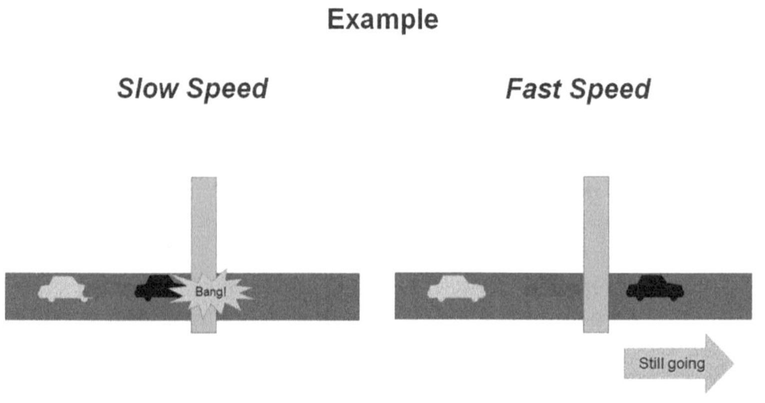

Example

Slow Speed   Fast Speed

Fig. 3.4 Example of tunneling. The *left side* has the car object moving slowly enough that the car collides with the wall. In the *right* example, the car is moving so fast that the collision is missed by the physics engine and the car tunnels through the wall.

These sections are the time steps that must be completed within the time of the swing. The length of the time steps is then

$$\frac{\text{swing time}}{\text{arc sections}} = \frac{0.25\,\text{s}}{300} = \sim 0.0008\,\text{s}.$$

That is one tiny time step!

Most engines have a default time step of 0.01 to 0.02 seconds. This is far larger than what is needed for a golf swing. As a result, any object carried by a person in VR is at high risk of tunneling.

These are some of the solutions to tunneling:

1. Increase object size: Make the collider object big enough to prevent tunneling. This is common where the collider is bigger than the object. However, this method doesn't work too well for movements like golf.
2. Decrease the time step: Change the default fixed update rate (edit > project settings > time > fixed time step). While this option does fix the fundamental tunneling problem, it also slows *everything* down, and many computers would not be able to keep up with the faster update rate.
3. Slow movement down: Capping the speed is also an option for this solution. The advantage is that the time steps can keep up and prevent the tunneling. The disadvantage is that some objects are meant to move fast, such as a rocket.
4. Hijack the engine for only the fast items: This has the advantage of fixing the tunneling problem for *only* the problem items and, therefore, will have less computational overhead. The disadvantage is that this method requires a much deeper understanding of the underlying physics engine. There are a couple of methods for this solution:
   • Check if the distance traveled is more than half of the smallest intersectable object, and then do the smaller time step until the current position is reached. This gives good physics but requires knowledge on what the smaller object is going to be and requires tuning. It is also still more computationally expensive.
   • Check a larger bounding box area made from the last update and this one, and only check items within that box in its travel area.

However, the only way to completely avoid tunneling is to ensure no time step is larger than what would allow the distance of half the smallest object in one-time step. In the golf example above, that would be 0.0008 s.

This is far too small for a real-time system such as VR. Therefore, VR applications have a few extra design considerations to help prevent tunneling situations from arising. First, it helps to keep objects larger in VR. This goes further than just for physics, as users tend to feel objects are smaller than they really are as well [1]! If possible, keeping hand interactions proximity-based eliminates the need for some physics responses. Finally, simplifying boundaries can help with the computations.

Hijacking the engine for only the problem items may be the only solution in some cases, but this requires deep understanding of the physics engine, how collision detection works, and the underlying mesh that makes up the models.

Reference

[1] Rebenitsch LR, Owen CB, Coburn S. "World and object designs for virtual environments". *Meaningful Play*, 2014 Conference proceedings, East Lansing, MI, USA. Hosted by Michigan State University.

4

Multiple System Interaction Frameworks

This chapter gives an overview of the interaction methods in virtual reality (VR) and then describes a framework to handle the varying VR controller input options across headsets. Specific interactions development is discussed in Chapter 5. The general topics here are basic interactions categories, viable interaction design for both three dimensions and VR, and structure for long-term use/maintainability.

Basic Interaction Types

At the most basic level, there are a limited number of interaction modalities for digital systems:

- Verbal commands
- Position (e.g., mouse or gesture)
- Key/button press/release

Any other form of interaction is built on these interactions. There are several standard combinations that are often categorized as a single interaction type with dedicated names. These interaction paradigms have developed over time to meet both hardware restrictions and ease of use. For example, a mouse drag is a very common interaction method that uses a combination of a specific set of buttons for press/release and positional data. It is sufficiently common to be considered its own interaction rather than a description of a sequence of buttons and positional data.

When changing from desktop to three-dimensional (3D) and 3D to VR, the earlier paradigms generally still hold. These paradigms have developed over time and breaking them will tend to make the application very difficult to use. Early systems, particularly in VR, often attempted to see if these two-dimensional (2D) paradigms were still needed. Menus were removed or gestures were attempted with no other input. With some exceptions, menus quickly returned and often in 2D format, no less. Drag and drop still exists, but camera movement is an addition in a 3D setting with the expected orientation control being on the right joystick and translation control on the left joystick. Key, or button, responses are still heavily used. Menus and "pointing to" selection come from older systems as well.

A Practical Introduction to Virtual Reality. https://doi.org/10.1016/B978-0-443-14036-5.00004-2

This chapter begins with an overview of a common paradigm that builds on the desktop setting and the input data types that a developer can expect. The changes in the new setting are also outlined. This is used to develop good interaction frameworks that allow use across different systems, which allows for better access to the developer's application.

3D Interaction and Input Types

Interaction methods in 3D typically use almost all desktop paradigms with a few additions due to the added dimension. The exception to this rule is the loss of some key options. When switching to a console controller, a full qwerty keyboard is lost. However, the paradigms of "do X on key press" and drag and drop still hold. This is simply a change in the standard choice of buttons to trigger, such an interaction change due to the change in the input device.

Just like the change from desktop to 3D kept certain paradigms, the change from 3D to VR also keeps the core paradigms from 3D. The main difference in VR is that there are some new additions due to more input dimensions. Like the shift from desktop to 3D, VR also simply narrows the control of some of these paradigms, such as camera orientation control, which is now almost exclusively down to head gestures. However, VR does add some of its own core paradigms, such as throw and two-handed interactions, that are less feasible in 3D but come naturally in VR.

Support for interaction combinations vary, but the input data type is usually more stable. When switching from desktop, the range of input data type changes. In desktop, values are usually limited to Boolean (is the button up or down) and integers/float for mouse movement. The controls of 3D and VR expand on that. The main input types and where they are present in 3D, which are also included in VR systems, are

- Boolean: button down/up
- Float
  - Mouse movement
  - Joystick
  - Smooth trigger
- 2D Vector in the range [–1,1]
  - Joystick
  - Positional tracking
- 3D Vector (often VR only)
  - Positional data

The exact input type can vary. An example of this is the joystick input, which can be used as either a float or vector type. Vectors can also be split according to the axis of movement (Fig. 4.1).

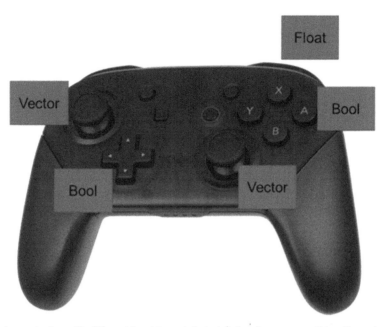

Fig. 4.1 Example of a controller with different input types labeled. (https://commons.wikimedia.org/wiki/File: Nintendo-Switch-Pro-Controller-FL.jpg.)

Handling Different Input Sources

Designing an application for both 3D and VR has a distinct advantage. There is a much higher number of 3D consoles than VR headsets, which means that supporting both VR and 3D is good for sales and development. Because there are only a few paradigms that do not shift between VR and 3D very well, designing for both is usually a reasonable option.

The challenges occur in areas where there is not an overlap, but often some added guidance in the interaction still allows for both to be supported. Throwing is a good example. Many 3D games have throwing in that a button click will result in an item being thrown. But the direction is restricted to the direction the player is facing, making the interaction close to just a plain button click. VR does not have that restriction and allows the user to pick whichever direction. 3D throw has help; VR does not.

Moreover, there are some challenges in using current VR interactions with direct mapping from button to event:

- VR is more difficult to debug.
- VR cannot easily support more than one system.
- VR cannot easily support changes in input preferences (3D example: choosing between space for jump or Z for jump).
- Input/reaction combinations are difficult to chain.

Some of these issues are becoming less troublesome as VR matures. OpenXR greatly aided in supporting different systems, but differences in button availability and even axis of control still exist. The difference in button availability is also why changes in input preferences are still troublesome. Trouble with chaining reactions is due to the triple proximity areas of the head, left hand, and right hand. There are more edges than before. For example, let's say that an interaction uses a left trigger and then a right trigger plus one proximity area. Which proximity area needs to be active?

A design solution for these challenges is to use best practices. Best practices take substantial upfront coding but then save a substantial time in the long run. In VR, best practices for interaction frameworks involve a combination pattern derived from the Observer (specialized callbacks), MVC (model-view-controller), and Mediator patterns For a deep dive on the original patterns consider Design Pattern: Elements of Reusable Object-Oriented Software by Gamma et. al. [1].

This section covers the structure of best practices, starting with an overview of two patterns used in the combination pattern. Once the patterns are defined, they are built up into the handler for VR interactions. This includes

- separating and registering event functions to and from input, and
- separating the device from input, making a class per input type and forwarding filtered data.

These best practices are starting to be integrated into mature game engines. Both Unreal and Unity now have Input Action assets. To best explain how these work, this chapter will begin with the interaction framework. The chapter ends with an example of building a button handler step-by-step.

The Observer Pattern

The Observer pattern attempts to answer the question, "How can the code monitor changes in the model?" It is extremely easy to forget to update a portion of the program that is dependent on a change event. The key issue that the Observer tries to solve is that an object needs to know about the change event, but it is not helpful to check for every single instance.

The pattern aims to resolve this issue by announcing that the model has changed to the designated "viewers." In this case, viewer means any observer, such as an online database. For our purposes, the viewers are any items that are affected if an input state is changed.

A major component of the Observer pattern is the callback. Callback is simply a function that is registered to be called on some event (Fig. 4.2).

Fig. 4.2 A conceptual explanation of a callback in tempo. (CC BY-SA 3.0 What is a callback? Post by cam, https://stackoverflow.com/questions/2139812/what-is-a-callback.)

The Observer pattern has three interrelated components (Fig. 4.3):
- Subjects—the item or items to be watched
- Observers—the items that are affected by changes in the subjects
- Callback—the function used to communicate changes in the subjects to the observers

The observer pattern has two key functions: (1) a notify function that should be called when the data have changed; its job is to notify all interested parties something happened, and (2) an update function that is called back when the data have changed.

The steps to create the Observer pattern in code are
- Make the observer and subject.
- Let the observer register with the subject.
- Run the callback when an event occurs.

An example of this in pseudocode, if there is no built-in language support, is

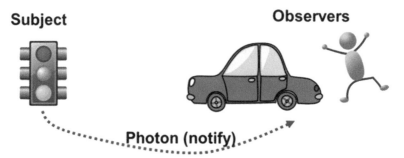

Subject

Observers

Photon (notify)

Fig. 4.3 A drawn example of the Observer pattern occurring in real life. Both cars and pedestrians (observers) watch for changes in the streetlight signal (subject). The signal change is transferred by the streetlight emitting photons in different colors (callback). (Created from https://openclipart.org/image/2400px/svg_to_png/195159/Traffic-light-icon. png and https://openclipart.org/detail/21980/toy-car.)

Subject

```
class Subject
  Observer[] viewers
  someData

  // registration and de-registration
  function AttachObserver( Observer o )
    viewer.Add(o)
    o.SetSubject( this )

  function DetachObserver( Observer o )
    viewer.Remove(o)

  // some editing function
  function DoSomething()
    someData.Foo()
    NotifyAll()

  // tell all observers
  function NotifyAll()
    for v in viewers
        v.Update( someData )
```

Observer

```
class Observer
  Subject subject

  function Update( someData )
  // … do something with someData
```

```
// registration, and reference to subject if needed
  function Detach()
    subject.DetachObserver( this )

  function SetSubject()
    o.SetSubject( this )
```

Callback Uses

```
// (1) make everything
Subject subject
Observer a
Observer b

// (2) register
subject.AttachObserver( a )
subject.AttachObserver( b )

// (3) edit data, and trust that the observers will be notified
subject.DoSomething();
```

> *The observer pattern, like many patterns, initially feel like excess work and complicated bouncing around. However, the alternative is a tremendous amount of special casing and even harder travel up and down the scene tree. Instead, the observer pattern is saying "trust me to notify you when something changes." and "trust me" is a scary thing for coders.*

Trace through the Callback Use code above and see what happens. At (1), an object that needs monitoring is made along with two objects that can be notified. At (2), the subject is told that these two observers should be notified if its data changes. At (3), the subject does some tasks that changes its data. Internally, the subject must remember to notify all its observers that it changed. The observer then is able to do what it needs to adjust to the data change. Many languages have a built-in form of this pattern. This includes Java and C#. Some languages also have an event data type that wraps most of the above in a clean fashion. The appendix has more details on the event data type, if desired.

The Mediator Pattern

The Mediator pattern is used when a number of callers are present and these callers may use different systems. Instead of building a unique class to link for each pair of callers, the pattern uses a "mediator" to standardize the links (Fig. 4.4).

This pattern is needed to handle the different types of inputs (keys versus buttons) and directs them to the classes that need to respond to said inputs.

Building the Handler

At a high level, a good interaction framework is that of the Observer pattern watching the input device subject and sending a

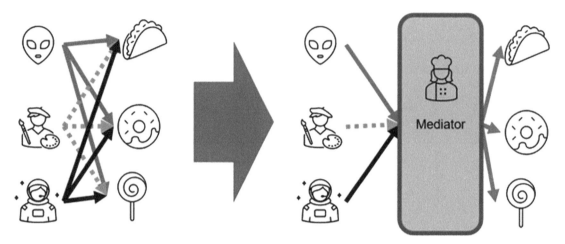

Fig. 4.4 Example structure of the Mediator pattern. The caller and data objects are linked by a standardized mediator (the chef) object.

callback or, in this case, forwarding, to the action. This action in turn is being watched and will send a callback to interested functions. Therefore, we have a double observer, being mediated by a central class. Another way to look at it is a C# style dictionary mapping from input to an action and then that action to a function.

This structure allows for expanding the input devices and resulting reactions. For example, if a new device is to be added, only the input device object requires updating. If the response needs to be changed, only the action object requires updating.

It may seem strange to have so many class transitions before our code for the effect. So, let us start with what we want to do and then identify maintenance issues with it until we are in a stable state.

Suppose our task is to perform a jump when a space is detected. A naïve solution to this may be something like this, which is largely how input has been handled so far:

```
class InputMapper
  function Update()
    if SpaceIsDown
      character.Jump()

  function Jump()
  character.ApplyUpwardsForce()
```

Here, we are checking the input state explicitly and then forwarding to the action object to generate a response. The method is error prone as the link to the response has been added manually. If something else needs to know if the space has been pressed, we need to add it in the Update function. That breaks the Open-Closed (O) principle in SOLID and causes maintenance issues whenever there is a new jump.

To fix this, we need to add a layer that holds all the jump functions that need to be called on space down. By doing this, the Observer pattern begins to appear.

```
class InputMapper
  ObjectsThatCareAboutJump actions[]

  function Update()
    if SpaceIsDown
      for a in actions
        a.Jump()

  function RegisterJump( Object o )
    actions.Add( o )

class Character
  function RegisterJump()
    InputMapper.RegisterJump( this )

  function Jump()
    ApplyUpwardsForce()
```

This version still has a restriction. What happens if there is a new event, like move? InputMapper would need to be reopened to add that, which would break O in SOLID. To fix this, the code needs to allow outside classes to state what they need, not have InputMapper control it. This updates the code to have input to function pair (Fig. 4.5):

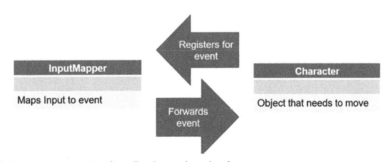

Fig. 4.5 Visual of class structure state after allowing registration for events.

```
class InputMapper
  Pair[ inputName, func ] actions[]

  function Update()
    for a in actions
      if a.inputName occurred
        a.func()

  function Register( String inputName, Object o )
    actions.Add( inputName, o )

class Character
  function RegisterJump()
    InputMapper.Register( "space down", this.Jump )

  function RegisterMove()
    InputMapper.Register( "rightArrow down", this.Move )

  function Jump()
    ApplyUpwardsForce()

  function Move()
    ApplyMoveForce()
```

This version is missing personalization options. There are many different keys that could be jump! Space, Z, and W are all common keys for jump. This will quickly happen if we want to support a console or VR as the buttons are not the same! Adding personalization options requires adding another layer between input-action pairs. That gives us the beginning of the Mediator.

```
class InputMapper
  Pair[ inputName, eventName ] events[]
  Pair[ eventName, func ] actions[]

  function Update()
    for e in events
      if e.inputName occurred
        for a in actions
          if a.eventName == e.EventName
            a.Func()

  function Register( String inputName, Object o )
    actions.Add( inputName, o )

class Character
  function RegisterEvents()
    InputMapper.Register( "jump", this.Jump )
```

```
    InputMapper.Register( "move", this.move )

  function Jump()
    ApplyUpwardsForce()

  function Move()
    ApplyMoveForce()
```

You can see the double mapping from the input to the event name, and then from the event name to the function. One last step remains: registering the event with the action (Fig. 4.6).

```
class InputMapper
  // other functions and variables are unchanged

  function RegisterAction( String inputName, String eventName )
    events.Add( inputName, eventName )

class Character
  // prior code is unchanged

class DeviceInput
  function RegisterActions()
    events.Add( "space down", "jump" )
```

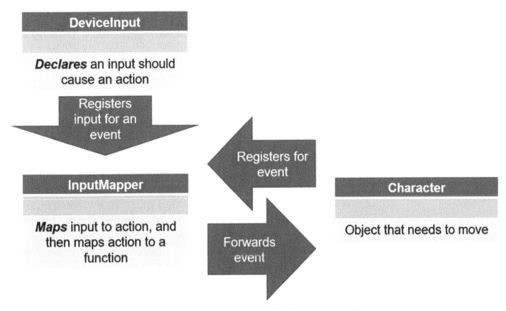

Fig. 4.6 Visual of class structure state after allowing registration for events and inputs.

Now, the mediator is complete. There is still an issue here that the pseudocode hid. We will not want InputMapper to know how to test for all events; that really should be the job of DeviceInputs. This will take just a little refactoring to make DeviceInput filter its desired input and forward it to Input Mapper's handler:

```
class InputMapper
  function Update( String inputName )
    for e in events
      if e.inputName == inputName
        for a in actions
          if a.eventName == e.EventName
            a.Func()

  // other functions and variables are unchanged

class Character
  // other functions are unchanged

class DeviceInput
  InputMapper handler

  function Update()
    if input is identified
      handler.Update( input.name )

  // other functions are unchanged
```

Thus, we have three classes to make this maintainable. When coding to support both a console and VR, this allows us to make a DeviceInput class for both VR and a controller, but for InputMapper our functions for our events remain unchanged!

InputMappers will largely support only the requested types of event combinations. The device's job is to format the state into the supported event combination. There are a couple of options for designing the InputMapper:

- Figure out all the combos you could possibly want and add them to the mapper—for example, OnDown, OnUp, etc. This has better clarity but limits extensibility.
- Make a top-level mapper, then make individual combos, and add them to the list. This has better extensibility, but it is easy to write a conflicting combo.

Most systems use a mix of these options. Events, such as OnButtonDown, are usually premade and mostly in the filter. Common events, such as collisions and proximity events, may have their own call-back. Specialty events, such as a two-handed grab, can be added later.

Test Your Understanding 4.1

Let's build a button handler/manager in pseudocode. Before writing any pseudocode, there are some questions that need to be asked:

1. What kinds of button events are allowed?
2. How does a device register to the filter?
3. How does an object register for the event?
4. How is more than one device handled?
5. How are subcategories or chains of events delineated, such as right-handed versus left-handed, handled (or how is the hotkey, ctrl + C combination, handled)?

Answering these questions gives the steps to develop the button handler. We will go through the questions individually.

1 What kinds of button events are allowed?

There are a large number of possibilities for button events. For now, let's assume a starting set of common button events:

- OnDown (buttonID)
- OnUp (buttonID)
- IsDown (buttonID)

This helps limit all of our input names and makes it easier to ensure the event is supported. For example, let's look at before the code allows for input strings of "A on down." After the change to restrict to some kinds of event, this becomes "A" with enum "OnDown." The advantage of the type check is clarity in purpose. The disadvantage of the type check is that adding different event types later becomes harder.

InputMapper is first refactored to use the new format. The larger differences are highlighted in the code. Rather than a single Update() function, it is separated into the subcategories of down, up, and held down. To avoid copypasting the check in action, it is separated into its own Notify function for each button event to call as needed.

```
// structure to aid in registering key events
enum EventType = { OnDown, OnUp, IsDown }
class EventCombo
  EventType event
  Key key

class InputMapper
  Pair[ eventName, func ] actions[]
  Pair[ EventCombo, eventName ] events[]

  function OnDown( Key k )
    // checks if the event list has this key and event type
    for e in events
      if e.combo.EventType == EventType.OnDown
        if e.combo.key == k
          // found a match! Run update
          Notify( e.eventName )
```

Continued

```
function OnUp()
   // same as OnDown, but filters on OnUp

function IsDown()
   // same as OnDown, but filters on IsDown

function Notify( eventName )
   // if this event has a callback, run it
   for a in actions
      if a.eventType == eventName
         a.Func()
```

2 How does a device register to the filter?

This task can be completed by creating a reference in the device code to the InputMapper filter. After this, events can notify the InputMapper on detection, which primarily occurs in Update().

```
class DeviceInput
   InputMapper filter
   Pair[key, boolean] keyState[]

   constructor Device()
      // add and set all keys states to false

   function OnUpdate()
      for k in keyState
         // find what event type it is, if any
         if GetKey( k.key ) == false && keyState[ k.key ] == true
            filter.OnDown( k.key )

         else if GetKey( k.key ) == true && keyState[ k.key ] == false
            filter.OnUp( k.key )

         else if GetKey( k.key ) == true && keyState [ k.key ] == true
            filter.IsDown( k.key )

         // update state of key for next frame
         keyState[ k.key ] = GetKey( k.key )
```

Where to register is system dependent. Some systems support a search method, while others allow for direct settings. Because OnDown/Up is not always available, these events need to be monitored. If converting the pseudocode into working code, the code can be checked by setting a break point.

3 How does an object register for the event?

This is similar to registering the devices, except the filter now holds the references. The InputMapper pseudocode now becomes the following:

```
// structure to aid in registering key events
enum EventType = { OnDown, OnUp, isDown }
class EventCombo
```

```
    EventType event
      Key key

class InputMapper
  Pair[ eventName, func ] actions[]
  Pair[ EventCombo, eventName ] events[]

   function OnDown( Key k )
      // checks if the event list has this key and event type
      for e in events
         if e.combo.EventType == EventType.OnDown
           if e.combo.key == k)
             // found a match! Run update
             Notify( e.eventName )

   function OnUp()
      // same as OnDown, but filters on OnUp

   function IsDown()
      // same as OnDown, but filters on isDown

   function Notify( eventName )
      // if this event has a callback, run it
      for a in actions
        if a.eventType == eventName
          a.Func()

   function Register( String eventName, function o )
     actions.Add( eventName, o )

class Character

   function Register()
     f = FindInputMapper()
     f.Register("foo", this.Foo)

   function Foo()
     // do something
```

At this point, everything appears to be connected. However, if this is converted to code and run, the action is never called. This is because there is no mapping from events to actions. So, where should the mapping go? The device's job is to collect input and to format as needed. Mapping does not go there. The object's job is to run actions when needed. Mapping does not go there either. That leaves the filter as the place to put the mapping, except this requires adding new functionality that affects existing code in the InputMapper class. That violates O in SOLID. As a result, the mapping does not fit in any of the previously created objects, which means that combination mapping gets its own class.

```
class InputMapper
  Pair[ eventName, function ] actions[]
  Pair[ EventCombo, eventName ] events[]
```

Continued

```
// ...prior functions and variables

function RegisterAction( EventCombo c, String name )
  actions.Add( c, name )

class Character
  function register()
    f = FindInputMapper()
    f.Register("foo", this.foo)

  function Foo()
    // do something

class ComboMapping
  function AddMap()
    name = GetName()
    combo = GetEventCombo()
    f = FindInputMapper()
    f.RegisterAction( combo, name )
```

Now the events are forwarded. Here are the steps for the forwarding so far:

- A device event occurs.
- The device sends the event to the mapper.
- The filter checks if any actions are connected to the event.
- If true, the filter looks up all the available actions and forwards the event to those actions.

4 How is more than one device handled?

How multiple devices are handled depends on the desired result. If only one device is used at a time, the different DeviceInput classes are swapped. If all devices can be used at once, then another Device object is added. In this case, we will assume a combination of buttons from different VR devices. The update function between VR buttons and the keyboard is highly similar. The near-identical code is highlighted to show the similarities.

The main difference is that VR has the extra challenge of the device availability being unstable. This means there is a potential set of input devices rather than a single keyboard. After adding and removing the devices as needed, the rest of the pseudocode runs about the same after being converted to code. However, this does not differentiate which controller is in which hand.

```
class ControllerButtons
  VRController device
  Pair[ button, Boolean ] buttonState[]

class VRDevice
  InputMapper filter
  ControllerButtons controllers[]

  function OnDeviceConnect( VRController c )
    temp = ControllerButtons()
    temp.device = c
```

```
    SetButtonstoFalse( temp.buttonState )
    controllers.Add(temp)

function OnDeviceDisconnect( XRController c )
    controllers.Remove(c)

function OnUpdate()
    for c in controllers
        for k in c.buttonState
            // find what event type it is, if any
            if GetKey( k.button ) == false && keyState[ k.button ] == true
                filter.OnDown( k.button )

            if GetKey( k.button ) == true && keyState[ k.button ] == false
                filter.OnUp( k.button )

            if GetKey( k.button ) == true && keyState[ k.button ] == true
                filter.IsDown( k.button )

            // update state of key for next frame
            keyState[k.button] = GetKey( k.button )
```

5 How are subcategories or chains of events delineated, such as right-handed versus left-handed, handled (or how is the hotkey, ctrl + C combination, handled)?

There are a couple of common methods to handle delineation:

- Make a list of all required, simultaneous true states that are allowed for events and add to the combination data structure. To support sequences instead of simultaneous states, a class is required to check and return true when the sequence conditions are met.
- Forward the events with all of these parameters and let each function in the chain decide.

Which method to use is context sensitive. For the button handler, let's allow for all button combinations. This is the complete version:

```
enum EventType = { OnDown, OnUp, isDown }
class EventCombo
    EventType event
    Modifier m[]
    Key key
    boolean active

class InputMapper
    Pair[ eventName, function ] actions[]
    Pair[ EventCombo[], eventName ] events[]

    function OnDown( Key k )
        for e in events
            if e.combo.EventType == EventType.OnDown
                if e.combo.key == k
                    Notify( e.eventName )

    function OnUp()
        //same as OnDown, but filters on OnUp
```

Continued

```
function IsDown()
  // same as OnDown, but filters on IsDown

function Notify(EventType type)
  for a in actions
    if a.eventType == type
      a.Func()

function Register( String eventName, function o )
  actions.Add( eventName, o )

function RegisterAction( EventCombo[] c, String name )
  actions.Add( c, name )

class Character
  function Register()
    f = FindInputMapper()
    f.Register( "foo", this.foo )

  function Foo()
    // do something

class ComboMappingHelper

  function AddMap()
    name = GetName()
    combo = GetEventCombo()
    combo2 = GetEventComboWithModifier()
    f = FindInputMapper()
    f.RegisterAction( combo, name )

  function GetEventComboWithModifier()
    Event Combo c
    c.event = GetEventType() // e.g. isDown
    c.key = GetKey()         // e.g. Ctrl
    while more modifiers
      c.m.Add( GetModifier() ) // e.g. IsCapitalized
    return c
```

Essentially, anything that requires more than one item is allowed an array. When running the confirmation check with this pseudocode, all possible states must be true.

Not all interaction combinations have been added yet. There is one missing: proximity.

A common interaction combination in both 3D and VR is proximity plus a button or snap placement. The challenge here, like the mapping in the handler example above, is where does this combination go? The mapper knows what combinations are needed to trigger an event. However, the proximity object knows the position of the player. The proximity combination can go in the Character class because the object was already registering for events.

Let's start with a proximity enter/exit event. In this case, proximity is registered when the player is sufficiently close to an object. The needed data to register this event are

- The maximum distance from the object to respond
- A list of close objects

- A way to register an object to a tracked item
- A way to unregister an object to a tracked item

```
class Character
  function Register()
    // permanent registration
    f = FindInputMapper()
    f.Register( "foo", this.Foo )

  function OnCollisionEnter( Object other )
    // in range, ask for callbacks
    if object == player
      f = FindInputMapper()
      f.Register("goo", this.Goo)

  function OnCollisionEnter(Object other)
    // out of range range, remove request for callbacks
    if object == player
      f = FindInputMapper()
      f.Deregister("goo", this.Goo)

  function Foo()
    // do something
  function Goo()
    // do something
```

This is very close to the Character class earlier. It still does not restrict to the controller, but that restriction can be added with an optional condition upon registering.

Another item to keep in mind is that if the same function is used across several objects, it's helpful to separate out that code. This allows for repeat action to be centralized and for the user to select an action from a given list rather than depending on correct typing, if that is helpful. The new class also gives a good place to put interaction helpers, such as outlines.

```
class Character
  function Register()
    f = FindInputMapper()
    f.Register( "foo", this.Foo)

  function Foo()
    // do something

class Proximity
  Object obj

  constructor Proximity()
    obj = FindProximityObject()

  function OnCollisionEnter( Object other )
    if object == player
      f = FindInputMapper()
      f.Register( "goo", this.Goo )
```

Continued

```
function OnCollisionEnter( Object other )
  if object == player
    f = FindInputMapper()
    f.Deregister( "goo", this.Goo )

function Goo()
  // do something with obj
```

Top-Level Organization of Interactions

After going through all of the interaction options and best practices, it is helpful to stop and take a top-level view of how to design an interaction scheme for an application. In general, any VR application must allow for

- Different device input
- Input to be filtered and mapped to actions
- Actions forwarded to the objects that respond

This means that there should be a minimum of three different classes. For more complex interactions, such as a two-button interaction or a left-hand-only button interaction, the information needs to be bundled in a useful way. At the high level, the interactions are organized as in Fig. 4.7.

VR engines do offer some built-in options for interactions with some caveats. In Unity, for example, proximity filters are not directly supported but can be worked around. Combination interactions are

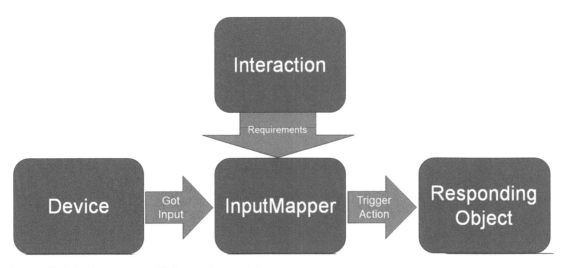

Fig. 4.7 High-level structure for VR interactions and classes.

supported, but sequence interaction is not. If the device is unique, the developer will need to create the interactions. If a custom gesture is required, a custom interaction will need to be developed.

Reference

[1] Gamma E, Helm R, Johnson R, Vlissides J. *Design Patterns: Elements of Reusable Object-Oriented Software*. Addison Wesley; 1994. ISBN 0-201-63361-2.

5

Virtual Reality Interactions

This chapter gives an overview of the available interaction methods in virtual reality (VR). The general topics are viable interaction design for both three-dimensional (3D) and VR applications, basic interactions categories, common code patterns for interactions, and template interactions.

Good Practices for Interaction Options

Because standardized and good practices for interaction options influence how the interactions are implemented, it's important to understand how interactions can work either with or against the user. It is difficult to overstate the power of familiarity with interactions even if the interaction may be, objectively, bad. Therefore, this chapter discusses common interaction paradigms and good practices specific to VR to aid in ergonomics and usability.

Some interactions overlap with 3D applications but often have additional considerations in VR. The chapter begins with an overview of the base interactions and ergonomics and usability in VR. Then, how to develop different interactions are discussed, building from old 3D paradigms to mostly VR-specific interaction paradigms.

Shifting From 3D to VR Interactions Paradigms

Interaction methods in 3D are typically derived from common desktop paradigms with a few additional items due to the added dimension of input. The exception to this rule is when a controller is used, which will restrict the number of buttons, so full-textual input is unwieldy. These additional interaction paradigms that are built up from the base desktop interactions include

- Button tap
- Grab
- Drop
- Camera control
- Proximity event
- Select from menu
- Point

Unity formally released their XR interaction kit in 2024, and there is some minor support built into Unreal. At a high level Unity's framework structure is similar to what is presented in this chapter. Understanding how this works allows for simultaneous 3D and VR support, and extensions when the base framework is not sufficient.

A Practical Introduction to Virtual Reality. https://doi.org/10.1016/B978-0-443-14036-5.00005-4

As an example of progression from desktop to 3D, consider "drag and drop." This is common in desktop, and is still common as "grab and drop" in 3D.

Just like the change from desktop to 3D kept certain paradigms, the change from 3D to VR also keeps the core paradigms from 3D. All of the above interaction paradigms are present in VR, with some new additional ones due to more input dimensions, such as hand tracking. However, like the shift from a desktop to a console controller, there is some narrowing in button input as well. For example, VR camera control is now almost exclusively done by head gestures.

Most paradigms in 3D shift well into VR with the caveat that there is more sensitivity in VR. One of the main differences between VR interaction and 3D interaction is that VR has multiple, fine-grained, tracked positions. This yields a few extra VR-only paradigms in bold below:

- Button tap
- Grab
- Drop
- **Throw**
- Camera control (head controlled)
- **Proximity (x3)**
- Point
- **Two-handed grab**

With the exception of the bolded elements, providing support for both console and VR are reasonably attainable. The challenges occur in the bold text interactions where there is not a direct overlap, but often some added guidance in the interaction still allows for both to be supported. Throwing is a good example. Many 3D games have throwing, in that a button click will result in an item being thrown. But the direction is restricted to the direction of a joystick's disputable direction indicator, making the interaction close to just a plain button click in the direction the player is facing. VR does not have this restriction and allows the user to pick a direction based on natural hand movements. 3D throw has help; VR does not. Shifting proximity and two-handed grab from VR to 3D take a bit more work. VR also has its own ergonomic and usability concerns.

Prominent VR Categories Differences

Of the listed basic interactions, proximity, pointing, and two-handed grab require some notable differences in approach from 3D console systems. Proximity includes grabbing with two-handed interaction being a special case. While pointing is still pointing, the effect of distance in VR has some effect.

Proximity Category

The biggest difference between 3D and VR interactions is that 3D has one interaction zone while VR has three. To shift proximity-based interaction in VR to 3D, either all three of the zones are merged into one or the interaction is shifted from "zone + specified button events" to non-intersecting separate events (Fig. 5.1). Consider an instance where the left and right hands are considered separately. In VR this occurs naturally with the "hand zone." In 3D, there is a "mode switch" to separate the events.

The additional areas allow for fine tuning grab and drop interactions that would otherwise not be possible. Holding different items in both hands becomes much easier in VR, but this also means users tend to expect it!

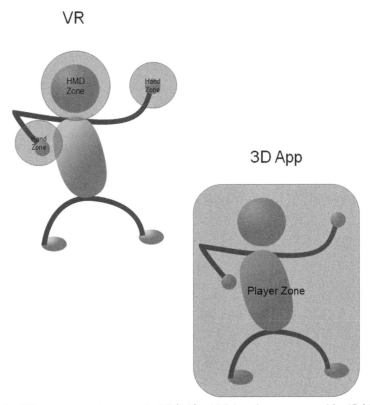

Fig. 5.1 Drawing of the different interaction zones for VR (left), which has three zones, and for 3D (right), which has one zone.

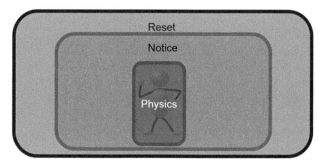

Fig. 5.2 Three collision areas.

Fig. 5.3 Detection in a 90° arc in front of the AI character.

Multiple Collider Proximity Interaction

Standard collisions fall into two categories: physics and trigger events. The challenge is when there is more than one type of trigger event. This isn't the same as the strategy or the visitor patterns where multiple classes interact to determine one event. In this case, there is one object or pair of objects that have different events depending on the context.

Consider a common application element where something becomes active if the player becomes close and inactive when the player leaves at an even further distance (Fig. 5.2). Combine this with physics, and we have three different events, all based on the proximity of the player!

Another common example in VR is the grab area versus the hand's physical area. In general, the area that a user is allowed to grab is much larger than their hands. However, to allow a hand to push open a door, a second collision area is needed that is fitted to the hands properly.

Both Unity and Unreal support multiple colliders. This allows different colliders to achieve different responses. Having multiple layers of collision is fairly common. The complex environment in games usually has a simplified structure for collisions compared to the level of detail that is seen.

Game engines' support for collision volumes can vary greatly. For the most complex response areas, rays may be needed. In this case, first, figure out the volume, and then shoot enough rays to guarantee a hit (Fig. 5.3). Combinations of volumes and rays to narrow the response are common, since a volume check can be faster. Consider an item behind a column. In this case, a volume is used to indicate whether an item is near enough to be of interest, and a ray is used to confirm if the item is in the line of sight.

Different systems will have different methods for handling multiple collision layers. Unity and Unreal can place additional colliders in children, or even within the same object, and then notify the main class for the character. Using purely the ray technique avoids this.

Usability Concerns

Shifting from 3D to VR for grabbing and dropping uses largely the same code but now there are two areas that can grab. That means there are multiple instances of the Grab code. However, the grab areas are usually much smaller than in 3D due to improved tracking with one caveat. Users typically underestimate distances in VR, so expect to pad areas to 50% to 100% [1,3]. As an example, if a hand is around 15 centimeters long, double that for ease of use.

In the case of throwing, changing to VR is the simpler task in some ways. If starting in VR and shifting to 3D, expect that a throwing "mode" will be needed to aid in choosing a direction.

The challenge when throwing in VR is that releasing from the controller may not be a completely natural movement as the controller must still be held. Users often feel there is no strength to their throwing, so adding a bit extra force to the release object is common.

Pointing

The ability to point and select is as important in VR as in 3D applications. The main difference here is that menus are usually no longer statically positioned and selectable items are in "real space." The challenges of placing menus are discussed in Chapter 6. However, there are pointing tasks not related to menus that have some unexpected usability concerns. The primary cause is that humans in general are not very good at estimating distances. Put a long thin stick in someone's hand in real life, and many would still have difficulty telling you if the stick is long enough to reach a specified point. Combine that will some loss in visual parallax and quality in VR, and straight pointers can feel unresponsive if the pointer simply does not reach the selectable item!

As a result, pointing in VR requires notable feedback to determine if the pointer has reached. There are several common techniques here. Highlighting in some fashion is common and is relatively easy to code. However, a long pointer still feels like carrying an extremely long stick, so reserving straight pointing to shorter distances like menus is preferred. Parabolas are commonly used in more modern systems due to the arc allowing easier identification of where the line ends. However, that, too, can require higher levels of fine motor control, which means they work best when narrow selection is not needed. An older, but less used, technique is to have a type of virtual hand where the distance is mapped to a nonlinear function. As the user reaches out, the hand gains greater distance. Because this is a 3D object, it is a bit easier for the user to identify relative distance, but this still only works in moderate ranges.

Two-Handed Grab Category

The two-handed grab is one of the most complex interactions in VR and is also the hardest to translate back into 3D interactions. To shift the interaction to 3D, the interaction has to be essentially shifted into an orientation/manipulation-type mode (Fig. 5.4).

There are a few additional subcategories of two-handed interactions. There are button combos that just happen to use both hands. This is simpler to map to 3D in that the interaction involves just two buttons down. Then there are interactions that just happen to be two-handed. This is like playing a guitar. The handle is in one hand, and brushing the strings to make a sound can be in the other. However, the sound still occurs even if the guitar is not held and the strings are touched. In 3D, this would need added help in that picking up the guitar would require placement relative to the player in code rather than being manipulated in real time by the user's hand.

Fig. 5.4 An example of VR interaction using two-handed grab to use a map.

Ergonomics

VR has a few additional ergonomic considerations, but there are two main ergonomic issues that are especially important to consider during development: gorilla arm and tactile feedback.

First, VR allows for a much larger range of motion, including arm motion. It may be tempting to add numerous gestures, but there are limitations to how much motion is helpful in longer use times. Motion that requires keeping the arms out is tiring. This is called "gorilla arm" due to the amount of strength required to maintain the motion.

In general, it's best to avoid gestures beyond typical motion in real life. Occasional pointing is acceptable, but sustained outreaching is not. In a situation requiring more sustained motion, restrict to forearm motion (Fig. 5.5) [2].

Second, while VR allows for greater interaction, tactile feedback is still limited, especially in the form of hand motion. Arcing motion is particularly difficult as this motion usually uses a push/pull pressing motion with notable pressure in the hand to indicate the distance that is not available in VR. Try moving a level in real life in a perfect arch such that the pressure remains at one point on the hand. It is very difficult! But, that is what the needs are in VR for this motion.

In general, it helps to restrict to linear motion whenever possible. Adding haptics or vibration can help, but those options are not full solutions. During play, most users will pause on collision if the

Comfort ranges

Acceptable

Ideal (not much past the shoulders)

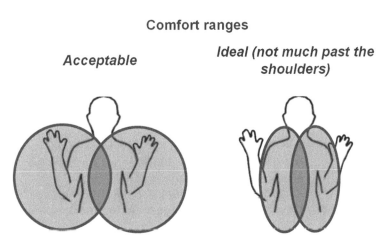

Fig. 5.5 Example of motion comfort ranges for extended VR use with the motion areas centered around the elbows. The left figure shows the acceptable range for short motions. The right figure shows the acceptable range for more sustained motion. (https://2.bp.blogspot.com/-PEw4R-XXfjE/UIOwZn6vOfI/AAAAAAAACW8/egT5cciXLcs/s1600/Outline-body.png.)

collision (a) is sufficiently slow and (b) has both a visual stop and a vibration. The typical VR options for vibrations are

- Left/right controllers
- Strength
- Duration

These options should be used judiciously as too much vibration can backfire. If vibrations are too heavily used, they lose their meaning and novelty. This is formally called repetition suppression. The insidious consequence of repetition suppression is when a user fails to notice something and the temptation to add more of the notification arises. What happens instead is that the brain decreases interest in the stimuli even further! Instead, notifications like vibration needs to match expectations. To give some examples of this, think about the needed vibration for the following scenarios:

- Earthquake
- Hammer strike
- Riding a horse

Each scenario requires determining where the vibration needs to take place, how strong, and for how long. An earthquake will be on both hands (and head if allowed), have strong strength, and last a few seconds. Compare that to a hammer strike, which will be one hand, short, and strong. A horse is in between. Both hands will be needed but the vibration will be minor to moderate, and the duration is pulsing.

Usability

Usability in VR is an active field of research. To cover all that is current in VR, user interface (UI) design would take multiple chapters and likely require substantial updates every year. Therefore, we cover a couple of UI design considerations that are more stable: selection indicators and button count.

Selection Indicators

First, one element in all UIs is to offer feedback for user input or selection. There are various options for this, but two that are commonly used are highlighting and decals.

To highlight an option for selection, simply change the color of the selected object, although more complex options are also available (Fig. 5.6).

Highlighting an object to select usually requires a selection collision. Here is some sample pseudocode for creating a collision-based highlighter.

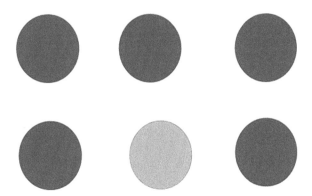

Fig. 5.6 An example of highlighting. The selected circle color was changed to yellow to show selection.

```
// A manager class for highlighting objects
class Highlight
  // A dictionary to look up an object's original color
  Pair[Object, Color] highlightedObjects

  // Make a new object-original color pair.
  // Recolor the object to the highlight color
  // Save the pair for later color reset
  function AddHighlight( Object o )
    temp = [ object, o.GetColor ]
    object.color = White
    highlightedObjects.Add( temp )

  // Find the original color of the object form the saved set
  // Recolor the object to the original color
  // Delete this pair for memory efficiency
  function RemoveHighlight( Object o )
    temp = highlightedObjects[ o ]
    o.color = temp.color
    highlightedObjects.Remove( o )

class HighlightCollider
  Highlight highlight

  constructor HighlightCollider()
    highlight = FindHighlightManagerObject()

  function OnCollisionEnter( Object o)
    hilighter.AddHighlight( o )

  function OnCollisionExit( Object o)
    hilighter.RemoveHighlight( o )
```

Decals are essentially virtual stickers. These can be any indicator that points to the object or child of the object. Because decals require

Fig. 5.7 An example of selection using decals. The left shows an arrow decal pointing to the parent box. The same selection can be achieved with a target decal placed on the parent box showing the current selection.

an orientation and position based on its target object, decals take more work than highlighting (Fig. 5.7).

Below is example pseudocode for creating and parenting a decal or a 3D arrow object to a parent:

```
function PlaceDecal( Object obj, Point p )
  normal = object.GetNormalAt( p )
  temp = MakeDecal( myDecal )  // create the decal
  myDecal.rotation.up = normal
  // place the decal a little higher than the target point
  // to avoid overlap
  myDecal.position = p + 0.01 * normal
  // make the decal a child so it moves with the object
  myDecal.parent = obj

function PlacePointer( Object obj )
  // get the world space volume of the object
  bound = object.Bounds( p )
  top = bounds.top
  center = bounds.center
  // the target point should be centered and
  // a tiny bit above the object
  p = ( center.x, top + 0.01, center.z )
  temp = makePointer( myPointer )
  // place temp assuming its origin is bottom centered
  makePointer.position = p
  // make the decal a child so it moves with the object
  makePointer.parent = obj
```

The decal position has a slight offset so that the decal and the object do not completely overlap. Overlapping can cause issues with the rendering, potentially showing the object over the decal. The pointer assumes that the bottom of the pointer is at (0,0,0). Parenting allows for the decal point to move with the object so that the position is updated at every update.

Varying Controllers

The last usability topic is button count. VR can support all of the button features of 3D applications in that most modern controllers use a similar button scheme for both VR and 3D:

- One or two bumpers per index finger
- One joystick per thumb
- Two or three menu or other option buttons

The challenge here is that there are two common differences in VR versus console controllers:

- Four buttons per thumb (console only)
- One VR grip per hand (VR only)

Some VR controllers do have additional buttons for the thumb but are often limited to just two more. Some rare console controllers do have a grip, but these are often mapped to have the same effect as other buttons on the controller. This makes designing an interaction scheme challenging in VR, especially if the application is designed to swap between 3D and VR. However, the above is not an official standardization, and some controllers can have fewer buttons. VR controllers are less standardized than console controllers which makes supporting ease of swapping interaction schemes nearly a necessity.

There is an implied restriction in the above button input being largely limited to two fingers: the thumb and the index fingers. Because the thumb has 2 degrees of freedom, each thumb can take either a joystick or a button group but can easily shift from one to the other as shown in Fig. 5.8. Index fingers have closer to 1 degree of freedom, so only two buttons are supported and often just one.

Even if the number of buttons stays the same, VR has more interaction options than 3D due to the added position input of VR. This means that not only does VR have the added option to use multiple proximity-based events but also the option to pair every button interaction with proximity.

Using all of these options may be tempting, but there is a human limit to how many interactions can be learned well at a time. Humans can learn about seven (give or take two) commands quickly. Unless already trained, that means that only five interactions can be assumed as readily learned and some will argue that number should be three. The reason for this limitation is chunking, which is a cognitive memory task [4]. Using more interactions requires additional training time or reminders.

Fig. 5.8 Example of controllers. Console controllers top row: Xbox, Switch Pro, Switch, PS5. VR controllers bottom row: Oculus Rift, Vive Cosmo, Vive wand, Oculus Go. (https://commons.wikimedia.org/wiki/File:Xbox-360-Wireless-Controller-White.jpg; https://commons.wikimedia.org/wiki/File:Nintendo-Switch-Pro-Controller-FL.jpg; https://commons.wikimedia.org/wiki/File:Nintendo_Switch_Joy-Con_Controllers.png; https://commons.wikimedia.org/wiki/File:DualShock_4.jpg; https://commons.wikimedia.org/wiki/File:Oculus-Rift-Touch-Controllers-Pair.jpg; https://commons.wikimedia.org/wiki/File:Oculus_Go_-_2.jpg.)

Event Source Consideration

Not all interaction events originate from the controller or have a direct connection with the controller. Often, there are events that require triggering from an interaction outside of the controller so the input device is not needed in these cases. In these cases, the event handling can be identical for 3D and VR development. Simple interactions may just be a function with the associated object, but more involved interactions can benefit from some OOP pattern(s).

Starting with a simple example, an event not originating from the controller would be other collisions, such as a ball bouncing on the ground. The bounce could trigger a collision sound (Fig. 5.9).

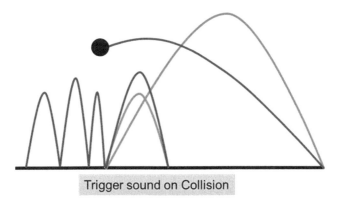

Trigger sound on Collision

Fig. 5.9 An example of an interaction event not originating from the controller: a bouncing ball.

A bouncing ball gives a simple example that can be added by merely checking for the correct collision pair and running the response as shown:

```
class MyObject

  function OnCollisionEnter( obj )
    if obj is correct kind
      obj.Foo()

  function Foo()
    // do something
```

However, this method is not very extensible. What occurs if there is one object that has multiple responses depending on what it hits? Let's illustrate with a gong example. The user has a selection of different objects to strike a gong, and each collision results in a different sound (Fig. 5.10).

We can use the action-to-function technique from the last chapter to refactor the code to allow for more flexibility. The function is still part of the object, and the action is called when needed. The information of which sound occurs with which object is stored with the gong, because the gong is common to all the interactions. However, determining what to call it is not as clear. Here is an example of the refactored code:

```
class MyObject
  function Foo()
    // do something

  function Goo()
    // do something
```

Fig. 5.10 A complex response example where a gong can be struck with different objects: a hammer, a mallet, or drumsticks. (Gong from HiltsSterre: https://media.sketchfab.com/models/0c694ee745fc46b79e4dc0f83784d041/thumb nails/82e4c8d6d492433ab414cec2fc2224db/d7212c3d3d62426a904c98661610f0ec.jpeg; Others are from open source: https://openclipart.org/detail/298644/drum-stick; https://openclipart.org/detail/196270/carpenters-mallet; https://open-clipart.org/detail/2555/hammer-3.)

```
class OtherObjectA
  function OnCollisionEnter( obj )
    if obj is MyObject
      obj.Foo()

class OtherObjectB
  function OnCollisionEnter( obj )
    if obj is MyObject
      obj.Goo()
```

This method still has a notable restriction. To make a more complex interaction, let's say that the user has not only the gong to play but also other percussion instruments (Fig. 5.11).

This is too complicated for the current interaction framework. However, this type of interaction is also very common in VR and games in general. Consider different characters responding differently to different powers in a game. This type of interaction is a very common requirement! A possible solution to this can be derived from the Visitor pattern, which is also very suitable for even more complex

Fig. 5.11 A more complex interaction pattern where the user has a selection of percussion instruments and percussion tools. (Created from https://openclipart.org/detail/298644/drum-stick; https://openclipart.org/detail/196270/carpenters-mallet; https://openclipart.org/detail/2555/hammer-3.)

cases where three or more different objects together decide the reaction.

There is yet another case where the above code would not be sufficient. Consider a snap placement of a released object. Snap placement is an in-between action that occurs after the item is released. Once the item is released, the controller is no longer involved in the interaction. This means that there are at least two potential release behaviors depending on the context. Either a normal drop occurs if outside of the snap area or the object snaps into place if the object is released within the snap area. However, there is only one release function. A possible solution to this is the Strategy pattern, which allows behaviors to be swapped out.

Let's look at these patterns in more detail.

The Visitor Pattern

The Visitor pattern is heavily used in VR and 3D applications in general. Here, a simplified version of the pattern is presented. However, if the responses require three or more objects to decide, the full pattern is better.

The Visitor's job description can be summarized as specifying how to work with different types of objects and performing type-specific operations in a type-safe way. This allows for doing interesting things with classes without modifying the classes.

Let's illustrate this through an example. A farmer has several opaque boxes. Each box contains one farm animal. The animals want to communicate with the farmer. Unfortunately, after years of operating large equipment with insufficient hearing protection, the farmer is mostly deaf. To solve the problem, a communication method needs to be created between the animals and the farmer.

This is where a special class comes in: call the visitor. The farmer hires an employee to talk to the animals. The employee is the visitor (Fig. 5.12).

The visitor is an instance of the Visitor class that can be passed to the box. An overridden function passes the visitor to the animal, who then calls a function specific to that animal type. Now, the visitor employee knows the animal type and more (Fig. 5.13).

Enabling the visitor to gather the animal information requires developing two interacting interfaces: Visitor and AcceptVisitor.

The Visitor interface contains the functions that map to the relevant types. This interface is placed in the object that can call the correct action functions.

The AcceptVisitor interface has only one function: accepting the visitor instance. This function then calls the associated function for the type.

The challenge with the Visitor pattern is that there are several moving parts and the control path is not straight forward. Let's start at

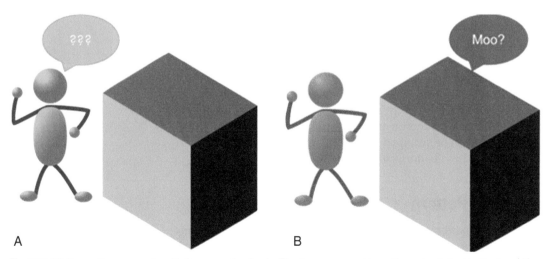

Fig. 5.12 Visitor pattern example with farmer and animals. The farmer cannot hear the animals inside the box (A), so the farmer hires an employee (the visitor) to talk to the animals (B).

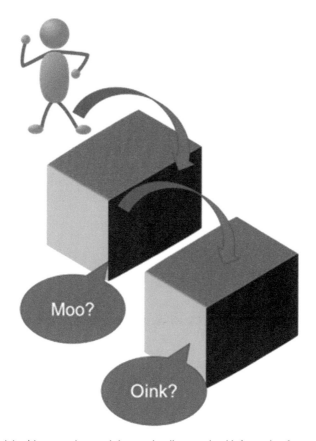

Fig. 5.13 The employee (visitor) is passed to each box and collects animal information from each box.

the top: the interfaces. In pseudocode, the two critical interfaces for the instrument example earlier look like this:

```
interface Visitor
  function GiveMeADrum( Drum d )
    // do something with the drum

  function GiveMeAXylophone( Xylophone x )
    // do something with the xylophone

  function GiveMeAGong( Gong g )
    // do something with the gong

interface AcceptVisitor
  function ReceivedVisitor( Visitor v )
    //call the matching type function in v
```

The Visitor interface must have an accept function per supported type. This is how the visitor will know what it is talking to. All supported types must implement AcceptVisitor so the instance of Visitor may enter into its "box." Expanding this method to work for the multiple instruments example simply expands on the above interfaces. Below is psuedocode for a Drum (who accepts visitors), and a Mallet who visits instruments.

```
class Drum implements AcceptVisitor
  function Foo()
    // do something

  function Foo2()
    // do something

  function ReceivedVisitor( Visitor v )     // 4
    v.GiveMeADrum()                         // 5

class Mallet implements Visitor
  function GiveMeADrum( Drum d )            // 6
    d.Foo()                                 // 7

  function GiveMeAXylophone( Xylophone x )
    x.Foo2()

  function GiveMeAGong( Gong g )
    g.Goo()          // not shown in psuedocode

  function OnCollisionEnter( other )        // 1
    if other implements AcceptVisitor       // 2
      other.ReceivedVisitor( this )         // 3
```

When the mallet collides with something, the call path starts at the line marked with 1. If the other object is a drum, the path follows the lines in the order noted in the comments. The benefit to the added bouncing around of classes, if done correctly, is that new behaviors are simple to add. Want a new drumstick? Make a new drumstick class derived from Visitor, but the Drum class remains unchanged.

Implementing the Visitor pattern well requires maintaining SOLID principles. Here are some of the common errors that can arise:

- If there is a parameter in a start up function that uses a specific type of Visitor and not the parent, D was broken. In the above example, that would be changing the if line to something like *if other implements Drum.*
- If there is more than one start up function for a visitor, O was broken. This does not include adding another function for a

singular item or range, which does not break O. In the above, that would be like adding a second OnCollision function.

- If the Visitor member variable is in the start up class, O was broken. In the above example, that would be like adding a Drum variable to Mallet and then *instantiating it*. The Drum should be created outside of Mallet.

The Visitor pattern comes with its advantages and disadvantages. One such advantage is that new capabilities can be added without changing the way data are stored. Another advantage is that for a complex task, all of the code for the task is in one place instead of being spread all over. A disadvantage is that the pattern requires extra code to support the pattern. Another is that the function names ReceiveVistior() and GiveMeX() are not meaningful. The meaning of the task is found in the concrete visitor, so good naming of the child class is needed to understand what is occurring. In addition, every time a new derived type is added, a new accept/visit function must also be added for that type.

In general, visitors are best used when the classes defining the object structure rarely change but new operations are often being defined over that structure. Visitors are particularly useful for simulations, which pull varying types of data, and games, which use complex interactions.

In the examples above, the interaction only works with two classes at a time. A full visitor pattern implementation allows for more complex interactions and for two or more contributing objects to control the effect.

Strategy Pattern

The simplest version of the Strategy pattern is to swap out a single function depending on the context. This can be illustrated with the snap placement interaction described above. In pseudocode, this appears as an if statement in the Object.Release(). The alternate snap functionality is then set or removed when within the Snap object's collision space:

```
class Object
  FunctionPointer releaseFuncPointer

  function Release()
    if releaseFunc != null
      // if there is an alternate release function, use it
      ReleaseFuncPointer( this )
    else
      UnParent()
```

```
function SetRelease(FunctionPointer f)
  releaseFuncPointer = f

Class Snap()
  // The actual snap function.
  // In this case, place this object in the same location
  // rather than just release it
  function Snap( Object o )
    o.UnParent()
    o.transform = this.transform

  // Set the alternative snap function
  function OnCollisionEnter( Object o )
    o.SetRelease( this.snap )

  // remove the alternate snap function
  function OnCollisionExit( Object o )
    o.setRelease( null )
```

The current pattern fails if the snap areas overlap. If there are overlapping areas, a list of pointers is required. The last or nearest pointer that had a collision is then chosen for the release.

Button Interaction

Button interaction in VR largely follows best practices with console controllers. The difference lies in the format of the controllers. As described in an earlier section, VR controllers are more varied than console controllers. As a result, only a joystick, a grip, a trigger, and one other open button per hand can generally be assumed, although some systems like an Oculus Go have less.

Users in VR tend to favor using the trigger and grip buttons for most items, so favoring those in interaction for "standard" tasks is ideal. A moderate exception is that heavy console game players may favor that one "open" button, as it is in a similar spot as the most used button in a console controller. Vive wand controllers do not have this button, but Oculus Quest, Rift, Valve Index, and Vive Cosmos do. Expect different button mappings to be needed in different systems. While these options give a workaround, they have a similar failing: users can only easily remember seven, give or take two, novel commands, according to Miller's law [4]. That number can increase with familiarity, so using standard mapping is highly suggested.

Combine this restriction with VR users expecting a higher level of interaction, and that button-only command can be oddly hard to remember. Therefore, buttons should be limited to items that truly have no 3D context such as opening a menu or activating a non-physical item like a laser pointer. Let's look at one such example, grabbing.

Grabbing and dropping are button commands but are paired with proximity events and may be paired with the grip button to ensure it feels natural.

Grabbing is the most fundamental interaction in VR and is a proximity-based event. Grabbing also has a fair number of edge cases so greater care must be taken. This interaction can be grab and hold, grab and collect, grab and play a sound, etc. Moreover, what if an object that could be grabbing, gets turned off during the run? Throw in snapping on release, more than one grab effect on an object, possible walls in the way, and two-handed interactions, and good grab code is not as simple as just parenting an object in the scene tree to the hand.

The key elements in the above are that the grab and release have times they need to clean up and filter what is legal to grab, that the effect is separated from "can I grab now?" and that there can be more than one effect on a grab. Combine this with a good interaction framework, and there are a few layers of code in creating good grab code. At a high level, this code flow will look as follows (Fig. 5.14).

The interaction framework was discussed in an earlier chapter, so the next step is the grab\release event code. This class's job is to collect information about the event that the effect may need and then determine what are the legal objects that should respond to the grab request.

At a high level, the logic to do that is

1. Get a list of grabbable objects.
2. On a grab event,
   a. If in VR, save which device triggered the grab.
   b. Clear out any "dead" objects that had registered.

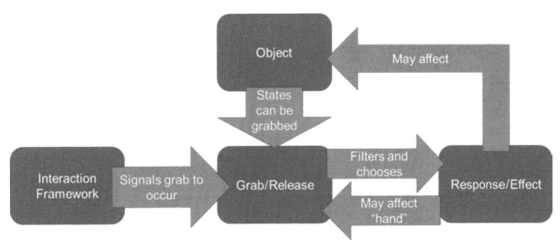

Fig. 5.14 Graphical representation of button interaction.

    c. If the hand is open,
      i. Find a list of valid grab effects.
      ii. Call that list of effects.
    d. Clear out any "dead" objects that may have happened after the grab.
  3. On release,
    a. Clear out any "dead" objects that had registered.
    b. If the hand has something,
      i. Find a list of valid release effects.
      ii. Call that list of effects.
    c. Clear out any "dead" objects that may have happened after the release.

Assuming that interaction framework is already set to trigger a function on the controller grab action, the grab code can focus on what to notify. To do this, the grab code must know the list of objects that are grabbable, the device that triggered the event if the response needs it (like haptics), and if a grab should be allowed at this time period (e.g., the hand already has something). This gives the code parameters and registration functions so objects can state whether they are grabbable. The Grab class belongs on the the user's hand\controller object and acts like a manager for the hand.

```
class Grab
  // what is currently held in the hand
  inHand = null

  //the device that triggered the grab
  sourceDevice = null

  // the list of objects, in range that have responses
  // to grabbing
  GrabEffect[] grabObjects

  function RegisterGrab( item )
    grabObjects.Add( item )

  function UnregisterGrab( item )
    grabObjects.Remove( item )
```

The next step is the grabbing. An OnGrab() function mirrors the above logic almost line to line. Cleaning up dead objects will vary with the system but can include removing objects that have been deleted, inactive, or simply in an invalid state.

```
function OnGrab()
    //get left\right controller that caused the action
    sourceDevice = GetDeviceForThisHand()
```

```
    // remove objects that "died" from last event
    CleanUpDeadObjectsInList()

    // sanity check, do not grab if hands are full
    if inHand == null && grabObjects.count > 0
      // check for all the objects that are to be notified
      list = GetGrabCallbackSet()
      for go in list
        go.OnGrab( this )

    // remove object that "died" when grab completed
    CleanUpDeadObjectsInList()
```

The more challenging function is getting the valid list. There are many choices here, so the GetGrabCallbackSet() function should be allowed to be overridden. As an example, assume that the goal is to get the closest object that is in line of sight. The pseudocode to do that is as follows.

```
function GrabEffect[] GetGrabCallbackSet()
  closest = null

  for obj in grabObjects
    // if there is nothing blocking us continue
    if !IsSomethingBetween( this, obj )

      // always store the first legal one,
      // and then update if closer later
      if closest == null
        || distanceBetween( this, obj ) <
          distanceBetween( this, closest )
        closest = obj.gameObject

  if closest == null
    return null

  else
    return closest.GetObjectGrabEffects()
```

Releasing parallels the grab code.

The large item missing from above is the grab effect. For example, at no point did the above code place anything into the hand! A grab effect may merely play a sound, after all, so that is not the Grab class's job.

GrabEffect registers on collision using the techniques from section Multiple Collider Proximity Interaction. However, given the failing of Physics engines, sometimes alternatives are used such as registering on enabling. This is slower but more reliable. Registering on activation is what Unity's XR interaction framework uses.

Instead, that responsibility is shifted to a grab effect. A grab effect's logic at a high level is

1. If an object is within grabbing distance,
    a. Let the **object** register if it wants to know if there is a grab or release event on it.
2. If an object leaves grabbing distance,
    a. Let the **object** deregister.
3. When notified of a grab\release on this object, do the task.

A grab effect is generic and incomplete by itself. For example, where did the "place reference into hand" go? That is a specific grab effect. This means a grab effect starts as an abstract class, but it can watch for entering and exiting the range of an object that has the Grab class.

```
abstract class GrabEffect

  // within range of a hand,
  // register desire for notification
  function CollisionEnter( otherObj )
    if CanCauseGrab( otherObj )
      // Check if the other object has a Grab class instance
      otherObj.RegisterGrab( this )

  // leaving range of a hand,
  // deregister desire for notification
  function CollisionExit( otherObj )
    if CanCauseGrab( otherObj )
      // Check if the other object has a Grab class instance
      otherObj.UnregisterGrab( this )

  // dedicated callback if this object is grabbed
  function abstract OnGrab( Grab controller )

  // dedicated callback if this object is released
  function abstract OnRelease( Grab controller )
```

By structuring the code this way, later code can focus purely on what to do when told the hand is trying to grab them. Take a "grab and hold" concrete implementation of GrabEffect placed on a grab-able object as an example. OnGrab and OnRelease could be implemented as follows:

```
class GrabEffectHold inherits GrabEffect

  function override OnGrab( Grab grabber )

    // turn off physics and parent to grabber
    // which is assumed to be the controller
    this.TurnOffPhysics()
    this.parent = grabber
```

```
// place this object neatly into the hand
this.transform.AlignTo( grabber )

// tell the grabber the hand is now
// holding something
controller.inHand = this.gameObject

function override OnRelease( Grab grabber )

// turn on physics and deparent
// which is assumed to be the controller
this.TurnOnPhysics()
this.parent = null

// tell the grabber the hand is now free
controller.inHand = null
```

Throwing merely adds a bit more to the release in that the physics must be transferred to the objects being dropped. But the Grab code already saved the controller, so it is ready for use. That adds only a few lines to OnRelease:

```
function override OnRelease( Grab grabber )

// turn on physics and de parent
// which is assume dot be the controller
this.TurnOnPhysics()
velocityDir = grabber.sourceDevice.GetVelocity()
force = |velocityDir| / deltaTime
this.ApplyForce( velocity.Normalize(), force )
this.parent = null

// tell the grabber the hand is now free
controller.inHand = null
```

The registration and deregistration are already handled in the parent, so this is rather short!

To continue with some of the examples, suppose that the same object wants to play a sound on grab. This would be a new GrabEffect that only cares about what happens in OnGrab:

```
class GrabEffectPlaySound inherits GrabEffect

function override OnGrab( Grab grabber )
// play sound on grab
SoundSystem.Play( "beep.mp3" )

// leave the hand open
function override OnRelease( Grab grabber )
// NOTHING!
```

Again, it's very short and allows the coder to focus on the response only. Having more than one GrabEffect is perfectly legal in the entity component structure of Unity and Unreal, and both will be called if using the example pseudocode for GetGrabCallbackSet() above, which calls all grab effects on the closest object. This is just the basics. Additional states such as Hover() and UnHover() can easily be added in a similar fashion.

Two-Handed Interaction

Two-handed interaction is largely unique to VR and other XR applications. This particular interaction is also difficult to convert to a comparable 3D interaction. Interestingly, gamers tend not to use this interaction very much initially, while nongamers do, possibly due to past training of controllers. Two-handed interaction tends to be applied in three categories of events:

- Two-handed task
- Two-handed action
- Transformation manipulation

This section covers what these categories entail and how they are applied in VR.

Two-Handed Task

There are a lot of day-to-day interactions that require the use of both hands, such as playing various instruments, picking up bulky objects, or using a rolling pin to roll out cookie dough. These are two-handed tasks. Applying this type of interaction in VR is fairly straightforward. Usually, only one object needs to be parented to one hand and the other hand runs the collisions like normal. To convert to a controller, the first grab would cause a change in modes (Fig. 5.15).

Fig. 5.15 An example of the two-handed task of playing a guitar. In a VR application, the guitar would be parented to one hand while the other hand interacts as normal. (Image from Pexels: https://images. pexels.com/photos/1751731/pexels-photo-1751731. jpeg?cs=srgb&dl=photo-of-person-playing-acoustic-guitar-1751731.jpg&fm=jpg.)

Two-Handed Action

Two-handed action is largely a logic gate for a particular action event. For example, if a large beach ball is tossed in real life, most players would try to catch the ball with both hands. A two-handed response can reuse the Grab class from one-handed grab to be notified when a grab occurred. A legal grab area is the same in both, so this avoids duplicating code. In this case an equivalent VR interaction would have a logic gate requiring that the ball can only be caught if both notified hands have caused a grab event without a release in between (Fig. 5.16).

The base of a DoubleGrab class is similar to the Grab class. However, to keep things smaller, let's assume at most one double grab effect is allowed on a double grab, so there is merely a single callback function rather than a list. Because there is only one, these callbacks are made abstract. DoubleGrab still has an OnGrab and OnRelease, but now the grabbed object must be paired to the hand. This doubles our parameters.

Fig. 5.16 An example of two-handed action. A player may catch a small ball with one hand, but both hands are used for a large beach ball.

```
abstract class DoubleGrab

  // the two grab points to activate
  GameObject grabPoint1
  GameObject grabPoint2

  // monitors what hand has what object
  Pair[ GameObject, Grab ] first
  Pair[ GameObject, Grab ] second

  // our callbacks for the double grab effect
  function abstract DoubleGrabEvent( GameObject in Hand1,
                                     Grab hand1,
                                     GameObject inHand2,
                                     Grab hand2 )
  function abstract DoubleReleaseEvent( GameObject inHand1,
                                        Grab hand1,
                                        GameObject inHand2,
                                        Grab hand2 )

  function OnGrab( GameObject obj, Grab grabber )
    // watches if both hands have grabbed the grip point

  function OnRelease( GameObject obj, Grab grabber )
    // watches if either hand has released
```

This code cannot be called directly from the Grab code as the parameters do not match. Instead, this task starts with a new single grab effect that will merely notify the double grab class that a grab request occurred.

```
class GrabEffectDetect inherits GrabEffect

  DoubleGrab doubleGrab

  function override OnGrab( Grab grabber )
    doubleGrab.OnGrab( gameObject, grabber )

  function override OnRelease( Grab grabber )
    doubleGrab.OnRelease( gameObject, grabber )
```

The effect is placed on the grabbable objects and has to register the *doubleGrab* variable with the associated DoubleGrab class. This can be completed at startup and will vary with the system. Following that, the OnGrab() and OnRelease() code can be completed for the DoubleGrab class. OnGrab() makes a pair of the object and hand (grabber) and saves a reference. When both are down, the DoubleGrabEvent() is fired.

```
function OnGrab( GameObject obj, Grab grabber )
    // no item grabbed yet, save it
    if first == null
      first = Pair( obj, grabber )

      // place objects in both hands
      grabber.inHand = obj

    // if the first hand if full,
    // and the same object is used for both grab points
    // OR the incoming object is a different grab point
    // from the first
    else if (first != null && grabPoint1 == grabPoint2)
           || obj != first[ 0 ]

// sanity check, this should be a different controller
       if first[ 1 ] != controller
         second = Pair( obj, grabber )

         // place object in both hand
         grabber.inHand = obj

         // both hands have something, trigger!
         DoubleGrabEvent( first[ 0 ], first[ 1 ],
                          second[ 0 ], second[ 1 ] )
```

Release takes a bit more logic as there are four cases. (1) Somehow release was called and nothing is held. Do nothing. (2) Both hands are now empty. Set hands to null\open. (3) The first hand released. Shift the second hand to the first and trigger the release because we do not have both hands grabbing anymore (4). The second hand is released. Set the second hand to null and trigger the release because we do not have both hands grabbing anymore. Here is the pseudocode with the four cases marked:

```
function OnRelease( GameObject obj, Grab grabber )
    // 1) sanity check, if there is nothing held, do nothing
    if first == null
        return
    // 2) last release
    else if obj == first[ 0 ] && second == null
        //release first hand
        grabber.inHand = null
        first = null

    3) second grab is still active, move it to first
    else if (obj == first[ 0 ] && second!= null)
        // went from both hands having something, to one, trigger!
        DoubleReleaseEvent( first[ 0 ], first[ 1 ],
                            second[ 0 ], second[ 1 ] )
        // shift second to first hand, and release second hand
        grabber.inHand = null
        first = second
        second = null

    // 4) first grab is still active, remove second
    else
        // went from both hands having something, to one, trigger!
        DoubleReleaseEvent( first[ 0 ], first[ 1 ],
                            second[ 0 ], second[ 1 ] )

        // release second hand
            grabber.inHand = null
            second = null
```

To convert this interaction to a 3D controller, the simplest solution is to create three overlapping colliders for the head and the two hands.

Now the code is ready to respond to two-handed interactions in the next section.

Transformation Manipulation

Transformation manipulation refers to moving, scaling, and rotating objects with two hands. This category requires more involved interaction *between* the hands. To illustrate, let's have a user grab a map with two hands and build the transformation manipulation interaction from there (Fig. 5.17).

Before any transformations can occur, the user must be able to grab the map with two hands. But that code is already done! All the coder needs to do at this point is override the DoubleGrabEvent() and DoubleGrabReleaseEvent() callbacks and focus on what happens *after* both hands have grabbed, and when one hand has released. Here is the starter pseudocode to override for the callbacks and save a reference to both hands for later use.

```
class GrabByBoth inherits DoubleGrab
  Grab gripHandA
  Grab gripHandB

  function override DoubleGrabEvent(GameObject inHand1,
                                    Grab hand1,
                                    GameObject inHand2,
                                    Grab hand2)

    gripHandA = hand1
    gripHandB = hand2

  function override DoubleReleaseEvent(GameObject inHand1,
                                       Grab hand1,
                                       GameObject inHand2,
                                       Grab hand2 )
    gripHandA = null
    gripHandB = null
```

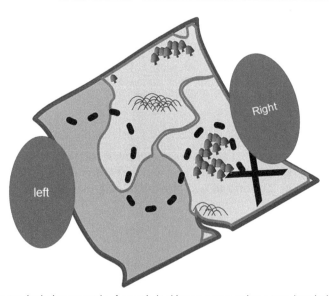

Fig. 5.17 Transformation manipulation example. A user is looking at a map using a two-handed grab.

Now to focus on the placement of the map. This is fairly straightforward. The object is placed at the midway point between the two controllers on every frame update. This assumes that the center of the object is at (0,0,0). Because this requires a reference, the booleans will need to be replaced with references in GrabByBoth (Fig. 5.18).

```
function Update()
   center = ( leftHand.position + rightHand.position ) / 2
   this.position = center
```

Next, let's add scaling. Scaling requires matching up the length of the object with the distance between the hands. This means that an axis needs to be chosen for aligning purposes. Because VR tends to use left-handed coordinate systems, let's set the left controller as the x-axis. Next, the percentage change needs to be computed using distance / initialWidth (Fig. 5.19).

```
Constructor DoubleGrab()
  initalWidth = this.bounds

function Update()
   center = (leftHand.position + rightHand.position ) / 2
   this.position = center

   leftToRight = leftHand.position - rightHand.position
   distance = | leftToRight |
   scale = distance / initialWidth
   this.scale = scale
```

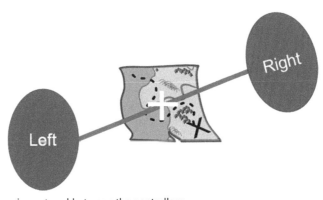

Fig. 5.18 The grabbed map is centered between the controllers.

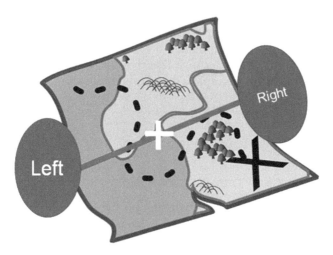

Fig. 5.19 The grabbed map is scaled according to the distance between the hands.

Finally, let's add rotation. Rotation requires two major axes:
- The axis aligning with the hands' vector
- The up vector or the x-rotation of the hands

This can be implemented using direct manipulation of the matrices or a quaternion. In this example, a mix is a bit simpler. Let's add this in steps. First, the axis of the hand's vector and the rotation quaternion is created. The rotation is also added but is not complete.

```
function Update()
    center  = ( leftHand.position + rightHand.position ) / 2
    this.position = center

    leftToRight = leftHand.position - rightHand.position
    distance = | leftToRight |
    scale = distance / initialWidth
    this.scale = scale

    right = leftToRight.Normalize()
    forward = Vector( 0, 1, 0 ) x right // x is the cross product op
    up = forward * right
    // make a quaternion aligned to the left-right vector
    q = MatrixToQuaternion( right, forward, up )
    this.rotation = q
```

The matrix to quaternion function is usually given in game engines, but if not, the proof is in the appendix.

Next, the pitch angle needs to be determined. The pitch angle cannot be assumed only from the controllers' pitch angles, because each controller may be held at different angles. There are some options from which to choose: minimum, maximum, or average pitch. The average is most likely the preferred case for the user and probably the most common solution.

```
function Update()
    center = ( leftHand.position + rightHand.position ) / 2
    this.position = center

    leftToRight = leftHand.position - rightHand.position
    distance = | leftToRight |
    scale = distance / initalWidth
    this.scale = scale

    right = leftToRight.Normalize()
    forward = Vector( 0, 1, 0 ) x right // x is the cross product op
    up = forward * right
    // make a quaternion aligned to the left-right vector
    q = MatrixToQuaterion( right, forward, up )

    thetaLeft = leftHand.rotation.localX
    thetaRight = rightHand.rotation.localX
    theta = ( thetaLeft + thetaRight ) / 2

    if hand order is flipped
        theta = -theta

    q2 = Quaternion( right, theta )
    this.rotation = q2 * q
```

This solution works if all of the objects stay in this transformation. If not, the target transformation will require saving and then is applied after the map is released.

Pockets

In most applications, there are quick access options to some elements, such as

- Hot keys
- Favorites
- Hot bars

In VR, quick access in the form of hot keys is no longer available. Instead, pockets, or proximity-based areas relative to the user, are used to provide quick access options.

Pockets are typically placed relative to the head and controllers. The head area typically has only one pocket, because two pockets relative to the head do not tend to work well. One of the pocket areas tends to move out of the user's range (Fig. 5.20).

When thinking about adding quick access to pockets, it helps to think about real life examples. For example, ear buds are placed in the head pocket. Typically, the hand-placed pockets are placed around the user like an innertube or inflatable utility belt. Interaction with the innertube is dependent on the hand-plus-button combination. The 2.5D metaphor is also used with pockets. For example, if the controller rotates upside down, the 2.5D hot bar shows tappable areas. Here are some examples of pseudocode pulling an object out of a pocket.

```
hand = null
function OnCollisionEnter( Object o )
  if o is controller
    hand = o

function OnCollisionExit( Object o )
  if o is hand
    if grabButton down
      PullFromPocket( hand )
  else
    hand = null
```

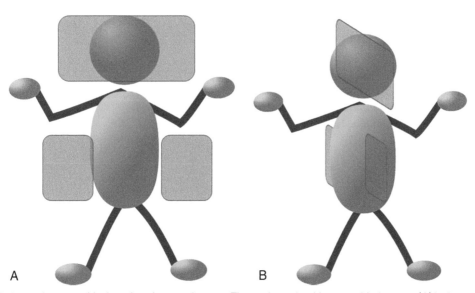

Fig. 5.20 Approximate positioning of pockets on the user. The pockets should move with the user. (A) is the pocket location if the user's head is the same direction as the body. (B) is if the body remains still but the head turns.

References

[1] Rebenitsch LR, Owen CB, Coburn S. *World and object designs for virtual environments. Meaningful Play,* 2014 Conference Proceedings, East Lansing.

[2] Hansberger JT, Peng C, Mathis SL, Shanthakumar VA, Meacham SC, Cao L, Blakely VR. Dispelling the gorilla arm syndrome: the viability of prolonged gesture interactions, *International Conference on Virtual, Augmented and Mixed Reality*, Springer, Cham; 2017.

[3] Jaekl PM, Jenkin MR, Harris LR. Perceiving a stable world during active rotational and translational head movements, *Exp Brain Res* 163(3):388–399, 2005.

[4] Miller G. The magical number seven, plus or minus two: some limits on our capacity for processing information, *Psychol Rev* 63(2):81, 1956.

## 6

Menus and Heads-Up Displays

Virtual reality (VR) applications, while three-dimensional (3D), have a number of two-dimensional (2D) objects. This chapter covers using 2D objects in 3D environments and available menu systems in VR. These topics are together since menu systems are the most common example of requiring 2D objects in 3D environments. The general roadmap of the chapter is as follows:

- types of 2D objects in 3D applications
- 2.5D in heads-up display (HUD) design
- canvasing, and scene changes

This chapter contains a large overlap with general graphics due to good practices for usability specific to VR applications. It covers the more common 2D-focused interaction methods used in VR.

At first glance, it may appear counterintuitive to add a 2D element to a 3D application, but several items in the real world are intrinsically 2D. For example, anything written on paper is in 2D. In VR, there are elements that remain primarily 2D, the most common of which are menus or inventories in game settings. From here, the most common metaphors are clipboards, painting canvas, heads-up displays and 2.5D cubbies or shelves. However, VR has some additional usability concerns beyond that of 3D console systems that must be discussed first to understand the limitations of 2D elements in VR.

Usability Concerns

Visual Acuity

When wearing a VR HUD, you may have noticed that when the eye shifts, but not the head, the screen becomes blurry. This is due to lens quality. Lens reshape the screen as shown in Fig. 6.1, from the original on the left to the more rounded version in the center. The greater issue is that the eye has a field of view of approximately 120° around the horizontal (wider for women on average) but high visual acuity (which is needed for reading) at only about 15°.

To be effective, individual elements (e.g., a single word) need to be near or even inside that 15° range to be comfortable. Due to the blurring and natural range of eye movement, the total arc of combined elements (e.g., a line of text) should be less than around 50°.

A Practical Introduction to Virtual Reality. https://doi.org/10.1016/B978-0-443-14036-5.00006-6

Fig. 6.1 Field of view example. The leftmost photo is an unchanged, flat lens image with a straight line of perspective. In the middle, the lens has been rounded and a vignette has been applied, but the line of perspective now curves at the edge. In the rightmost image, the area of highest acuity is outlined. This area must have the sharpest focus. (Derived from https://pixnio.com/free-images/2017/09/23/2017-09-23-16-10-09.jpg.)

Past that, head movements will be needed, which can act like standing too close to a billboard and trying to read it.

Most VR headsets have field of view (FOV) ranges far wider than the 50° preferred limit. Here is the horizontal FOV of some common headsets:

- Vive Cosmo (~84°)
- Oculus Rift S (~86°)
- Oculus Quest (~95°)
- Vive Pro 2 (~107°)
- Valve Index (~109°)

To illustrate how this can be applied, let's say that an application requires having a Sun icon at the bottom of the 15° arc at a visual distance of 2 m away (Fig. 6.2).

Calculating Position for Menu Icons

The position of the Sun icon can be computed in pseudocode.

```
up = < 0, 1, 0 >
// find the axis perpendicular to the view direction
rotateAxis = up * lookAt
quaternion = CreateQuaternion( axis, -15.0 / 2 )
place = < 0, 0, 2 >
// rotate a point 2m out according to the quaternion
finalPlace = quaternion * place
//rotate object to face the user
finalPlace.rotation = -lookAt
```

Any rotateAxis is determined from the cross product of the up vector and the direction of the center of vision. The up vector has the y-axis as up.

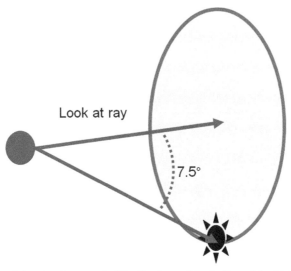

Look at ray

7.5°

Fig. 6.2 Calculation for determining the placement of the Sun icon at the bottom of the high visual acuity range.

Any position can also be computed according to the distance from the eye and the vertical and horizontal angles from the gaze direction, which here are (θ_{right}, θ_{down}) with the differences highlighted.

```
up = < 0,1,0 >
dist = < 0,0,z >
rotateDownAxis = up * lookAt
quatDown = CreateQuaternion( rotateDownAxis,θdown )
quatRight = CreateQuaternion( up,θright )
quaterion = quatDown * quatRight
finalPlace = quaternion * dist
finalPlace.rotation = -lookAt
```

Here, the rotateDownAxis is determined from the cross product of the up vector and the direction of the center of vision. The up vector has the *y*-axis as up.

Calculating a Point on a Sphere

Alternatively, the position of the icon can also be calculated from a point on a sphere around the user. In a left-handed system with the *y*-axis up, the coordinates can be calculated from

$$x = r \sin\theta \cos\phi$$

$$y = r \cos\theta$$

$$z = r \sin\theta \sin\phi$$

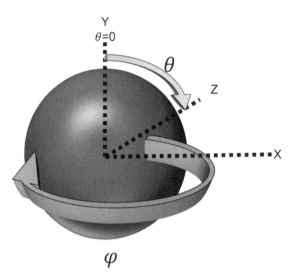

Fig. 6.3 Finding a point on a sphere in a left-handed coordinate system.

This is basically converting between spherical and Cartesian coordinates. To review spherical coordinates, let's assume a Unity coordinate system. The calculation of the position starts with the direction pointing up or along the y-axis. The direction is then rotated down by θ, which here has a range of $[0°, 180°]$. This is the same as rotation around the z-axis. The direction is then rotated clockwise (this is left-handed) by ϕ, which has a range of $[0°, 360°]$. This is the same as rotating around the y-axis. The position finally shoots out a distance of r, giving the position. The motion is shown in Fig. 6.3.

One item of caution: if $\theta = 0°$, then the ϕ value becomes irrelevant. Try tracing out the position on your left hand to see why.

Font Size

Font size requirements are larger in VR than in other 3D applications. Some of this is due to the current resolutions available in VR being insufficient to clearly read small text. To give some context, font size on signs in real life are typically *easily* readable at 1 inch per 10 feet of distance (or roughly 0.83 cm per 1 m of distance) [1]. In VR, the suggested font size is 4 to 5 times the real-life height. In addition, each individual word width needs to meet the 15° arc width, with a line width total of less than around 50°, or the text becomes distorted.

Fig. 6.4 In a VR application, the clipboard virtual monitor cannot be assumed to be in a static position. The player can rotate and, as a result, the virtual monitor can be rotated out of the player's line of sight. (Created from https://svgsilh.com/svg/151791-e91e63.svg.)

Menu Location

Second, while the virtual monitor stays in place in 3D, this is not true for VR. The position of the player also does not stay in place in VR. There are some solutions to this location issue (Fig. 6.4):

- Pause and fade out the rest of the screen so that only the menu is visible.
- Rotate the virtual monitor with the user.
- Use both of the above methods.

These solutions have some needed design considerations in order to be effective.

The pause and fade-out option works best with a main menu with a large number of options. This method can still be jarring, however, and if the user rotates 180° at the start of the fade-out, the menu is still out of the user's line of sight. The solution for both of these side effects is to center the main menu in the user's line of sight at the start of the fade-out.

The main challenges with rotating the virtual monitor are how to rotate and, in particular, how fast to rotate. Parenting the virtual monitor to the user's centered line of sight can be both jarring and problematic if the user needs to make a comparison between the menu and the environment but the menu blocks the view of the environment. This can be resolved with two suboptions:

- Parent the menu to one hand and then have the hand pull the virtual monitor into view.

- Connect the menu to a spring animation to smoothly pull the virtual monitor into view with a delay.

Using a spring animation to rotate the virtual monitor is not a simple linear interpolation (LERP) or spherical linear interpolation (SLERP). The animation smoothing takes some extra steps:

1. Add a time delay from when the user turns.
2. Spring quickly at first and then slow down.
3. Add a buffer zone to minimize jitter.

Step 2 is not strictly needed but provides an anticipation of motion technique that is commonly used in smoothing motion animation to reducing jarring effects. The time delay and buffer are to account for the natural small movements of the user, such as glancing toward a new object and then switching back to the original object. For a user motion like this, a delay works well. The buffer zone is particularly critical for normal small head movements. If the menu is placed at the edge of the view, the menu will appear to jitter during the rotation animation.

At a high level, the buffer and timer for the animation follow these conditions:

- If the user is in range and stable, reset, and do nothing.

```
delayElapsedTime = 0
```

- If the user leaves the buffer range, increment the delay timer.

```
delayElapsedTime += deltaTime
```

- If the delay elapses, start the animation timer, and save the current location.

```
startTransform = item.transform
animationElapsedTime = 0.0f
```

- If animation timer is active, animate every update until done.

```
function OnAnimation( percent)
  target = trackedObject.position // if target is changed
  progress = Progress( percent)
  position = Lerp( start, target, progress )
```

To animate the motion to move quickly and then slow down, the LERP progression needs to be adjusted into a nonlinear formula using the techniques discussed in the transformation chapter. A formula that will start fast and end slow could be $f(x) = x^{1/n}$ where higher values of n will give a greater difference between slow and fast periods.

A final note on the menu position relates to the distance. On a desktop, the user can move the screen to a comfortable distance. In VR, the application places the menu distance from the user. If the menu is too close, this can cause a sensation of violating the user's personal space. In general, the menu should be placed just past arm's length or farther.

Metaphors

VR user input is in 3D but the following metaphors are in 2D. Converting from 3D to 2D requires mapping user input. This can be and often is done with button presses, but most menus today support both pointing and keyboard input. The mouse equivalent of selecting a button is simply pointing in VR. Keyboard controls can be mimicked with the joysticks. There is good reason to support both. Points allow quick, broad movement but are unsuitable for fine-grained movements. Joystick taps are good for fine-grained movement but can become irritating if there are numerous other elements to bypass.

This leads to the original 2D metaphor for menu layouts: Canvases.

Canvas

A canvas is a 2D area for menu items and is inspired from the painter's canvas. At a high level, it is simply an area to put menu elements. A canvas typically supports basic menu items, such as

- buttons,
- lists,
- text information, and
- check boxes.

In a console system, the canvas may overlay the entire screen, allowing the placement of user interface elements throughout.

Layout options in variation systems can vary tremendously in what is supported, and how elements are added. Most systems allow for absolute positioning and automatic linear (column, row) type layouts. For more complex layouts, most systems use one of two paradigms: percentage-based or nested tree of layouts like grids, stacks, etc. However, Unity and Unreal only use the percentage-based paradigm, so only that paradigm will be discussed here.

There are a few unintuitive points on a canvas. For one, the dimensions of a canvas are $(-\infty, \infty)$, but the user only sees finite dimensions of [w, h] as a window into the canvas. Another is that the anchors and origin of the window in the canvas have different placements. The origin is traditionally placed in the upper left corner of the window similar to line character placement when reading from left to right. The anchor is where the object is pinned relative to the object, not the window (Fig. 6.5).

At a high level and knowing these unintuitive points, how is a canvas menu made with four buttons placed in a horizontally centered column and having the column begin at the top? If the button height

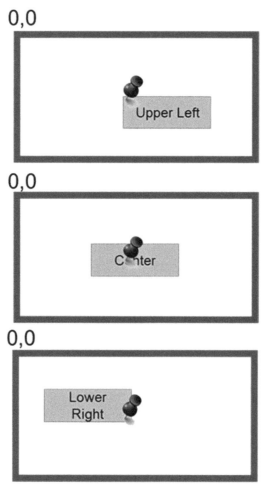

Fig. 6.5 Examples of the placement of the origin and the anchors. The text in the yellow box notes where the box is anchored. In each of the three examples, the origin of the window is placed in the top left corner. The yellow object's anchor, represented by a pin, does not change position relative to the window. However, the relative placement of the anchor to the object does change.

is B, the spacing between buttons is S, and absolute positioning can be used with a window size of [w, h], then the following pseudocode will place the buttons in a canvas:

```
centerH = w / 2
for i from 0 to 3
    down = S * ( i + 1 ) + i * B
    button = Button()
    button.SetAnchor( TOP_CENTER )
    button.SetPos( centerH — button.width / 2, down )
```

Both Unity and Unreal have Canvas objects, and they work very similarly. They use percentage-based anchors to determine where and how to place objects, and they use a Pivot to define where rotations are centered and where the object is "pinned." This is the only layout, and thus, it lacks the typical linear layout option.

There are four anchor values to set: minimum (x, y), and maximum (x, y). If min and max along a dimension **match**, this represents a set location at that point. As an example, if minX = 0.25 = maxX, the element would place its horizontal pivot point directly at 25%. If the pivot point was centered vertically, it would be placed as shown in Fig. 6.6.

Offsets are also allowed in the layout format. Using the above example, the user may choose to add a horizontal offset of a few pixels to give a buffer space as shown (Fig. 6.7).

If the anchors do not match, the object is stretched to fill the space in between. As an example, if minX = 0.25, and maxX = 0.75, the element would stretch to 50% of the horizontal width. If the pivot point was centered vertically, it would be placed as shown in Fig. 6.8.

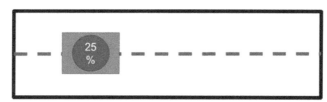

Fig. 6.6 The orange area is the element, placed at 25% horizontally if the anchors minX = 0.25 = maxX.

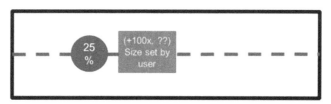

Fig. 6.7 The orange area is the element, placed at 25% horizontally if the anchors minX = 0.25 = maxX, and then pushed to the right with an offset of 100 px.

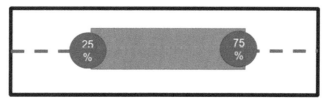

Fig. 6.8 The orange area is the element, stretched between the horizontal anchors minX = 0.25, maxX = 0.75.

Fig. 6.9 An example of a curved clipboard from the Vive home menu.

When elements are nested, such as buttons inside a panel, the composite object acts like a scene tree and the transforms chain in the same way.

Clipboard

The clipboard metaphor for 2D menus is essentially a canvas with much smaller boundaries than the entire screen and "floats" in space so that the user may pick up and move the menu. It is far more common than traditional canvases in VR, as it works well with the usability limitations explained above rather than against them. The clipboard is usually shown as a popup virtual monitor (Fig. 6.9). Any of these clipboards are now curved due to the limited high visual acuity area mentioned above.

2.5D

2.5D refers to elements that are in 3D but interaction occurs in a 2D manner. A real-life example is the floor plan. Building spaces are

Fig. 6.10 An example of a 2.5D implementation. The shelf displays items in different boxed areas. Selection can be simplified to the square over the boxed area. (https://pixabay.com/illustrations/salon-shadowbox-barber-sales-decor-1149913/.)

in 3D, but floor plan dimensions are given in squared feet or squared meters. In VR, 2.5D allows for more sophisticated menus, which are often shown as 3D elements in cubbies or 3D elements on a shelf. Some UI points to consider when designing a 2.5D menu are that

- 3D recognition can be harder or easier depending on the element.
- Text should always be in 2D.
- Selection areas can be harder to implement.
- Menus should not be in full 3D in most cases.

Two other considerations are that 3D elements are usually less recognizable than their 2D counterpart in many contexts. Pointing selection can also be harder as the bonding bounds may block the pointer from reaching the desired element. Consider Fig. 6.10. The selection areas are shown as transparent boxes. Selection, being the square rather than cubes, would be simpler to implement and display as more contiguous to the user.

Fig. 6.11 Two examples of HUDs: the left shows a car HUD, and the right shows a percentage process bar. (A, Derived from https://www.pexels.com/photo/car-side-mirror-showing-heavy-traffic-191842/ B, Derived from https://openclipart.org/detail/181040/sky-and-moon.)

Heads-Up Display (HUD)

In this case, a HUD refers to icons overlaid on many 3D applications. These icons are useful for reminder information, warnings, attention direction, and cybersickness mitigation (Fig. 6.11).

HUDs are used regularly for many, many applications. For example, think of using Microsoft Word without the Ribbon, which comprises all of the top bar of buttons, and instead having to use Word with required memorization of all of those buttons.

Yikes!

This illustrates a principle of good UI design:

Avoid memorization when possible.

HUDs enable this principle heavily. However, it still must meet the usability requirement mentioned above, and the distance can be a challenge to keep the elements out of the way, while still not being so close to feel intrusive.

Scene Changes

One of the most common uses for menus is a scene or level selector paired with the system settings. For a scene change, the menu part stays the same. However, there are a few more development questions beyond the basic menu:

- How does the application transition from the main menu scene to the application scene?
- How is information, such as system-wide settings, transferred to the new screen?
- What are some good practices for a main menu?

This section goes over each of these questions at a conceptual level.

Scene Swap

Most systems have a built-in method to swap scenes. The typical method is to build two scenes and to point to the scene currently in use, while the other is temporarily inactive. The scene breaks shown in several games is where a new section is loaded and follows this same scene swap process.

Lightweight applications can manage this by turning some elements on or off without the scene overhead. Others may have streaming systems to load and unload sections as needed without needing the scene break. This can be done by clearly designing the area to disallow views of far-off locations and varying levels of detail models, as discussed in a later chapter.

Most systems have a method built in to do this that follows this format:

1. Register the scenes.
2. Save anything required for both scenes.
3. (Ideally) Unload the prior scene.
4. Switch to a new scene *when it is ready*.
5. Reload anything from the prior scene.

The scene breaks you see in games where a new section is loaded follows the same process.

The less intuitive portions of these steps are the saving and loading.

Transfer Information

The transfer of information between scenes varies more than the loading of a new scene. Singletons, (with caveats) long-lasting dictionaries, files, database push/pulls, and custom systems are all possible. However, there are some common steps to each of these methods:

1. Copy the needed information into a place or object that exists both before and after the scene change.
2. Make the scene change.
3. Copy the needed information back.

Singletons

Singletons are classes where the code enforces the existence of only one instance. They are very good if some data are used across multiple classes and that data must stay synced, so there is only one instance! However, singletons tend to be extremely finicky in entity-component systems like Unity and Unreal. The reason is that singletons are embedded in a component, and there is no restriction that a user can only add one of a certain type of component. The instant a duplicate component is added, the singleton will break.

However, some systems have an alternative that gives a similar effect. Unity has this with its ScriptableObjects and Unreal with its SaveGame object, but this can be mimicked elsewhere. A ScriptableObject fakes a singleton by essentially creating a shared resource. Just like a material that may be reused across objects and changing the base material changes them all, this resource is shared, and updating it means all later reads will have the new data. This shared resource technique can generally be accomplished even if there is no dedicated method.

Dictionaries

Some systems provide a specialized built-in dictionary where key-values pairs can be stored across scene changes. This is common in systems where user access tends to be transient, like in the web (web storage) and mobile systems (Android has bundles). This technique is good when there are only a few values that are needed. Unity has this built-in with PlayerPrefs.

Files/Databases

Files and databases are good when there are very large amounts of data and they do not have to be update regularly. However, many game-focused systems often have specialized formats for speed. Databases also have the synchronization issue to consider, but these are largely out of scope of this text.

Do Not Destroy the Data on the New Scene

This last method can occur when the data that need to change may be too erratic or time-consuming to save and then reload. Consider the VR player rig. It seems illogical to destroy and remake every scene. However, this method has a risk. Let's start with an example to better explain where these risks are. Assume this scenario:

1. Make a scene called *A* with the VR player rig and system-wide scripts.
2. Load scene *A* with the main menu scene called *B*.
3. To load the user-selected level, scene *C*,
   a. Start loading *C* in the background.
   b. When ready, switch to scene *C*.
   c. In the background, unload *B*.
4. The user wants to go back to the main menu, so
   a. Start loading *A* in the background.
   b. When ready, switch to scene *B*.
   c. In the background, unload *C*.

In this case, we never have more than two scenes: The current active scene, and our permanent entities.

The first problem can occur in step 4. If scene *B* adds some data to the long-term area, when we come back to *B*, that same data gets added again! And we have duplication.

While this method has many benefits, it does require upfront consideration to ensure the long-term data are accessed in a manner that remains consistent.

Good Practices

There are a number of good practices to make scene changes smoother for the user.

The foremost recommendation is to make the first scene calm. This is the first thing your user sees and will give an impression for the entire application. A good question to ask is, "What are the first and most common things a user does?" Only that should be in the initial menu.

The next large suggestion is to limit scene changes when possible. Numerous scene changes tend to be more disorienting in VR than in 3D.

If a scene change is absolutely required, have a transition to mitigate the disorientation nature of the scene change. Most modern systems have scene-loading windows. A caveat is the "loading percentage" bar. Users become irritated if this is off, with contention on the "hanging at 99%." Conservative estimate is highly suggested.

There is one more good practice that is worth going into detail: the MVC pattern. This chapter focuses on the concepts particular to VR, with more details in the appendix.

MVC in VR

MVC stands for Model-View-Controller. At a very high level, this simply means that the components should be able to be swapped out without affecting other components. This becomes critical if viewing modes or controllers need to change.

However, the Controller aspect of the MCV pattern has already been decoupled previously in the interaction framework chapter. The input system thus far allows for a fairly easy swap between Desktop and VR scenarios. This was accomplished by mapping the actions to run from the input, so it did not matter where the input (controller) originated.

The next MVC challenge is to section out the View. If you have ever played a game that has both a first-person view and a behind-person view, this change in view should be familiar. The data does not change, but the view does! While this type of change in view is less common in VR, mini-maps, which are as valuable in VR as they are in console applications, also use this pattern.

The tricky part of pulling out the view for many is usually one or both of these two questions:

- What is the "pure" model?
- How can the data be used to present the view if the data is not part of the view? The same issue exists with the controller, which affects both the view *and* the model in many cases.

Specifically, the pure model can generally be found by asking these two questions:

1. If changed to the command line, what data would still be needed?
2. What goes into a save file?

Answering these question gives the pure model, *and nothing more.*

This means MVC only works well if the open-closed principle from SOLID is applied well.

If needed, there is more detail of the event data type and the observer pattern in the OOP appendix.

There is one more very common variant of MVC in VR that needs to be discussed: the MVVM (Model-View-View-Model). The controller is not entirely missing in this form, it is just hidden in the View-Model combination. This combo is basically a subsection of the full view that requires some model information to work. Normally, this should be temporary data. For example, if the application is restarted, the elements that use the MVVM format are reset to their initial state.

As another example, consider a multiple selection box. The box has a view (the presented list of items), a model (what items are selected) and a controller (how the items are selected and deselected). However, if the application was restarted, the box is expected to reset to its initial set of selected items, not save and load the last set of selections run after run! Basically, MVVM is MCV in miniature form.

This is *very* common in VR and games in general. Both MVC and MVVM are often used in the same application. MVVM would be largely the self-contained widgets that reset on run, and MVC would be the application as a whole with data that last across runs.

Inventories

With the MVC pattern and scene changes, there is a new common need. That is saving data to review at a later time, or in game terms, an inventory. Good inventory code closely follows the MVC pattern with observer support and can provide data consistency across scene or level changes.

An inventory is fundamentally the model part of MVC as it is pure data. If looking at a real-world consideration, an inventory can simply be a list of parts. This is what the user currently has. At the most basic, an inventory could be as simple as the following code, where InventoryObject is just an interface to give a consistent API to the items in the inventory:

```
class Inventory
  InventoryObject[] stuff

  function AddStuff( InventoryObject s )
   stuff.Add( s )

  //various getters and setters
```

However, an inventory is often used by multiple objects. If this is to stay synchronized, the observer pattern should be used. This merely adds an event (which is a specialized observer) to the class that should trigger anytime there is any change to the inventory.

```
class Inventory
  InventoryObject[] stuff
  event NotifyMe

  function AddStuff( InventoryObject s )
    stuff.Add(s)
    NotifyMe()


  // various getters and setters
```

For a view to use an inventory, it simply needs to register and store any information needed to perform its job on notification. In the example below, the view saves a reference of the inventory rather than relying on data being sent.

```
class View
  Inventory model

  // various references to its components
  function Setup()
    // make components
    model = FindInventory()
    model.NotifyMe += GotNewData

  function GotNewData( )
    // update by pulling from model
```

Suppose that a different view now needs these data. Its code could look like this:

```
class View2
  //SAME
  Inventory model

  //SAME
  //various references to its components
  function Setup()
    //make components
    model = FindInventory()
    model.NotifyMe += GotNewData

  //WILL BE A DIFFERENT IMPLEMENTATION
  function GotNewData( )
    //update by pulling from model
```

It is almost identical. There is a new name and how the view's appearance will look will be different. The variable and functions needed are identical to support an inventory.

There is one other common variation of this pattern, and that is pushing the data through. In the prior example, the inventory reference was saved. Instead, the needed data could be sent instead. Suppose that a view only needs to know the last item added to this model. That results in the following highlighted changes:

```
class Inventory
  InventoryObject[] stuff
  event NotifyMe ( InventoryObject item )

  function AddStuff( InventoryObject s )
    stuff.Add(s)
    NotifyMe( s )

  // various getters and setters

class View
  // Inventory model

  // various references to its components
  function Setup()
    // make components
    model = FindInventory()
    model.NotifyMe += GotNewData

  function GotNewData( InventoryObject s )
    // update by pulling from model
```

Effectively, this shifted from a **pull**-based observer to a **push**-based observer. Which is better depends on the code's goals. Pull-based allows the most access, while push-based can restrict access better.

So where is the controller? That is the interaction framework discussed in earlier chapters and what actually adds the Inventory item that starts up the event notification.

The greatest advantage of a pure model inventory is the ease of saving the data. There is no concern of the controller or hooking up the view. It is just a straight save of all variables in the class. Getting everything back into synced order just requires triggering the event after the load is complete!

Reference

[1] Arthu P, Passini R. *Wayfinding: People, Signs, and Architecture,* New York, 1992, McGraw-Hill Book Co.

## 7

Models and Animations

This chapter covers the topics of model formats, choosing models, and animation topics. The topics and techniques are limited to what is used in virtual reality (VR) rather than an in-depth discussion on model file formats that would be needed if working deeply with a three-dimensional (3D) model editor software like Blender or 3DS Max. For a more in-depth discussion, please refer to a graphics textbook. If you have had a previous course in graphics, this chapter presents some details on importing models into VR engines but is otherwise a review. This chapter focuses on the model's structure, and later chapters go into more detail on texture, animation, and more.

Introduction to Models

Models are made up of triangles. Collections of triangles are called polygons and collections of polygons are called meshes. The corners of these triangles are called vertices, and these vertices can be shared among triangles. For example, in Fig. 7.1, the model contains 26,907 vertices shared by 52,896 triangles.

In general, this text does not work directly with triangles because that topic veers into graphics, but some basics are worth defining here in the event that some mesh manipulation is required.

First, any shape can be defined with triangles, so long as the vertices are known. However, how the vertices are stored and supported varies. A common, noncompressed storage format has the following characteristics:

- The model is composed of a list of vertices.
- A triangle points to the three indices in the list of vertices.
- The indices are listed in *clockwise* order.
- The ordered index list is then composed into a list of triangles.

Some formats also support higher-level groups (e.g., shading groups) that then have a list of triangle indices (Fig. 7.2).

As an example, let's approximate the image in Fig. 7.3 into triangles.

A Practical Introduction to Virtual Reality. https://doi.org/10.1016/B978-0-443-14036-5.00007-8

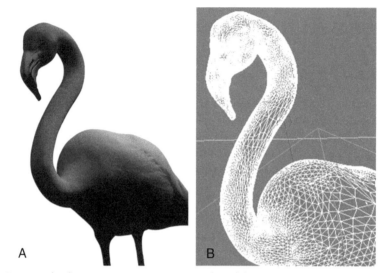

Fig. 7.1 Example of a model (left) and its triangles and vertices (right). (Courtesy of Charles Owen, used with permission.)

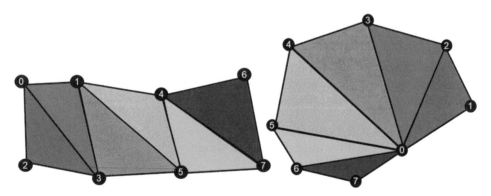

Fig. 7.2 Two examples of indices and triangles to create different shapes. Notice the ordering of index numbering.

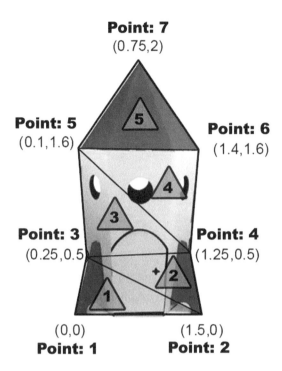

Point: 7
(0.75,2)

Point: 5
(0.1,1.6)

Point: 6
(1.4,1.6)

Point: 3
(0.25,0.5)

Point: 4
(1.25,0.5)

(0,0)
Point: 1

(1.5,0)
Point: 2

Fig. 7.3 Image of a rocket approximated into a set of triangles. (Courtesy of Charles Owen, used with permission.)

With the triangles drawn and the vertices labeled, the vertices are then placed in an array of vertices:

Index	Location
1	(0, 0)
2	(1.5, 0)
3	(0.25, 0.5)
4	(1.25, 0.5)
5	(0.1, 1.6)
6	(1.4, 1.6)
7	(0.75, 2)

This gives each vertex a reference index. The triangles are then defined through the vertex indices in their own clockwise-ordered list:

Index	Triangle Vertices
1	1, 3, 2
2	2, 3, 4
3	3, 5, 4
4	5, 6, 4
5	5, 7, 6

The reason for focusing on having the lists in clockwise order comes from culling. A triangle that is covered by another object does not need to be rendered, but how does the system tell if a triangle is covered? Let's look at this from the perspective of the user to an object and let's say that the object is a ball. The side of the ball that should be rendered has clockwise triangles and the back side has *counterclockwise* triangles. This is commonly seen in games where if the camera accidentally exits the world boundaries, most items are see-through.

Other Components of Models

In addition to triangles, models are composed of other components:
- Normals
- UV maps and textures
- Bones and rigging
- Animations

These other components are what make models so useful. Going into detail on each component veers into graphics and is not strictly necessary for VR development. The reason for this is that often, application development is separated into different graphics, level design, and development teams, where the development team imports the graphics into the application and support-level design *requires coding skills* by the designers. If you take a close look at large console game credits, you may notice this divide and that there are far more artists and designers than coders. Since the focus here is on development, each of these components are discussed briefly below from that point of view.

Normals

At a minimum, the normal refers to the direction that a vertex is facing. If you ever took a physics course where you had to define the normal of a surface, where the "normal" is at a right angle to the surface, this is very similar but applied to a vertex. Normals are needed for both shaders and some physics. For example, flat shading adjusts the normals to be identical across the triangle. Simple smooth shading adjusts the normals into an average. A normal mid-triangle is then calculated as a weighted average of its vertices' normal, as shown in Fig. 7.4.

UV Maps and Textures

Textures are essentially stickers placed over a model. The UV maps are used to determine how the texture is applied. These maps essentially act like pins that pin the locations of a two-dimensional (2D) image on a 3D surface based on their coordinates. UV is nearly equivalent to XY on a 2D image, but different letters are used to differentiate

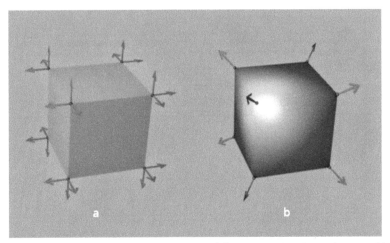

Fig. 7.4 Example of flat shading (a) and simple smooth shading (b). Note the direction and composition of the normals at each vertex. (https://commons.wikimedia.org/wiki/File:Vertex_normal_%E0%B8%81%E0%B8%B1%E0%B8%9 A%E0%B8%81%E0%B8%B2%E0%B8%A3%E0%B9%80%E0%B8%9B%E0%B8%A5%E0%B8%B5%E0%B9%88%E0%B8%A2%E0%B8%99%E0%B9%81%E0%B8%9B%E0%B8%A5%E0%B8%87%E0%B8%81%E0%B8%B2%E0%B8%A3%E0%B8%AA%E0%B8%B0%E0%B8%97%E0%B9%89%E0%B8%AD%E0%B8%99%E0%B8%82%E0%B8%AD%E0%B8%87%E0%B8%9E%E0%B8%B7%E0%B9%89%E0%B8%99%E0%B8%9C%E0%B8%B4%E0%B8%A7.png.)

between the vertex and the texture coordinates. There are several UV map options:

- Albedo (base color)
- Normal (use a normal per pixel rather than by vertex)
- Specular (shininess per pixel)
- Alpha (transparency per pixel)

And so on. These options are almost always computationally faster than adding more vertices (Fig. 7.5).

There are 3D textures in special cases, but the vast majority are 2D. Details on texture mapping are provided in Chapter 9 Textures.

Bones, Rigging, and Animation

Bones and rigging are components placed in a model for generating motion in the model for animations. Bones have a similar meaning as in real life. They describe the underlying "stiff" components that the model's surface should follow when the bone is moved. They also tend to map to individual children nodes in the scene tree. The actual assignment of the model's surface, or "skin," is called rigging. This text does not go into creating rigging as that is a topic for model creators. However, it is important to note that if a model does not have rigging, there will generally be no animation when the model is imported. If models do come with built-in animations, they can then be played in the engine on command. Some examples include an avatar that can walk or jump (Fig. 7.6).

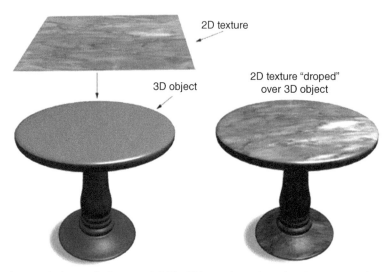

Fig. 7.5 Example of texture being applied to a model. The UV map determines the placement of the texture. (https://www.pcmag.com/encyclopedia/term/texture-map (Intergraph Computer Systems [Hexagon BX]).)

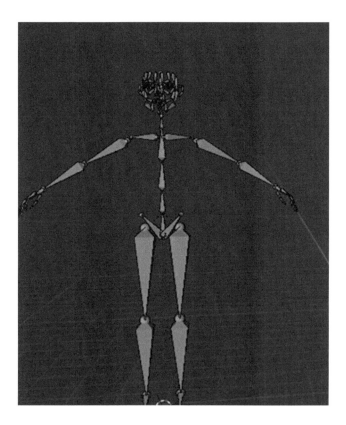

Fig. 7.6 Example rigging for a model.

Details on animation are provided in later chapters as triggering and interpolating animation can be the developers job.

Models for 3D Applications

Good models for VR applications have more requirements than other applications. In general, most of the models found online will not be suitable for a VR application as of this edition. However, because there are so many models, there are still plenty of options to try [1].

When choosing a model, there are some characteristics that help determine if the model is suitable for 3D:

Good Model	Bad Model
Low polygon count, or low poly.	High polygon count, or high poly.
Detail is even.	Detail is not even.
Normals and UV coordinates exist.	Normals and UV coordinates do not exist.
No embedded polygons (no wasted polygons).	Objects inside of objects.
Triangles are all connected.	Objects are separated.
Textures are included.	Textures are shown but not downloadable.
Models are placed at the "feet" or centered at (0,0,0).	Model centering is not known.
Models are composed of a consistent unit (ideally meters).	Model sizing is erratic.
No unusual materials.	Unsupported materials except in the modeling software.

Often, these characteristics cannot be checked until after the model is downloaded. Switching the model to the wireframe, as in displaying the underlying triangular structure, or checking the UV map can help for an initial check. Let us go through some examples.

Example of Model Review

Hidden Polygons

Let's start with a fairly simple hamburger, shown in Fig. 7.7. From the fully rendered image, the model gives an initial impression of having a low polygon count. However, this model is listed as having 1034 polygons! Switching to the wireframe shows where all those polygons are hidden: inside the burger. Unless these extra polygons are necessary for an effective animation of the model, such as pulling the burger apart layer by layer in an animation, this model's excess polygons will never be seen. Therefore, this model has an unneeded polygon count for most purposes.

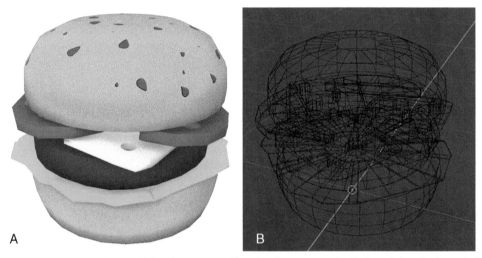

Fig. 7.7 This is a simple model with a high polygon count. The visual representation is A, and the wireframe is B. (https://www.turbosquid.com/3d-models/3d-low-poly-hamburger-2005008, n.d.)

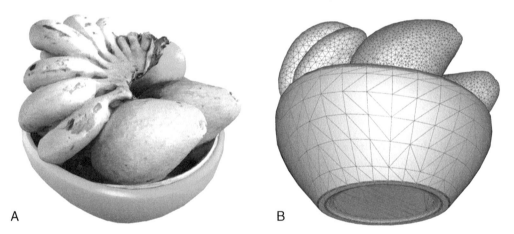

Fig. 7.8 Example of uneven detail. The visual representation is A, and the wireframe is B. (https://www.turbosquid.com/3d-models/3d-low-poly-hamburger-2005008, n.d.)

Uneven Detail

In the next example, Fig. 7.8 shows a bowl of fruit. But while the fruit is very detailed and realistic, the bowl is not. This is an example of uneven detail. The polygon count is also telling, 26,667 polygons, which is very high. Having one item in a model with a very high polygon count can also easily overrun the rendering software.

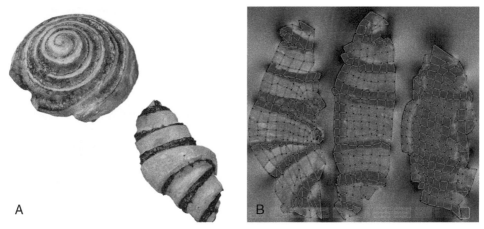

Fig. 7.9 Sample model with UV meshes. The visual representation of the models is A, and the UV coordinates for the croissant are B. (https://www.turbosquid.com/3d-models/chocolate-croissant-cinnamon-roll-3d-model-1853110, n.d.)

Normals and UV Coordinates Exist

The next example is of a potentially good model. Fig. 7.9 shows two pastry models, which come with UV coordinate maps. The presence of a UV map is generally a sign of a good model.

Game-Ready Model

The last example is that of a possibly good model. "Possibly good" is used here as the needs of the application can put additional restrictions on the models not referenced here. The model in Fig. 7.10 has a relatively low polygon count. Extra polygons are used only as needed, such as for the cherry decorations, so there are no embedded polygons. The online description also lists the texture sizes, which is a good sign. This particular model was also listed as game ready.

VR Engine Model Requirements

In addition to the general application/game requirements of a good model, VR engines have their own extra requirements for importing.

In Unity, only 3D files are supported for direct import:
- .fbx (Autodesk, Unity's preferred format)
- .dae (Collada)
- .3ds (old 3DX Max)
- .dxf
- .obj (3D object version of .ppm)
- .asset (Unity Asset)
- .unitypackage (Unity Asset Package)

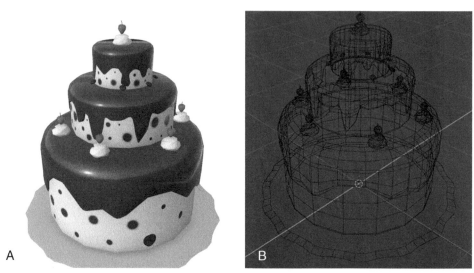

Fig. 7.10 Example of a game-ready model. The visual representation is A, and the wireframe is B. (https://www.turbosquid.com/3d-models/3d-cake-model-2004756, n.d.)

In Unreal, the range of supported 3D files for direct import is shorter:

- .fbx (Autodesk, Unreal's preferred format)
- .obj (3D object version of .ppm)

While more formats are officially supported, both Unity and Unreal handle these other files by converting the files into .fbx format during import. Unreal also supports more file types for textures only, although .fbx is still preferred.

Even if the models are already in .fbx format, import problems can still arise, such as missing components or incorrectly importing. In general, these components of a model are more likely to import correctly:

- Meshes (the structure of the model)
- Textures with caveats in Unity (the surface colors of the model)
- Smoothing groups (a group will average the normals for each vertex within that group)

Animations are more likely to import incorrectly. If the model and animation are *baked* before importing, they are more likely to import correctly. Baking refers to converting the high resolution/memory items, where the processing calculation functions are run each frame, to a more static, low memory option. There are many different options for baking.

Unity has some additional caveats for importing textures. Namely, Unity prefers textures in the form of a linked file. If the modeling engine, such as 3DS Max or Blender, exports the absolute file paths to the texture, which many engines do by default, path problems are to be expected. Embedded textures will also either not load or double the size upon import.

Specific details on importing models into a designated VR engine are covered in the associated tutorial.

Animation

Other than the absolute basics, creating base animations are largely out of the scope of the course for the same reason as stated in the section on Other Components of Models. The focus here is on the development side, not graphics. This section discusses some terminology, blending animations, animation state machines, and triggering animations in VR engines.

Animation Terminology

Procedural animation refers to animation performed in the code. Code is written to move the different objects and parts of a model. These animations are typically restricted to simple linear motions, such as path following. Another common use for procedural animation is for automatic functions, such as walking or jumping.

As an example, take a car model with turning wheels. What would it take to animate the automobile wheels? Find the bone/rigging that maps to a wheel child in the scene tree and set its local rotation (Fig. 7.11).

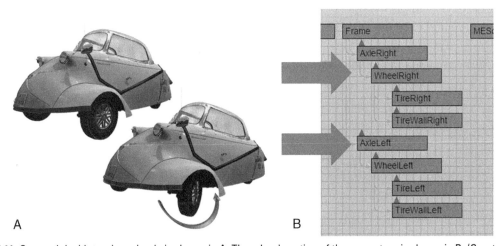

Fig. 7.11 Car model with turning wheels is shown in A. The wheel section of the scene tree is shown in B. (Courtesy of Charles Owen, used with permission.)

Keyframe animation is the built-in animation that sometimes comes with a model. This type usually uses rigging to describe the animation. Here, the model interpolates between the key points in the animation. At a high level, the animation has fixed points in time and transformations for a given joint. The transformations may come in the form of

- Matrices
- Euler angles
- Position
- Scale
- Quaternions

Making a custom keyframe animation is largely out of the scope of the text. Usually, the model can be imported and then a specific animation can be chosen from the VR engine's import settings.

Blended animation is what it sounds like—two animations blended together. There are two common forms of this:

- Blend: permanently blends two animations together
- Cross fade: blend as a transition between one animation to another

Blending offers the additional benefit of creating new animations without starting from scratch. Since this can occur on the developer's side, this type of animation is discussed in more detail in the next section.

Blending Animations

As a reference, let's take a robot samurai model with keyframe animations (Fig. 7.12).

For a blending example, if a model comes with both a walking animation and a crawling animation, a blended animation of both motions produces a crouching animation. Granted, this may not always be perfect, and the less tweaking required, the smoother the final animation (Fig. 7.13).

Fig. 7.12 Model with keyframe animation. (https://www.turbosquid.com/3d-models/charecter-anim-rigs-3ds/1089543, n.d.)

Fig. 7.13 Conceptual example of blending animations. (Created from TurboSquid model.)

This model comes with walking and crawling animations, so creating a crouching animation can be done on the developer's side.

For an example on cross fade animations, let's suppose an animation where the robot samurai walks, then runs, and finally walks again. Stopping the walk to start the run animation is jarring. A solution to this is to cross fade between the animation transitions. The transitions can be handled with state machines.

State Machines

More modern animations often use state machines. Using the walk-run-walk example above, the motion can be understood as a character that starts walking immediately but can transition to or from running. This is just a specialized flow chart.

Transition rules are used to determine when the transitions are allowed. No rule is equal to an instantaneous transition, such as the first walk animation. When there is a rule, there is a condition that must be met before the transition can occur. For example, the transition from walking to running could be set to occur when the character hits a speed threshold of 0.5.

Unity and Unreal have fairly similar state machine development for animations. Both engines have states and transitions and both have a way to handle three or more transitions from a state, although this varies more in use. In VR-specific terms, Unreal uses Conduits and Unity uses Blend Trees.

As an example, consider a simple state machine where the character can only transition from walk to run, and back again. The state machine would begin with three states of start, or the entry point of the machine; walk; and run, as shown in Fig. 7.14.

Fig. 7.14 Graphical representation of a state machine with three states.

These are initially disconnected, and merely state that there are walk and run animations. If run now, the model would not animate at all since it is stuck at start (Fig. 7.15). Using the samurai model, as an example, it would do this:

Fig. 7.15 Model stuck in base pose state. (From TurboSquid model.)

The model is not walking and is instead in its base pose.

To start the state machine will immediately switch the model to walk because there is a connection from start to run (Fig. 7.16).

Fig. 7.16 State machine with a connection from start to walk.

The key element here is that there are no restrictions on that transition, which means to transition immediately.

For the walk and run transition, a parameter would need to be created called "speed." Both Unity and Unreal support such parameters and allow outside access to them. The state machine then monitors these variables per frame update, and if the conditions are met, the effect is triggered (Fig. 7.17). After these transitions are added, the state machine may look like this:

Fig. 7.17 State machine with all necessary connections.

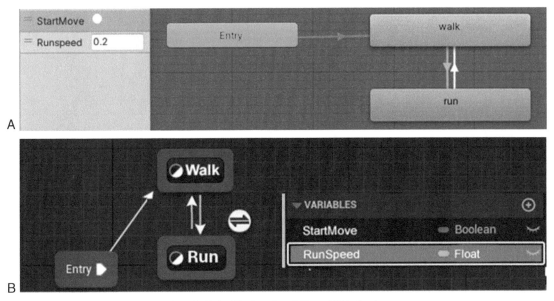

Fig. 7.18 State machine representations in Unity (A above) and Unreal (B below).

As an example, this is how it would look in Unity and Unreal (Fig. 7.18).

At this point, the development merely needs to set the speed variable and the state machine will do the rest.

Reference

[1] TurboSquid has a large number of models available for noncommercial use (https://www.turbosquid.com). All models in the chapter are from TurboSquid.

## 8

Terrains

This chapter introduces terrain models. While this topic may give an initial impression of being graphics focused, this topic is important for the development side of an application. Importing, creating, or tweaking a terrain is embedded on the development side of virtual reality (VR) engines where computational efficiency is critical.

What Are Terrains?

Terrains are a special type of model. Rather than being composed of only a volume of space, a terrain is a plane with raised points. Some systems treat terrains largely as models; others give terrains special treatment. Unity is between both approaches, while Unreal uses the latter approach. Terrains can be chained, have a height map applied, and have physics materials added.

Terrains use height maps to determine the raised points. The height map is not a texture unto itself but the mapping of the height of the terrain's base plane vertices. This mapping can be temporarily rendered as a gray scale image. These images typically have 16-bit depth to allow values between 0 and 65,535 and may require special software to view. Brightness is a characteristic used to describe the height of the vertices. This works similarly to a color-coded topographical map, like in Fig. 8.1. Applying the height map to the base terrains conceptually works like a push-pin toy (Fig. 8.2).

Creating a New Terrain

Creating a base terrain is fairly straightforward. Since terrains are objects, a new one can be added in the same way as other three-dimensional (3D) objects in Unity with Create > 3D Object > Terrain. In Unreal, a terrain is added by going to the Landscape tool (Mode > Landscape) and then selecting New under the Manage mode tab. In both cases, the terrain starts as a bare, flat plane. From here, the plane can be tweaked to

- be raised or lowered,
- make holes,
- be smoothed, and
- set to a specific height.

A Practical Introduction to Virtual Reality. https://doi.org/10.1016/B978-0-443-14036-5.00008-X

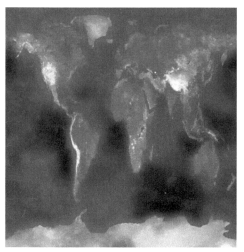

Fig. 8.1 An example of a height map. The lighter, brighter areas are higher in altitude. (https://commons.wikimedia.org/wiki/File:Approximate_Earth_Heigh_Map.png.)

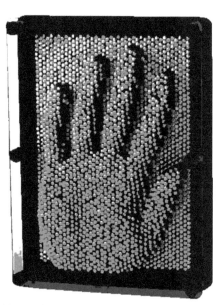

Fig. 8.2 Example push-pin toy.

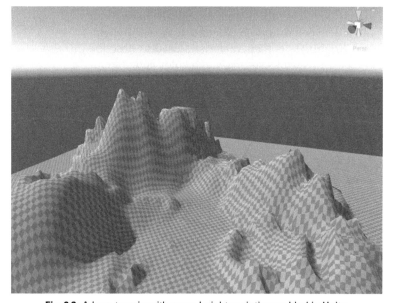

Fig. 8.3 A bare terrain with some height variations added in Unity.

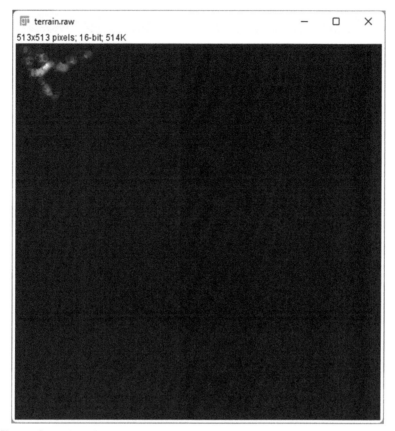

Fig. 8.4 Example of the resulting height map from Fig. 8.3 derived from a Unity terrain.

From here, the quality settings can be used to create the height map from the texture resolution

The base mesh can be saved and loaded into a height map. Fig. 8.4 shows an example of a height map of Fig. 8.3.

Terrains also can be patched together if more than one is needed. This is common in open world applications where a single terrain could not give sufficient detail. Both Unreal and Unity support this, and the key element here is that the edges must match exactly. Consider the example below with three terrain squares. The boundaries in orange match in height and resolution. This can be a challenge when using different levels of detail (LOD) to adjust the quality of the landscape at a distance. This is also shown below where the detailed areas have more triangles but the boundaries have the same resolution. Thus, the reason why terrains are usually handled in a special way compared to other models is to ensure that the locations where terrains connect stay synced (Fig. 8.5).

Fig. 8.5 Example terrain with three terrain squares patched together.

Adding Textures

Terrains normally have multiple textures, so the texture and material setup is a bit different. In Unity, the Edit Terrain Layers option allows for adding one or more textures to the list. Fig. 8.6 shows an example list with five images. In Unreal, the list is available in the Landscape tools > Paint mode tab as the Target Layers.

The textures are then painted onto the terrain. However, the textures are painted on in a grid pattern that is usually noticeable at far distances but is less apparent when zoomed in (Fig. 8.7). There are some size settings available that can help to mitigate the grid effect.

Adding Foliage

Trees can be extremely high in memory use. For this reason, there are a number of shortcuts to mitigate the effect. Before, Unity had a few built-in trees that came with a terrain. While this is not the case anymore, Unity still offers some premade models in their Asset Store. These models can be dragged and dropped directly into Unity. Unreal has a Foliage tool for adding trees with a large number of models available for free or for purchase in the Unreal Engine Marketplace.

After importing a tree, the trees can be painted onto the terrain. This is mostly just selecting an area and clicking on the tree option as shown (Fig. 8.8).

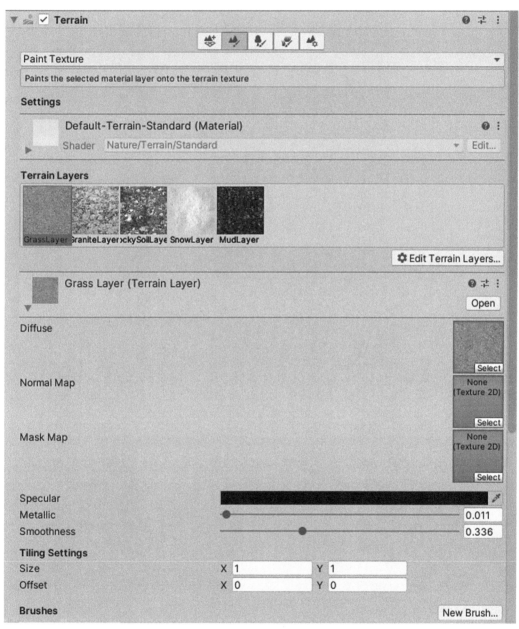

Fig. 8.6 Example of Terrain Layers list with five textures in Unity.

Fig. 8.7 Textures painted onto the terrain. A grid pattern to the texture shows at a distance but is not apparent up close.

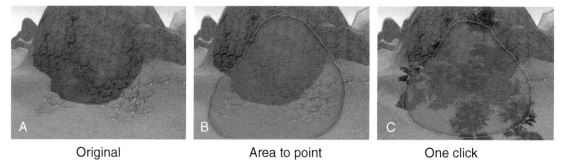

Original   Area to point   One click

Fig. 8.8 Steps to add Trees added to the terrain in Unity. (A) shows the area where trees are to be added. (B) shows the selection area to place trees. (C) shows the result after populating the selected area with trees in one click.

Fig. 8.9 Grass billboarding and rocks added to the terrain in Unity.

Rock and grass can be added as either a texture or a mesh. Grasses are thin, so billboarding (a textured panel often forced to face the user) with a texture is effective and some foliage models do come with billboarding. Rocks usually need meshes, as in 3D meshes. After adding the billboarding, the grass and rocks are painted on the terrain as before (Fig. 8.9).

Wind can also be added to the terrain. In Unity, there are two wind settings: speed and size. The grass texture has the wind settings under the Terrain settings. Trees, however, need a Wind Zone, which can be created as a 3D object (Create > 3D Object > Wind Zone). The Wind Zone object has two modes:

- Directional: global to whole system. Direction is set by the transform.
- Spherical: limited area. Direction is outward.

In Unreal, wind settings are available in the material's Functions > World Position Offset. Which function to use depends on the needed level of detail. There is a SimpleGrassWind function, which can be used as a shortcut for grasses and gives a nondirectional wind effect to foliage. Otherwise, the Wind function provides more settings and the PivotPainter_PerObjectFoliageData function is for customizing the wind for individual foliage objects, such as a detailed tree.

Even with these shortcuts, trees are particularly expensive. This can be further mitigated by adjusting the LOD according to the user's perspective.

Level of Detail

Think about how many details can be seen close up or far away, such as a pile of pebbles. Details that are distinct close-up blur together at a far enough distance. Close up, details of each pebble can be seen. At a distance, the pebbles blur into a rocky pile. Since these details become blurred at a distance, there is no need to render those distinct details. This natural variation in detail can be used to skip the blurred details in the rendering and reduce the computational load. It is used in computing as a characteristic called the level of detail or LOD. In VR engines, LODs have two main parts:

- Models of multiple, varying detail.
- Distance thresholds for shifting between models. This is usually measured in terms of how much screen space the object takes up.

As an example, let's take a tree model with four distinct LODs, as shown in Fig. 8.10.

In Unity, the LOD for an object is added by first creating an empty game object. The different LOD models are then added as children of the game object. An LOD group component is then added to the parent object. In the component, the children renderers are attached with the cutoff adjusted as needed.

In Unreal, the LOD models are stored as meshes. First, the object asset is opened in the Static Mesh Editor. LOD model options are imported under the Details panel in LOD Settings > LOD Import > Import LOD Level <number>. The LOD model can then be selected for import. The distance thresholds are also set in LOD Settings > LOD <number>, although the default setting auto-computes the thresholds.

There are some caveats to using LOD on terrains. First, items made directly on the terrain should be controlled by the terrain. As a result, detail meshes cannot have LODs. There are means to adjust materials and textures in terrains, but they require different function calls.

Navigation

Larger spaces require more advanced movement. Simple teleportation works well in mid-sized areas but can be jarring and decrease a user's wayfinding ability. Wayfinding here means the ability to navigate to a desired location, even when the location is out of view. Steering navigation, or the type of navigation in most 3D console games where the character moves smoothly over the ground, can be tempting here. However, steering navigation, and in particular rotation, is extremely prone to causing cybersickness without extreme care.

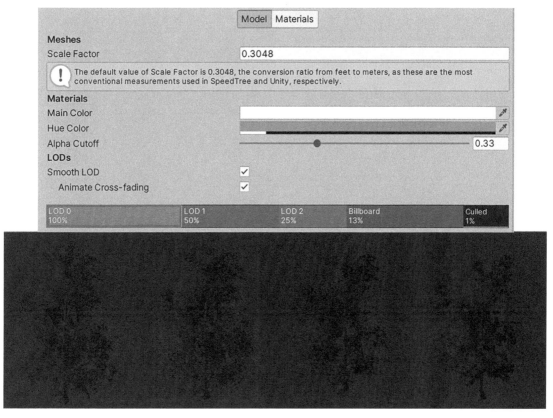

Fig. 8.10 Example of LOD in Unity. The tree model is presented with four LODs presented with decreasing LOD from left to right. The window above shows the distance specification for rendering which LOD model.

Wayfinding is its own field of study and is largely not discussed in this book as it involves cognitive science. However, better movement techniques are presented in the walking chapter, which is next.

9

Textures

While textures were introduced in the previous chapter, there are additional effects available through textures that are worth illustrating. The main topics covered in this chapter are the definition of a texture, UV coordinates, and texture special effects (normal maps, specular maps, and alpha maps). While not a VR topic, knowing what to request or what may have gone wrong in textures are valuable skills. This chapter is also heavily graphics focused, so those with a graphics background may find this chapter familiar.

Texture Mapping

Texture are images mapped onto the surface of a triangle. The most common textures are in 2D and have a file format of .png, .bmp, .fig, etc. These are usually applied by plastering a model with 2D stickers (Fig. 9.1).

In Unity and Unreal, these can be called textures, albedo maps, or diffuse maps. One of the advantages of using textures is that the appearance of a model can be changed by changing the texture settings or underlying mesh. An example of this is shown in Fig. 9.2.

Textures can be applied as a single map over the entire model, over portions of a model, or even repeated in a pattern. An example of this is shown in Fig. 9.3. The basic techniques in applying these textures are described in this chapter.

Those coming from a 3D modeling background may be surprised that texture images rather than materials with physical properties are still heavily used, and may even be required, in game engines. Textures render far faster than physics based materials. In fact, most of the fancier materials from 3D modeling software will not import! Instead, game engines typically use textures to store information about how to render whenever possible as will be shown in this chapter.

UV Coordinates

Textures are mapped onto models using UV coordinates. UV coordinates are similar to the X,Y location on a 2D image, but different letters are used to differentiate between texture coordinates and vertex coordinates. The main difference is that UV coordinates act more like

A Practical Introduction to Virtual Reality. https://doi.org/10.1016/B978-0-443-14036-5.00009-1

Fig. 9.1 A real-world example of applying 2D textures (stickers) to a 3D object (computer). (Attributed to Blake Patterson. https://www.flickr.com/photos/blakespot/3871908897/in/pool-laptopstickers/lightbox/.)

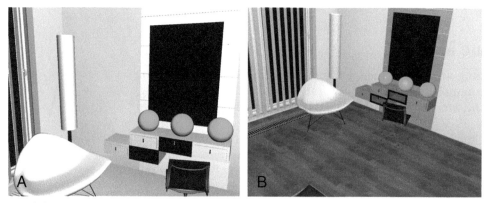

Fig. 9.2 The (A) image is a room without any textures. The (B) image is the same room with a few textures added. (Courtesy of Charles Owen, used with permission.)

a percentage on the image. The UV point of the texture is pinned to the UV-specified vertex on the model. Fig. 9.4 shows an example of this mapping.

Tiling

Tiling refers to repeating the texture. There are two options for tiling. One is to set the mapping to higher than one or the unit texture. The other option is to set the tiling options when importing. The options can vary, but repetition or tiling, clamping, and size adjustments are common.

Consider the image in (Fig. 9.5) (left) and a square (right) that can hold exactly four of those images.

Normally tiles would mod the square's UV coordinates by 1 to determine the image location per vertex, which would result in the image shown in (Fig. 9.6).

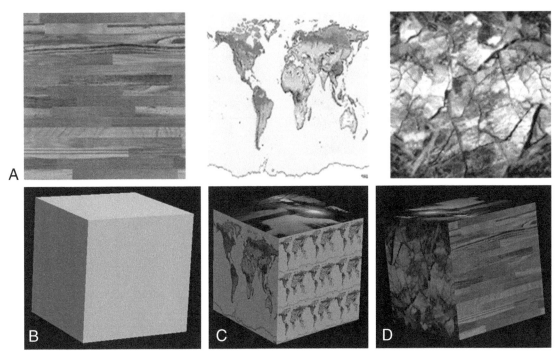

Fig. 9.3 Shows an example of applying different textures in different ways to the surface of the cube. The A row of images show the textures to be applied to a cube. The B image is the base cube. The C and D images show different sides of the cube to show the textures applied to different surfaces of the cube. (Courtesy of Charles Owen, used with permission.)

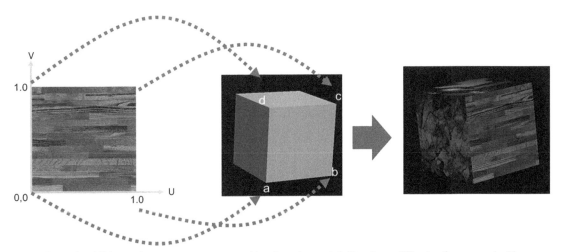

Fig. 9.4 Example of UV mapping a texture onto one side of a cube model. (Courtesy of Charles Owen, used with permission.)

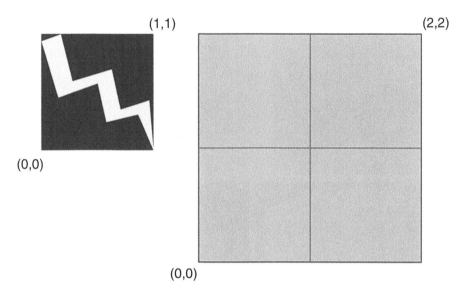

(1,1) (2,2)

(0,0) (0,0)

Fig. 9.5 Example tile texture and tile map.

Fig. 9.6 Example of applying a texture tile to the tile map.

Fig. 9.7 Example of tearing caused by stretching the boundary pixels to the edges.

Clamping and mirroring are also commonly supported. Clamping means the image can only be placed once. In some engines, this means fitting the texture to the full object, but in others, the texture size is set, and the color at the edge is stretched. This stretching is also called a "tear" and is shown in Fig. 9.7.

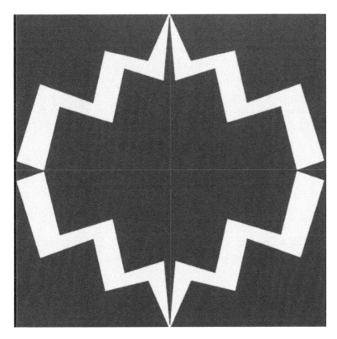

Fig. 9.8 Example of mirroring.

Mirroring is similar to normal tiling but flips the image on each repeat (Fig. 9.8).

More wrapping options are available but vary between VR engines.

Animating Textures

Textures can be animated by adjusting the UV coordinates at a much lower cost than a model animation. Consider moving water. The texture can be animated to show the water moving down a river. As an example, let's take a texture applied to a plane. The texture pattern is repeated and pans to the left. Here is the pseudocode to do that:

```
class AnimateTexture

  animationSpeed = Vector( 1.0, 0.0 )
  uvOffset = Vector( 0.0, 0.0 )

  function FrameUpdate()
    uvOffset += ( animationSpeed * deltaTime )
    textureRenderer = GetTextureRenderer()

    if textureRenderer != null
      textureRenderer.setTextureOffset( uvOffset )
```

Non-Grid Textures

While tiling can be helpful for filing in textures, repeating texture can give a grid effect, which humans are very good at spotting. There are some methods to resolve the grid effect:

- Detail/secondary map: This method uses a higher level of detail (LOD) texture up close and a lower LOD farther away.
- Random overlays: This method places textures over textures, similar to the haphazard layering of stickers.
- Skinned model: This method has the texture sectioned so that the different parts of the texture can be peeled and placed on the model.

An example of a detail map would be trim on a character's sleeve. At a distance, the trim may be solid, but closer, it may show embroidery (Fig. 9.9).

Random overlays are regularly used in terrains. Consider the example in (Fig. 9.10). The (A) image clearly shows a repeating pattern. The (B) image mitigates it.

Fig. 9.9 Example of LOD on a character's sleeve. The (A) image of the sleeve shows a low LOD texture with a solid trim at a distance. The (B) image of the sleeve shows a high LOD texture with detailed embroidery at a closer distance. (https://pixabay.com/illustrations/wizard-fantasy-magic-mystery-spell-4417430/.)

Fig. 9.10 Example of using a random overlay in Unity. (A) image does not use the random overlay while the (B) image does.

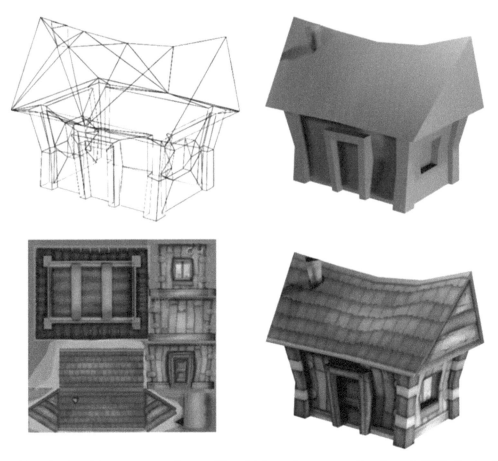

Fig. 9.11 Example of applying texture mapping to a 3D model. (https://commons.wikimedia.org/wiki/File:Hand-painted_house_3D_model_stages.png.)

Texture mapping essentially acts like applying 3D modeling paint over the surface and then peeling off the surface (this is called skinning) and putting it in a 2D texture. (Fig. 9.11) shows where the surface was lifted and placed into a single 2D image.

More Texture Types

Game and VR designers generally stick to low polygon counts in their models and use materials that do not require math beyond basic linear algebra to keep the computational load down. However, the resulting application can still require a high LOD. Designers get around this dilemma by using more texture types. So far, only the base color (Albedo, Diffuse) has been used in this chapter. Here are some additional texture types:

- Shininess or specular: This is the level of brightness of light reflected at a designated pixel.
- Occlusion/Ambient: This sets the ambient or minimum light over an object. There is more on this texture type in Chapter 11.
- Transparency: This sets the transparency. Also called alpha mapping.
- Normal maps: This sets the perceived angle of the designated vertex.

Normal and alpha maps are the most common mapping after the base color map.

Normal Maps

Normal maps are used to create bumpy surfaces on objects but do not affect the object's displacement. The more normals used in the map, the more detail is shown on the object. However, normals are usually associated with vertices in graphics. This means that more normals need more vertices, which in turn requires more triangles and becomes computationally expensive.

Let's illustrate this with an example. Fig. 9.12 shows two images: one with a wrapped texture and one with both a wrapped texture and a normal map.

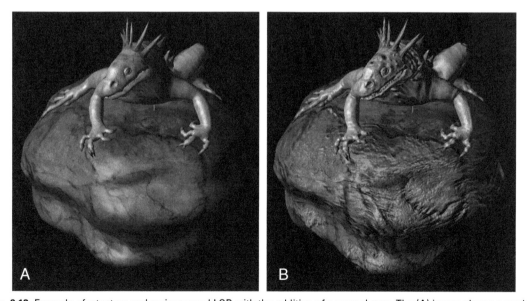

Fig. 9.12 Example of a texture and an increased LOD with the addition of a normal map. The (A) image shows a model with a mapped texture. The (B) image shows the same model with wrapped texture but also with a normal map applied. (Courtesy of Charles Owen, used with permission.)

Figure 9.12B shows more detail due to the normal map. What the normal map does is add angle variations between the model's vertex normals. A new normal is then calculated for each pixel; that is then used to compute the color (Fig. 9.13).

The texture and normal map used for the example are shown in Fig. 9.14. The normal map shows a pink color between parts of the texture. In a normal map, each pixel RGB value is a normal vector relative to the surface at that point. The range is typically [–1,1] but is mapped to [0,1] so that the normals become colors.

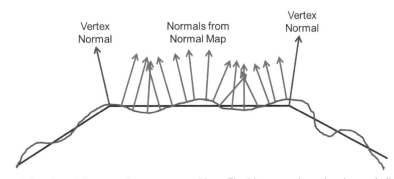

Fig. 9.13 Conceptual drawing of the normal map over an object. The blue rays show the change in light direction from the normal map effect.

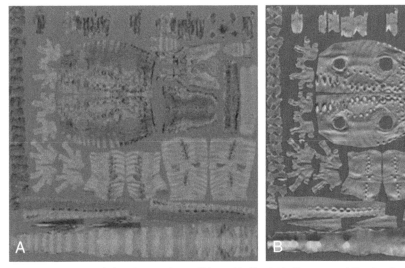

Fig. 9.14 The base color (A) and normal map (B) used in Fig. 9.12. (Courtesy of Charles Owen, used with permission.)

Alpha Maps

Basic transparency is fairly straightforward in most graphics systems. Each color has an associated alpha value (RGBA). An alpha value of 1 is opaque, while an alpha value of 0 is transparent. Values in between blend the alpha map values with the underlying color in a linear blend equation,

$$c_{\text{pixel}} = \alpha c_{\text{new}} + (1 - \alpha)c_{\text{old}}.$$

An alpha value of 0.8 means that 80% of the new color from behind the object is blended with 20% of the preexisting color.

There are some caveats to using alpha maps. For example, the alpha map only blends with a color that is preexisting. Transparency is drawn last This means if the transparency was drawn first, there is nothing behind the object and only the sky is shown. Another caveat occurs when a transparency map is placed over another transparency layer. Doing this several times is called Overdraw. There are several methods to handle multiple transparency layers, but they all follow a similar approach. Draw transparent objects last. This means that one transparency layer is drawn first and then the second layer in order. Unity has a Layer option in the Inspector that enables this ordered rendering. Unreal uses the Translucency Sort Priority under Rendering. Deeper details on handling this challenge are more of a graphics topic and thus out of the scope of this text.

Shininess and Occlusion Map

While these maps are less common, they are used for higher-end graphical applications. Normally how shiny a model is depends on its material lighting parameters at a given area. This, again, would result in more triangles if only some subareas needed to be shiny. As an example, consider the somewhat matte base sphere and possible raindrop texture in the top row of Fig. 9.15. In the shininess result, the areas marked in white are much smoother and look wet in the bottom left image. The occlusion map has a smaller effect, but note that the dark areas are darker, while the raindrop areas are the same as before as shown in the bottom right. They only look brighter due to an optical illusion given that the outer area is now darker.

Original   Texture

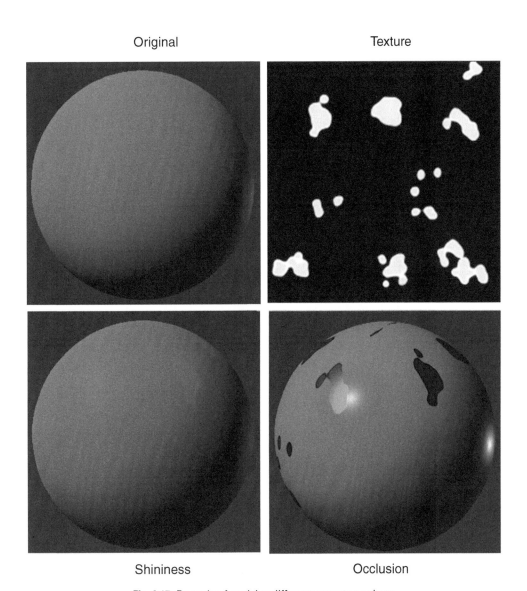

Shininess   Occlusion

Fig. 9.15 Example of applying different maps to a sphere.

10

Walking and Navigation

This chapter covers various walking and navigation designs and controls. While some of the materials may be covered in a game design course, virtual reality (VR) requires a number of specific navigation options. The general topics of this chapter are camera settings and models; walking options, which include three types of teleportation (instant, blink, node), steering, and other more physical methods, navigation combinations plus variants (arm swinger and snap movement) and special hardware; and finally locomotion on non-flat surfaces. This chapter also includes some suggestions for mitigating potential cybersickness. Reviewing the Model-View-Controller (MVC) pattern is suggested.

Cameras

Unlike other applications, cameras are largely controlled by the VR engine and predominately by aligning to the head on the head-mounted display (HMD). However, there are a few settings to discuss to better support walking. This is largely focused on situations where the user is in settings with closer walls.

First, let's discuss the camera configuration and the required information to describe a camera. The area that the user can potentially see is called the *frustum*. Most systems have options to choose how this frustum is to be shown to the user (Fig. 10.1).

With rendering, the objects that are to be selected for rendering must be within the range of the near-clipping plane and the far-clipping plane (Fig. 10.2). The aspect ratio of the screen is determined with width over height of the distance from the field of view and is similar to the aspect ratio of screens and monitors,

$$\text{aspect\_ratio} = \frac{w}{h}.$$

The aspect ratio is normally controlled by the system in VR but is settable in 3D applications. The common setting in 3D is to set the horizontal range to 60°. In VR, the range is usually set to match the HMD settings.

A Practical Introduction to Virtual Reality. https://doi.org/10.1016/B978-0-443-14036-5.00010-8

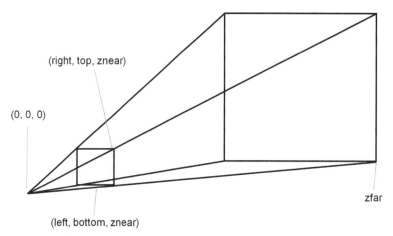

Fig. 10.1 Drawing of a squared volume range of a user's frustum. Here, the forward direction is in the positive *z*-axis. (Courtesy of Charles Owen, used with permission.)

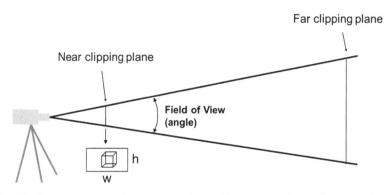

Fig. 10.2 Example of frustum with near- and far-clipping planes. (Courtesy of Charles Owen, used with permission.)

The clip planes are the start and end locations that objects must be in to show to the camera. Too close or too far and the object will not be in the final image. There are some limits in their settings. The near-clipping plane, for example, should not be set to the camera's origin, as this can cause the image to converge. Close distances are also not advised since the user can feel as though objects get too close. If the near-clipping plane is too far, however, the user will see through an object, which is generally not recommended unless the application requires seeing through walls. Due to the increased control of the VR camera, the near-clipping plane can generally be set closer than 3D applications, however. The far-clipping plane is more so for efficiency so that some objects can be ignored and allows a switch to a skyline rendering if nothing is hit.

There are two main modes for the camera: orthographic and perspective. An orthographic camera changes the frustum into a perfect box. A common case of using this is isometric visualization. Consider the example below in Fig. 10.3. The (A) image with the perspective camera has a vanishing point on the cube. The (B) image with the orthographic camera has the side parallel. While the orthographic camera is not typically used for HMDs, it is still used on occasion for elements like mini-maps. A perspective camera uses the frustum dependent of the field of view and the clipping planes discussed above. This is "natural" viewing as if through a real-world camera.

Another setting is the view port area. This refers to the amount of the virtual scene to use and is normally only used in orthographic cameras to set the scene size. However, the view port area is sometimes used in perspective cameras to change the amount of used screen space. These settings are available in the camera object in the VR engines, although Unreal has additional places to set the clipping planes.

Fig. 10.3 The (A) image uses a perspective camera, while the (B) uses an orthographic camera with the camera as the same point.

Walking Considerations

The instant a VR play area is larger than the user's play space, some sort of long-distance movement will be needed. Given that most users have little more than a living room–sized space, this occurs quite quickly. Walking has two requirements: locomotion method and navigation protocol. Together, these requirements are called wayfinding. In close spaces, direct walking works in VR. However, that changes once the user needs to move distances farther than a living room. One concern that pops up in large-range wayfinding is potentially walking through walls (or into physical walls). While boundaries may be active and prevent the feet from crossing that boundary, the user may still push their head through the wall. The head can be stopped in code, but this can be jarring. It is better to design levels to avoid this when possible. Another concern is spacing. Users tend to underestimate distance in VR [1]. For this reason, usability suggests bumping up the size of the environment by about 50%. The last concern to mention here is cybersickness.

For our purposes, cybersickness is the feeling of motion sickness due to visuals in a VR system. That is an incomplete definition, but this is sufficient for VR development. Cybersickness is an extremely common issue that develops as soon as the user starts moving in larger virtual spaces with current rates estimated at 60% of the population, but some very sensitive persons will notice it even in standing-only applications. More details are covered in Chapter 18, but for now keep the following in mind when developing wayfinding:

- Swaying *increases* the potential for cybersickness.
- Jitter with motion or visuals *increases* the potential for cybersickness.
- Greater user control *decreases* the potential for cybersickness.
- Allowing the user to see out to the horizon *decreases* the potential for cybersickness.

In general, the closer the application meets the user's real-life motion expectations with the inner ear, the better. Unfortunately, this means that steering locomotion—the smooth movement over the ground, which is typical in 3D console systems and VR rollercoasters have a higher risk for cybersickness due to the combined excess of visual feedback and the lack of inner ear feedback.

This chapter covers three of the main types of walking used in VR:

- Teleportation: jump to location
- Steering: virtual slide to location
- Physical: real movement to location

Most systems use a combination or variants of the above.

Teleportation

The wayfinding method used so far here and in the tutorials has been instant teleportation. This method uses a pointer and instant teleport to the target area interaction. There are some variations to this. One is to use super speed. This is when the transition to the target area is sliding to the location at extreme speed rather than moving instantaneously. Blink, which has some similarities to super speed, uses an animation to temporarily black out the user's view and then fade the user's view into the new location. Another is node-based wayfinding. This works the same as the instant teleport, but the target location options are limited.

There are advantages and disadvantages to using teleportation. Some advantages are ease of coding, fast navigation, and a lower probability of cybersickness due to the lack of sway. Some disadvantages are disorientation or lack of spatial awareness [2,3], decreased navigation ability, and errors with mid-grain movement. The issue with navigation is easy to see in the maze example (Fig. 10.4). Some of these disadvantages can be somewhat mitigated by requiring smaller hops.

Steering

Steering involves moving the user's position forward but with turning options. Steering is often used in movies with the control of the camera completely determined through code. This method is also frequently used in 3D games. This is usually done by having

Fig. 10.4 Example of navigation causing position confusion. (https://openclipart.org/detail/11476/rpg-map-symbols-maze.)

the position move according to the joystick orientation in console controllers. Variations in steering usually originate in the direction method source. The joystick method uses a joystick to directly map the motion in 3D. The head method uses the direction of the headset to determine the steering. Where the user looks is the direction of motion. Pointing works similarly to a joystick, where the user points to the target direction and is pulled forward.

This method has some advantages and disadvantages. This first advantage is familiarity. Between movies and 3D applications, this method is often familiar to users. This method also allows for better wayfinding support and good mid-grain motion. The main disadvantage is a high probability of cybersickness. Some variations increase the probability. For example, a movie on rails application, such as a rollercoaster video, has a higher probability. The pointing and head navigation methods are less prone to causing cybersickness [4]. There are some steering navigation methods that are notably lower cybersickness, but they meet the rules given above. For example, flying generally causes less illness but this is a very low jitter motion, and the horizon can be seen.

Physical

Physical walking is also an option with VR. HMD tracking is the most basic form of this wayfinding method. For a wider range of motion, however, gestures are used. For example, the user can signal to move forward by leaning the controls forward. Basically, the user becomes a human joystick. Balance boards and variations of walking in place are very common.

The advantages to using physical locomotion is that it offers fine-grain to mid-grain motion and low cybersickness. The disadvantages include difficulties with long-range motion and physical fatigue.

Navigation Combinations

The methods mentioned can be combined or varied for additional wayfinding methods. These methods may be complete wayfinding protocols or a supplement to one of the above methods.

One method that works as a supplement to add in some mid-grain motion is snap movement. Essentially, this is short-range instant teleportation and turns.

Another method is the arm swinger. This is implemented by using the direction and speed of the controllers' swing to calculate the movement. In other words, the motion of the controllers when walking in place is used to determine direction and speed. Super-speed teleporting is then used for the steps. Using an arm swinger typically makes locomotion a dedicated interaction mode. At the moment, there is not a large body of research on cybersickness potential, but it appears to be at least less prone than steering.

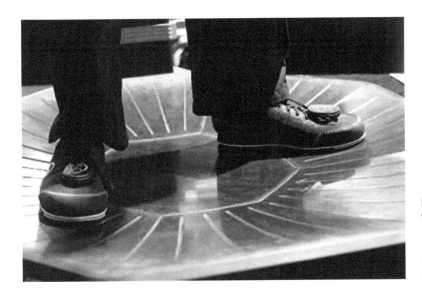

Fig. 10.5 Example of a 2D treadmill. (Fig. 10.5. Maurizio Pesce from Milan, Italia. (https://commons.wikimedia.org/wiki/File:Virtuix_Omni_VR_tread-mill_(16656146507).jpg.))

Special Hardware

There are some additional wayfinding options that use special hardware or spaces.

First, humans tend to have trouble walking in a straight line with their eyes closed. Redirected walking uses this to distract the user to turn while giving the impression of still moving forward. Unfortunately, this still requires a space much larger than a normal living room.

Another expensive method is to use 2D treadmills or VR chairs. This uses special hardware to strap the player into one location but allows for more intuitive physical motion. A 2D treadmill most often uses a slippery concave area that slides the foot back into place as shown (Fig. 10.5). The hardware has the benefit of preventing the player from walking into physical walls with intuitive wayfinding. However, the cost of the additional hardware is high.

An in-between option for the 2D treadmills is to use sensors for in-place walking. Additional sensors or trackers are added to the VR setup. The player can be either sitting or standing. The cost is lower than a 2D treadmill or full VR chair, but availability is limited as of this writing.

Teleportation Enhancements

Let's walk through developing some of the teleportation variants. Both super speed and blink require adding a given animation to the teleport. The general setup to add these variants has four steps:

- Choose a new target point.
- Disable input.

Unity's XR interaction framework has similar functions with similar purposes for locomotion. The main difference is that Unity's includes more transition states. For explanatory purposes, this chapter limits the number of states.

- Animate (using either linear interpolation [LERP] or spherical linear interpolation [SLERP]).
- Enable input.

Like grabbing, having base code can aid in later development. The main steps in the teleportation are the following functions.

```
target = null
function IsLegalToTeleport( Point target )
    // helper function to confirm target is legal

function FindTarget()
    // code to search for teleport target,
    // and saves a possible location in "target"

function OnTeleportStart( )
    // setup for teleportation

function OnTeleportEnd()
    // clean up teleportation

function TeleportTo( Point target )
    // actual teleport code

function OnUpdate()
    // any animation updates
```

This code starts with FindTarget(). If there are no visuals attached, this merely searches for a potential point in the world.

Upon selecting a point, IsLegalToTeleport() can apply any rules needed to state if the location is legal or not. Items that could stop teleportation are if the height difference is too high, too close to something else, the location is currently disallowed, and so on.

After a legal target is selected, OnTeleportStart() can be set up for any animation desired. For example, during animation the function can disallow for new teleport targets. When done, OnTeleportEnd() can clean up, and Update() is simply any frame by frame updated. TeleportTo() is a helper function again to do the actual teleporting (Fig. 10.6).

Visually the code path will look like this:

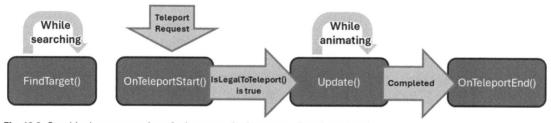

Fig. 10.6 Graphical representation of teleport method setup to allow for animations.

The code is intentionally very generic at this point to allow for later customization. For example, visual feedback in not included yet, but could reuse functions like IsLegalToTeleport(). To reach the same level of functionality of the original teleport code from the beginning of the book, these functions can be refactored with the following highlighted changes.

```
target = null

function IsLegalToTeleport( Point target )
  return target! = null

function FindTarget()
  // starting and direction would be the hand and its forward
  r = Ray( starting, direction )

  // shoot out a ray
  hit = r.FindHit( maxDistance )
  target = null
  if hit.location is legal
    target = hit.location
    // TeleportTo( target ) teleport no longer occurs here


function OnTeleportStart( )
  // setup for teleportation
  if IsLegalToTeleport()
    TeleportTo( target ) // teleportation now occurs here
    OnTeleportEnd()

function TeleportTo( Point target )
  // offset between play area and head location
  Point offset = head.position - feet.position
  // ignore changes in y right now,
  // to keep the head at the same height!
  offset.y = 0
  // final position
  feet.position = target + offset

function OnTeleportEnd()
  // not used as there is no animation

function OnUpdate()
  // not used as there is no animation
```

This does the same things as before—the target selection and teleport calls are separated. However, to animate, there needs to be a flag to indicate if it is currently running. This will not be much of a change.

```
animatingTeleport = false

function OnTeleportStart( )

  // setup for teleportation
  if IsLegalToTeleport()
    // TeleportTo( target )
    // OnTeleportEnd()
    animatingTeleport = true

function OnTeleportEnd()
  animatingTeleport = false

function OnUpdate()
  if animatingTeleport
    // do animation using teleportTo
  else
    OnTeleportEnd()
```

The above will serve as the base for the later example.

Super Speed

The first step to adding super speed requires two items: where the player currently is, and how far the player has been traveling. The last item, although not strictly needed, and an "is it animating" flag that can be checked if a user tries to pick another location during animation.

```
animatingTeleport = false
animationStartTime = 0
startLoc = null
void OnTeleportStart( Point target )
  if !animatingTeleport
    // note that we are currently moving
    animatingTeleport = true
    animationStartTime = 0
    // we should move along the ground,
    // so find the location directly under the head
    startLoc = LocationOnGround( head.position )
```

The second step is largely a LERP animation between locations. This can be done using the instant teleport code, which means there are zero changes to the TeleportTo() code. The teleport time, however, needs to be short to prevent cybersickness.

```
function OnUpdate()
  if animatingTeleport
    // calculate current position
    startTime += deltaTime
    target = Lerp( startLoc,
                   target,
                   startTime / teleportTime )
    TeleportTo( target )
```

After the transition comes the final step, reenabling input. This only requires resetting the flag.

```
function OnUpdate()
  if animatingTeleport
    // calculate current position
    startTime += deltaTime
    target = Lerp( startLoc,
                   target,
                   startTime / teleportTime )

    // same teleport code as before
    TeleportTo( target )
    // if movement has ended, and allow a new teleport
    if startTime > teleportTime
      animatingTeleport = false
```

Blink

Blink follows the same steps as super speed with one difference. The animation is blacking out the screen instead of using LERP between target points. This animation usually uses a shader although it is also doable with a transparent sphere that is turned opaque around the user. The teleport code is then called at the blackest point of the animation.

Survey of Other Wayfinding Options

Beyond simply enhancing instant teleportation, some of the other wayfinding methods mentioned above are worth outlining in detail. This section covers some of the conceptual coding required for snap motion, node wayfinding, and arm swinger.

Snap Movement

Snap Movement is commonly paired with other navigation to add some mid-grain motion. Snap movement is a short teleport or instant turn based on the head direction of the user being forward. This usually entails set rotation angles or strafing steps per click. As an example, if a user taps the up direction on the controller's joystick, the user will instantly be teleported a meter in the direction they are looking. This also supports turning, where a right tap on the joystick could turn the user instantly 20° to the right of their current face. Using the classic paradigm from 3D console games, both strafing and turning could be supported by having the left-hand controller's joystick be strafing and the right be turning.

Let's walk through the steps of adding snap movement for strafing and then rotating. First, the motion assumes a direction parameter of a unit vector:

```
function OnStep( Vector direction )
  // figure out new target
  target = head.position + direction * stepDistance
  // where would our teleport point be on the ground
  r = Ray( target, down )
  hit = r.FindHit( ∞ )
  // If legal to teleport, teleport!
  if IsTeleportTarget( hit.location )
    TeleportTo( hit.point )
```

The function only performs a tiny teleport based on a relative distance from the head. To make this smoother, it is helpful to add partial steps for a jump if the full distance is too close to a boundary.

Adding snap rotation takes a bit more. The head is being turned; however, the head *transform* is affected by the feet. This takes four steps:

1. Find the distance between the head and feet.
2. Find the new feet location. Recall that for a rotation $(x', y') = (x \cos(\theta) - y \sin(\theta), y \cos(\theta) + x \sin(\theta))$.
3. Place feet.
4. Rotate in reverse.

An illustration of these steps is given in Fig. 10.7, and the pseudo-code is given below.

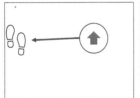 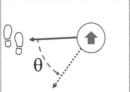 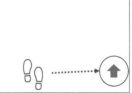 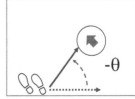

Fig. 10.7 The steps for adding a snap rotation. From left to right: (1) Find the distance between the head and feet. (2) Find the new feet location. (3) Place feet. (4) Rotate in reverse.

```
// Rotate the user by a set negative or positive angle
// (as indicated by leftRight)
function OnRotateSnap( leftRight )

  theta = leftRight * turnSpeed

  // shift to "origin"
  pointOffOrigin = feet.position - head.position

  // rotate around "origin" to find the new location
  newX = pointOffOrigin.x * Cos( theta )
       - pointOffOrigin.z * Sin( theta )
  newZ = pointOffOrigin.z * Cos( theta )
       + pointOffOrigin.x * Sin( theta )

  newPoint = Point( newX, pointOffOrigin.y, newZ )

  // shift back
  finalPoint = head.position + newPoint
  feet.position = finalPoint
  // add (not directly set) rotate in reverse to place head
  // in the same spot
  feet.AddEulerRotate( Vector( 0, -direction, 0 ) )
```

The sequence of shifting to the origin, applying the transform, and then shifting back is a common combination.

Node Wayfinding

Node wayfinding uses teleportation but has the restriction that the teleport locations are predetermined. The user is still teleporting. Setting up node wayfinding may require determining the graphs of potential target locations and adding checks to determine whether to teleport. Snap rotation is often paired with this.

At minimum, the teleport points are predetermined. As an example, spheres were added to Fig. 10.8 to note the allowed locations. Changing the spheres to decals in a full system is more common (Fig. 10.8).

From here there are a number of teleport options:
- Changing orientation to view a particular direction or distance
- Using the trackpad click direction or distance
- Pointing with a large selection area
- Predefining orders

Determining the distances or direction may not be sufficient to deny all desired cases. One example is moving around a sharp corner. One more design consideration is to define the connections and use that as a final validity check for the teleportation. These extra rules are simply appended to the FindTarget() function as needed (Fig. 10.9).

Fig. 10.8 Spheres are added to the path as node locations in Unity.

Fig. 10.9 Virtual map with teleport nodes as spheres and the valid teleport paths as dotted lines.

As an example, the FindTarget() from the above teleportation code could restrict selection to be within a certain distance, angle of the line of sight, and within a minimal height difference. The below code restricts to a 5m distance, 45° angle from the line of sight, and 2m height difference.

```
maxHeightDiff = 2
maxDistance = 5
maxAngle = 45

function FindTarget()
  wayPoints = GetDistanceSortedWaypoints( head.position )
  for g in wayPoints
    // make sure the node is within distance
    distance = Distance( head.position, g.position )
    if distance > maxDistance
      break


    theta = Angle( head.forward, g.position - head.position )
    heightDiff = | feet.position.y - g. position.y |
    isShortEnough = heightDiff < maxHeightDiff
    if theta < maxAngle && isShortEnough
      return g

  return null
```

The rest of the teleport code remains the same.

Arm Swinger

Arm swinger motion is based on the natural swing of the arms. In some more extreme cases, movement is a pulling motion. While this works as a variant of steering, the accompanying natural motion tends to lower the probability of cybersickness. Arm swinger has not been fully standardized yet, so the following is only an overview.

First, the direction of the user can be estimated to be the vertical planes the arms are largely moving within. Sometimes, extra sensors are added to the biceps, which has less movement outside of the plane during normal walking. However, controllers are used more often due to availability.

There are three general methods of approach. First, a cylinder is sometimes placed around the user to indicate active and inactive zones. This is helpful if the motion has a lot of starting and stopping. However, shifting from standing to sitting is much more difficult. The second approach uses the axis of the controller. The forward/backward swing determines the speed. However, it is harder to define the zone area for

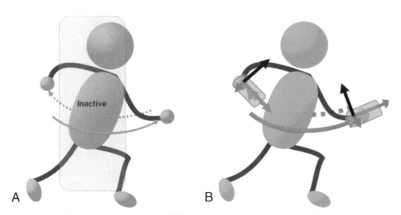

Fig. 10.10 Two conceptual methods for arm swinger. (A) is the method using the vertical planes of reference, and (B) is the method using the axis orientation of the controllers.

Fig. 10.11 One of the challenges of arm swinger is shown. The user picked up a bowl of fruit. While the bowl was parented, the fruit was not. As a result, the fruit flies out of the bowl during arm swinging.

standing still (Fig. 10.10). The last is the pulling motion where the user grabs the air and pulls themselves toward this invisible point.

One of the current challenges is with modes. The user can grab an object, but if the object is not parented to the avatar, the object can go flying (Fig. 10.11). The pull variation avoids this since the hand is stationary, but now has the "gorilla arm" issue.

Graded Surfaces and Walls

So far, all the virtual environments assume a single flat surface for wayfinding. There are two main reasons for this:

- Ease of coding.
- Up-and-down movement increases the probability of cybersickness.

Some grading can be added with ramps. The instant teleportation already handles some changes in vertical positioning:

```
function TeleportTo( Point target )
  // offset between play area and head location
  Point offset = feet.position - head.position
  // ignore changes in y right now,
  // to keep the head at the same height!
  offset.y = 0
  // final position
  feet.position = target + offset
```

The offset.y = 0 line handles minor topological changes. However, a tunneling issue can arise. If the target is selected using a parabola to point, which is very common, the user can point over a wall and use super speed to plow through the wall (Fig. 10.12).

With the current teleportation code, there are no restrictions on where the user can teleport other than checking if the target object actually exists. Some options can add the needed restrictions to prevent tunneling:

- Additional ray checks: This option can solve the above by checking for a line of sight between the initial position and the target position.

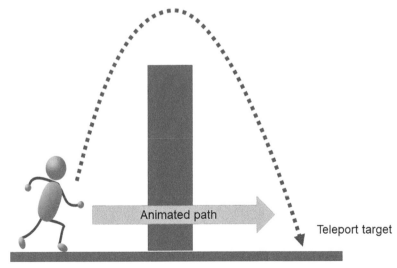

Animated path

Teleport target

Fig. 10.12 Example of potential tunneling using a parabola pointer for teleportation.

- Clear area checks: This option scans the target area for close by objects.
- Normals

Even with these checks in place, the user can potentially teleport close to a wall and inadvertently walk through the wall by moving their head in real-life. This also has some solutions.

The first option is to push the user back into the correct space. This is commonly done in 3D games. A collider is added to the camera or head position. When a collision occurs, the camera is pushed out of the wall and often slides along the wall. This offers an effect of using physics. However, the push can cause jittery unexpected motion, which can increase cybersickness. As a general rule, this option should only be used for small overlaps between the user and another object.

The second option is to put in buffer walls. Areas that cannot be accessed are flagged as no-teleport zones. In turn, a wall is added to outline the physical space for the user to interact to limit the user's distance to physical walls. In general, the physical space can be assumed to be roughly a maximum living room size. In the United States, living rooms are 10 to 12 feet long on average. Removing furniture space and adding in the wall buffer gives an area of about 7 feet by 7 feet (or about 2.1 m by 2.1 m)

The last option is to restrict based on the surface normals. If the normal at the target is too steep, no teleportation is allowed (Fig. 10.13).

To add these solutions to prevent tunneling, a new distance function to the head is needed

```
function FindDistanceToHead(Point target)
  // make a cylinder area around the head
  cylinder = Cylinder( head.height, maxCheckDistance )
  playerHeight = head.y - feet.y
  cylinder.position = target
  cylinder.position += playerHeight

  // check for overlap
  hit = cylinder.FindNearestOverlap()
  if hit has something
    return ( hit.location - cylindar.position ).magnitude
  return ∞
```

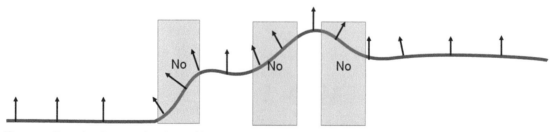

Fig. 10.13 Example of a rugged surface with normals and excluded areas of teleportation based off the normals. The gray areas exclude teleportation.

The above pseudocode adds the wall check by placing a cylinder around the head and checks for the closest point in the overlap between the cylinder and the wall. Not all systems support this. However, the area to check is about the same. In the worst-case scenario, the wall check may need to be performed manually with rays and sufficiently small steps.

Then this distance can be checked in IsLegalToTeleport() along with a secondary line-of-sight check:

```
function IsLegalToTeleport( Point target )
  // check if too close to a wall
  distance = FindDistanceToHead( target )
  if distance < minDistanceFromWall
    return false

  // check if in line of sight
  r = Ray( head.position, target - head.position )
  hit = r.FindHit( target - head.position.magnitude )
  if hit has something
    return false

  return true
```

The line of sight is the ray between the target and the head and the axes at the distance between the two. If the ray finds a hit between these two points, the target is not in sight.

Finally, the normals can be checked, again in the IsLegalToTeleport() function:

```
function IsLegalToTeleport( Point target )
  // check if too close to a wall
  distance = FindDistanceToHead( target )
  if distance < minDistanceFromWall
    return false

  // check if in line of sight
  r = Ray( head.position, target - head.position )
  hit = r.FindHit( maxDistance )
  if hit has something
    return false

  // check how flat the interaction plane is.
  groundAngle = | AngleBetween( up, target.normal ) |
  if groundAngle > maxSteepness
    return false

  return true
```

The angle between two-unit vectors at the target location is determined. If the angle is too steep, teleportation is not permitted.

References

[1] Jaekl PM MR, Jenkin MR, Harris LR. Perceiving a stable world during active rotational and translational head movements, *Exp Brain Res* 163:388–399, 2005.

[2] Langbehn E, Lubos P, Steinicke F. Evaluation of locomotion techniques for room-scale VR: joystick, teleportation, and redirected walking. March 2018. ACM Virtual Reality International Conference; Laval. doi:10.1145/3234253.3234291.

[3] Rebenitsch L, Delaina E. The effects of steering locomotion on user preference and accuracy in virtual environments, *Presence*, 2021.

[4] Habgood J, Moore D, Wilson D. *Alapont S. Rapid, continuous movement between nodes as an accessible virtual reality locomotion technique.* In *Virtual Reality*, Reutlingen, 2018, IEEE.

## 11

Lighting and Shaders

This chapter covers the basics of illumination, shading, and shaders. The concepts in graphics are included to describe the associated terminology. The types of lighting covered are basic lights, diffuse and specular illuminations, and light animations. The types of shaders covered are shaders, Lambertian illumination, and pixel shaders. Beyond the basics, a few more advanced topics are discussed. This includes an overview of lighting models, some postprocessing options, and, finally, a brief overview of the key components when coding shaders. However, this is all from the viewpoint of the developer, not the graphics designer. The focus is on understanding what a developer needs from a graphics designer, so that the correct items can be requested, limitations of the software can be explained, or how to support the designer. All that requires an understanding of the basics of lighting. A very brief overview of how shader code is added, as this is commonly referenced in game engines, although building them is typically a graphic specialist's task.

Lighting in Graphics

Lights in a computer graphics system are designed to mirror real-world lights. When speaking about lighting, there are often comments about the graphics pipeline. Rendering usually takes several steps where information and objects are piped through the step. The number of steps can vastly vary. There are three basic operations:

- Vertex processing
- Geometry processing
- Fragment (pixel) processing

Most systems have these and more steps. For example, Unity's built-in can have 35 steps. Unless writing a full lighting model, it is unlikely that vertex and geometry processing stages will be needed. After this, postprocessing takes the results and makes some final adjustments using the fragments, or pixels. Since postprocessing can use elements created in the pipeline, some of the basics of how lighting works need to be discussed. Some terms of note are

- Illumination: what gives a surface its color based on lighting components.

A Practical Introduction to Virtual Reality. https://doi.org/10.1016/B978-0-443-14036-5.00011-X

- Material: Description of the surface; includes one or more colors.
- Reflection: reflection of light from a surface; this is simulated to compute the illumination.
- Shading: Settings of the pixels to the illumination.

"Reflection" and "illumination" are often used interchangeably as both can be the final color of the light returned by a surface point. Details about the graphics pipeline, which go far beyond the three steps mentioned, are more of a graphics topic and thus mostly out of the scope of this text. However, a basic understanding of the vertex and geometry is needed to understand lighting and what a shader is and when it is used, so an overview of those is provided.

System Limitations

Depending on the system, many different lighting options are available. However, the expected minimum offers directional and point lights. Lighting always involves some light-to-surface physics interactions.

What occurs when light strikes a surface is quite complex. For one thing, the interaction is a continuous process. Light from an infinite number of angles can be reflected in an infinite number of directions. Computers cannot handle infinity, so some compromises are in order. The intensity, or illumination, of a pixel has to be computed with a

- *Finite* number of lights
- *Finite* number of reflections into space
- *Finite* number of illumination directions

This means using a discrete model for lighting and illumination. At a high level, the amount of light hitting a point is summed to be presented on an associated pixel.

When rendering a frame, the light, material, and surface direction affect the end result. Lighting models are the math behind this initial rendering. While the focus later in the chapter is more on postprocessing, some basics are needed to understand what options are available and how to get started on shaders.

Elements of Illumination

There are three fundamental elements of illumination: ambient reflection, diffuse reflection, and specular reflection. How each type of illumination is used, and if there are more elements, is dependent on the virtual environment. Let's outline each of these elements and how they are implemented into a virtual environment.

Fig. 11.1 Orange sphere with just ambient lighting.

The first is ambient reflection. This is the background light in the environment. The ambient reflection essentially simulates light bouncing from the various surfaces. Essentially, a small amount of light is assumed to hit all surfaces. Consider the image in Fig. 11.1 with only ambient lighting. It is dark, and there is no indication the object is a sphere. It could very well be the end of a cylinder.

Next is diffuse reflection, which refers to light reflected in all directions equally or close to equally where the intensity of the diffuse reflection is dependent on the impinging angle of light. This gives the color depth of the surface and the overall color of the object. Most objects have a component of diffuse reflection, other than pure specular reflecting objects like mirrors. In Unity, this is included in the albedo color. In Unreal, this is in the diffuse or base color. Since the intensity is the same in every direction, the only other characteristic is the angle between the incoming light and the surface normal. The smaller this angle, the greater the diffuse reflection. This consists of several components, but what is relevant is the amount of light reflected to the eye. As a result, objects of the same color may reflect different amounts of diffuse light (Fig. 11.2).

Last is specular reflection. This comprises the shiny reflections caused by bright highlights on objects. Here light hits the surface and bounces mostly in the reflection direction. The farther the user gets from the reflected direction, the less the specular reflection shows (Fig. 11.3).

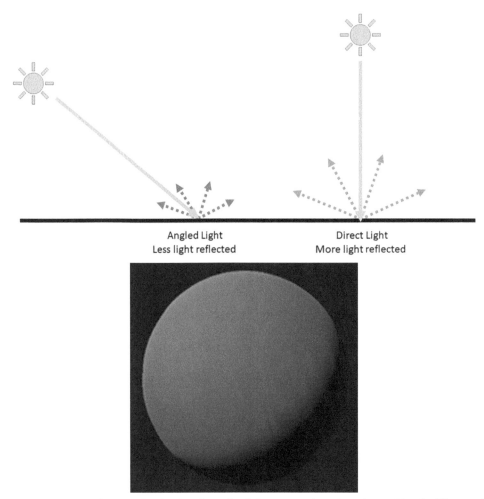

Fig. 11.2 Approximation of diffuse reflection from incoming light at an angle and a sphere with only diffuse and ambient lights.

To demonstrate this, let's walk through two examples: one where the user is at the position to see maximum specular reflection and one where the user is a bit off from maximum specular reflection.

In the first case, the light largely reflects symmetrically on the surface so that the incoming angle of light is the same as the outgoing, reflected light. In optics, the interaction is often drawn in a manner akin to Fig. 11.4.

The user is at position V. The light source is coming from direction L. In this case, the user receives the entirety of the reflected light.

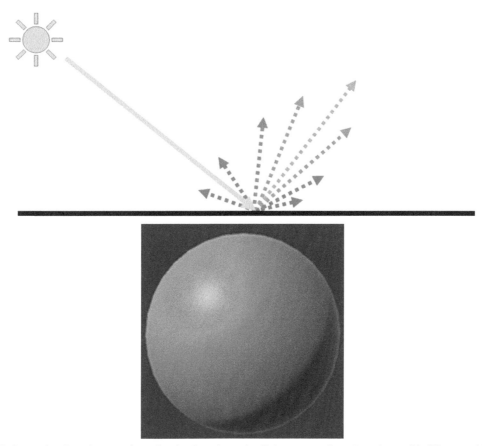

Fig. 11.3 Approximation of a specular reflection from incoming light at an angle and a sphere with diffuse, ambient, and specular lighting.

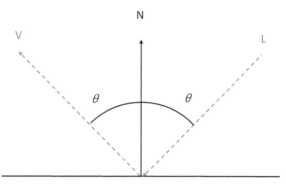

Fig. 11.4 Reflection of light as is often drawn in optics. *L* is the incoming light, *V* is the reflected viewed light, and *N* is the normal from the surface.

Notice that the normal of the reflected surface bisects the angle between the L and V vectors shown in Fig. 11.4. This means that N is the half-angle, H, vector between L and V. This half-angle vector has several uses in graphics and will be important for the second case. Before moving on to the second case of the user not being at the perfect reflection angle, though, it is helpful to see what happens when N ≠ H as shown in Fig. 11.5. H is still halfway between V and L, and N remains the same.

By considering the light-normal of the interaction this way, the half-angle vector, H, can be found by adding V and L and normalizing,

$$H = \frac{L + V}{|L + V|}.$$

This is shown visually in Fig. 11.5. With this vector and V, an estimate between these two vectors can be found, which leads us to the second case (Fig. 11.6).

When the user is not directly in the path of the reflected light, how much light the user receives depends on how close to the reflection direction the user is placed, which is the angle between the normal and the half vector. If the angle is zero, the user is looking at the light's

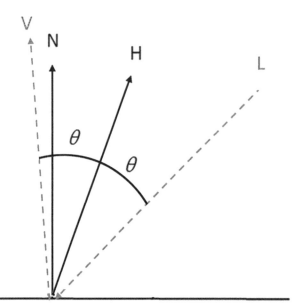

Fig. 11.5 Reflection of light as is often drawn in graphics. *L* is the incoming light, *V* is the reflected viewed light, *N* is the normal to the surface, and *H* is the half-angle vector that bisects L and V.

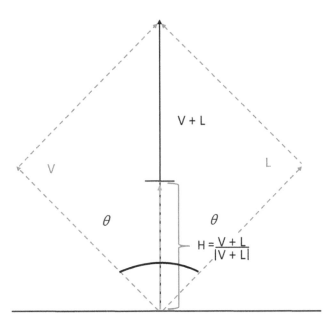

Fig. 11.6 The addition of the *L* and *V* vectors gives the non normalized *H* vector.

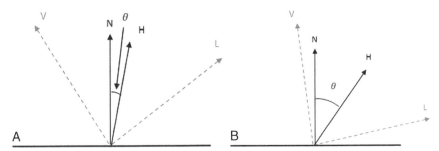

Fig. 11.7 (A) Example of where the user is slightly off from the direct reflected light. (B) Example of where the user is farther from the direct reflection. *L* is the incoming light, *V* is the reflected light, *N* is the normal to the surface, and *H* is the half-angle vector.

direct reflection (Fig. 11.7). Otherwise, the user is off the angle a bit. This angle can be determined with the dot product:

$$\cos \theta = N \cdot H$$

Another term often arises with specular reflection: glossiness. Specular lighting has both a strength of reflection and a rate of fall-off. Think of a glossy metal ball versus one with lots of small scratches. They both reflect a lot of light, but the spot of light is wider in the scratched ball. The strength of the reflection is called Metallic in Unity and Unreal. Glossiness, or the rate of fall off, is called Smoothness in Unity and Specular in Unreal (Fig. 11.8). An example of the interaction of the two is shown in Fig. 11.9.

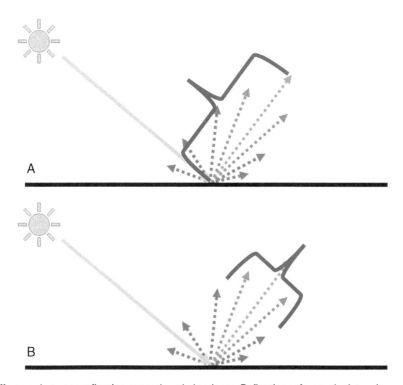

Fig. 11.8 The difference between reflection strength and glossiness. Reflection refers to the intensity or strength of the reflected light and glossiness refers to the spread of the reflected light. (A) is the reflection strength of the light or "Metallic." (B) is the reflection falloff or "Glossiness" or "Smoothness."

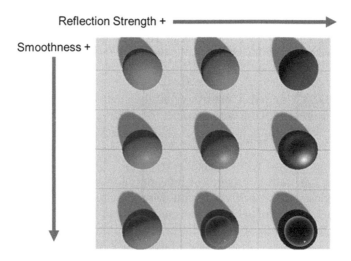

Fig. 11.9 Example of increasing smoothness and specular reflection for a sphere object in Unity.

At a high level, the illumination of a pixel is a sum of the ambient, diffuse, and specular reflections. Each of these can be expressed mathematically.

First, the ambient contribution is

$$I_a = M_d C_a,$$

where I_a is the ambient contribution, M_d is the diffuse material color, and C_a is the light ambient color.

Next is the diffuse contribution:

$$I_d = M_d \sum_{i=1}^{m} C_i \max (L_i \cdot N, 0),$$

where I_d is the diffuse contribution, M_d is again the diffuse material color, C_i is the color of light i, L_i is the vector point at light i, and N is the surface normal. This is summed over m number of lights.

The third is the specular contribution:

$$I_s = M_s \sum_{i=1}^{m} C_i \max (N \cdot H, 0)^n,$$

where I_s is the specular contribution, M_s is the specular material color, C_i is the color of the light i, N is the surface normal, H is the half vector, and n is the shininess or specular power. This is summed over m number of lights. The n term can have several names such as specular reflection highlight coefficient, shininess, or specular power.

A last addition is emission. Emission, or glow, is also commonly used. However, because emission does not illuminate nearby surfaces without extra help, it is not a true light. Emission is frequently used and therefore is also added as a constant:

$$I_e = M_e$$

This gives the final illumination setting of each pixel:

$$I_f = I_a + I_d + I_s + I_e.$$

This is the most basic form of illumination and the progression is shown in Fig. 11.10.

Beyond these elements, additional lighting effects can be applied. Some of these are emission glow, shadows, sky boxes, reflection, refraction, and radiosity. A more advanced illumination model is shown in Fig. 11.11. These additional effects bring increased realism and detail to an environment. These effects also require more computations. However, this is a good starting point for many postprocessing shaders.

Fig. 11.10 An environment where the elements of illumination are progressively applied. From left to right: ambient reflection applied, ambient and diffuse reflection applied, and all elements applied.

Fig. 11.11 Example of environment with numerous additional lighting effects applied. (From Unity docs. https://docs.unity3d.com/Manual/built-in-render-pipeline.html.)

Baking Light

Baked lighting refers to calculating the amount of light that reaches a point before running, saving the resulting lighting, and is then looked up and applied like a texture. If the lights in the environment do not change, this can help with run time if there are many little point lights. This can be seen in some applications where the environment has complex lighting but when a character walks through, their lighting is not affected by nearby point lights.

Shadows

At a high level, shadows offer a degree of realism as well as depth cues. This is implemented using shadow mapping, which is essentially rendering the scene from the viewpoint of the light and tells what the light can see. To limit the cost, it is helpful to keep track of only the depth to each point the light can interact with. Then, when rendering, points that are farther away from the interaction range of the light can be seen. Full shadow mapping is a graphics topic and is largely out of the scope of this chapter.

Summary

In summary, most surfaces have deep color and surface reflection characteristics. The deep color can be from the color of the paint, finish, material, etc. This is set in the Diffuse Material Property, Diffuse Color, or Albedo if using Unity or Base Color if using Unreal. The surface reflection characteristics can be varnish, polish, smoothness, etc. This is set in the Specular Material Property, Metallic/Specular Color, or the Metallic/Smoothness Color if using Unity. If using Unreal, the settings are under Material properties and set in Metallic, Specular, and Roughness, but there are also some presets in the Shading Model list.

Basic Lighting

Standard Lights

As mentioned earlier, almost all systems have directional and point lights. The directional lights are global vectors, and the point lights can be likened to a lightbulb. However, adding a directional or point light does not necessarily update the shadows.

Adding a directional light includes a few common settings:
- Direction: Orientation vector of the light.
- Color: Modern systems may have this in Kelvins, which would be based on a star's temperature to determine the color.
- Intensity: The color is rescaled from [0,100]% to 0 to another number. If the intensity is greater than 100%, then larger areas start shifting into the light's color rather than the diffuse color.

Unreal and Unity add a directional light by default to new scenes. This normally acts as the sun in the environments. This means all the light reflection uses the same lighting angle (Fig. 11.12).

A point light also has a few additional common settings:
- Position
- Range: maximum distance the light reached

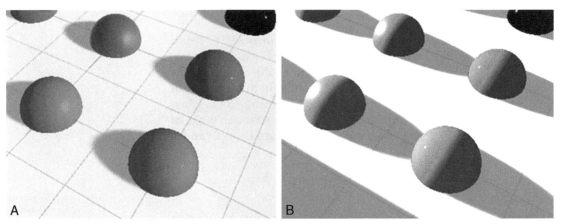

Fig. 11.12 The (A) image uses the default directional light. The (B) image rotated the light and increased the intensity by 2-fold.

Fig. 11.13 A point light placed between the four spheres shows the lighting angles changing per vertex.

Fig. 11.13 shows a point light centered between the four closest spheres. Here, the lighting angles change per vertex.

Spotlights and area type lights are also supported in both VR engines. Which lights need to be baked depends on the engine. Spotlights act like a point light but have an angle limitation. Area lights act more like typical fluorescent lights in an office building. They have similar settings as point lights (Fig. 11.14).

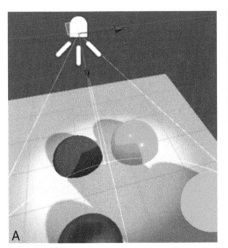 

Fig. 11.14 The (A) image is a spotlight, and the (B) image is an area light.

Skyboxes and Fog

Two more items that many lighting systems have are skyboxes and fog.

Skyboxes are for when there are areas with no light interactions hitting an object. While one option is to choose a default background color, skyboxes offer a set of textures to represent the sky. Skyboxes are relatively hard to make but can be added to the application. They are made by either a specialized shader or by creating six images, where each side lines up perfectly and has the correct perspective, or by creating a panorama, or possibly a sphere. Then, if the camera does see an object at a given pixel, the color is pulled from the skybox. Many modern systems prefer a sky sphere instead due to the ease of having a skewing effect along the boundaries of a skybox. Many times the terms are used interchangeably.

Let's walk through the steps of creating a basic skybox with the 6-sided box technique. Step 1 is to collect the images for the skybox. This means making six sides and making sure that the import settings have these sides set to clamp. Step 2 is to make a box using the images for each side. Finally, step 3 is to place the box to be always centered around the user, and when a sky pixel is needed, pull from the box (Fig. 11.15).

There is no sun at this point in the example. Normally, environmental lighting can come from several sources. Adding a sun varies drastically between Unity and Unreal. Unreal has direct support, but Unity does not.

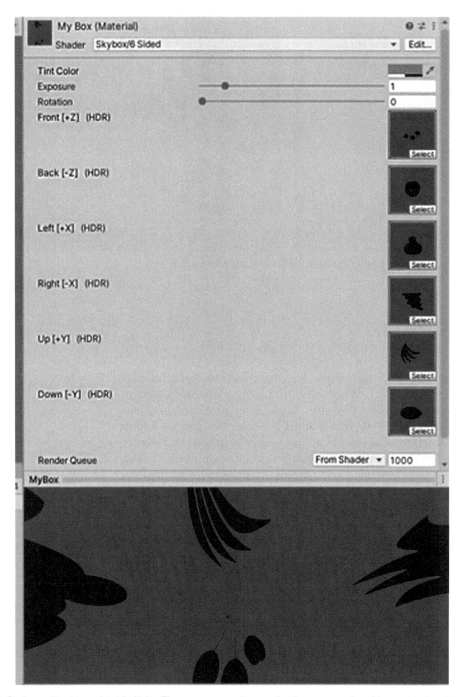

Fig. 11.15 Skybox with sides added in Unity. The upper area shows what images are the sides and below is what looking up to the sky would be when running.

Another element of environmental lighting is fog. Fog is a color overlay based on distance (Fig. 11.16). It may initially seem odd to place this with the environmental lighting, but adding fog to the entire environment includes setting the environmental settings, which includes lighting. In Unity, this requires going to the rendering settings under Lighting > Environment and going to the Other Settings. Fog can be enabled there. In Unreal, height-based fog is enabled under the Project Settings under Rendering, by enabling Support Sky Atmosphere Affecting Height Fog.

Reflections

Calculating true reflections requires ray tracing or more. However, a one-bounce reflection can be calculated with far less cost. This method uses reflection probes.

Fig. 11.16 Environment without fog (A) and with fog (B). Note that the skybox was unaffected.

Reflection probes, or reflection cubes, place a camera at the center of the object and then create a texture of the light interactions looking out in a sphere. When seen in code, the reflection map is wrapped, rotated to the correct orientation for the viewpoint, and blended (Fig. 11.17).

Reflection is computationally expensive to run in real-time. Because of this, it is important to bake light for reflections whenever possible. That does mean using restrictions and setups like baking area lights. To save time, engines often skip what they can. As seen in Fig. 11.17, the orange spheres on the ground are all missing in the probe because they were not static!

Reflection probes usually act in volumes. These are designated areas where the extra lighting effects are applied. This can cause some unexpected effects. Consider the example of the two capsules where the farther one has a lighting probe centered at its location (Fig. 11.18). Since the nearer capsule is within the volume, it is applied to the reflection probe. But that reflection probe has the nearer capsule in its saved texture. This results in a "ghost" capsule applied to the near capsule, itself!

Fig. 11.17 Example reflection probe.

Fig. 11.18 Example of an extra ghost reflection in the capsule.

Postprocessing

Postprocessing takes the result of the rendering and then applies some effects toward the end of the rendering pipeline. Overly simplified, these effects can be seen as image filters added to each frame. However, because these effects are still part of the pipeline, postprocessing can use elements created earlier in the pipeline to get much more nuanced effects than what is normally available on a smartphone.

Not all systems provide built-in postprocessing filters. However, there are a few common ones. Here is a set of options supported by both Unreal and Unity for VR.

1. Color grading
2. Chromatic aberration
3. Graining
4. Depth of field
5. Bloom
6. Exposure
7. Ambient occlusion
8. Vignette

As a starting example, let's look at volumes or the areas where the post-processing may be applied. Fig. 11.19 contains a green box. This green box marks where the user may be and where to apply postprocessing effects. This is formally called a volume.

There are three spotlights in the scene: one white lamp, one red lamp, and one yellow floor spotlight. The red spotlight does not have emission. The sides of the red light also show black. In the sub-sections below, the postprocessing options used came from Unity's Post-process Volume component, which is available from Unity's Post Processing Stack v2 library. All the options were selected from the predefined list of available effects. Unreal has these same effects.

Color Grading

Color grading has a broad range of effects but primarily involves tinting the final colors. This tends to be important for context, such as differentiating day and night or wet and dry surfaces. Color grading can adjust the white balance, contrast, saturation, tone, gamma, and color shifts. Shadow, mid-tones and highlights are often adjusted separately.

Here are some of the definitions to these settings:
- White balance: adjusts the balance of colors to match the light source and is like the white balance of a camera
- Tone: combined color tint, saturation or grayness, and contrast
- Color shifts: hue change
- Gamma: overly simplified, improved contrast correction

The names and level of control of these settings vary with the system. An example of a color shift and saturation change are shown in Fig. 11.20.

Chromatic Aberration

Chromatic aberration gives a prism-like effect. This may appear to be like wearing the older style of 3D glasses that were red and blue. The effect tends to show more in whiter areas. The settings often include the displacement amount and whether the color shifts are blurred. An example of this is shown in Fig. 11.21.

Graining

Graining largely adds noise that gives an effect like an old television. Some of the settings include adjusting the size of the grain and the intensity of the grain. Sometimes graining can include a setting for coloring or brightening the grain. An example of this is shown in Fig. 11.22.

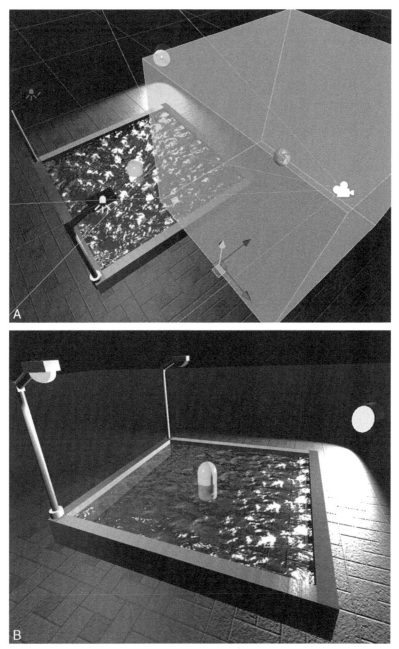

Fig. 11.19 Scene for postprocessing examples. The (A) is the scene with the postprocessing volume shown. The (B) right is the base image for postprocessing. The green box in (A) is the volume for postprocessing effects. The red spotlight does not have emission as can be seen in (B).

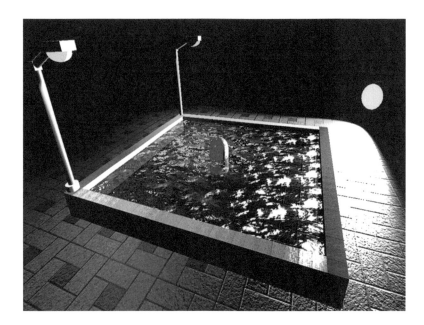

Fig. 11.20 Scene with the hue shifted and both the saturation and contrast are maxed.

Fig. 11.21 Scene with chromatic aberration applied.

Depth of Field

Depth of Field refers to blurring objects that are too close or too far. The settings can include adjusting the focus distance, the blur start range or aperture and the blurring radius or focal length. An example of this is shown in Fig. 11.23.

Fig. 11.22 Scene with graining added.

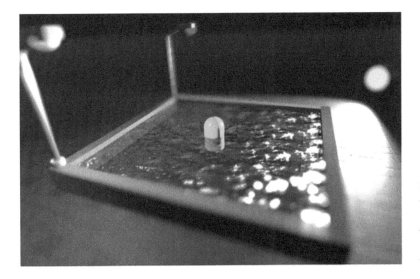

Fig. 11.23 Scene with depth of field added. The object of focus is the capsule, while the aperture is narrowed and the blur radius was decreased (or the focal length was increased).

Bloom

Bloom makes well-lit areas have a glow effect. More specifically, the strongly lit areas have the edges blurred to fake a light source. Settings can include intensity, light cutoff, blur setting, and color overrides. The light cutoff is available to prevent dim items from glowing. An example of this is shown in Fig. 11.24.

Fig. 11.24 Scene with bloom added. In (A), the intensity was turned up and set to spread. Note that the red light is unaffected. This is due to the red light having no emission and thus is not lit. In (B), the intensity of the white spotlight was turned down and emission was added to the red light.

Exposure

Exposure is like exposure of a camera; it is the amount of light collected for the scene. The more light collected, the lighter the scene appears overall. Settings can vary widely from system to system but usually have at least one setting for the minimum brightness to cause an effect and one setting for the maximum brightness to adapt. An example of this is shown in Fig. 11.25.

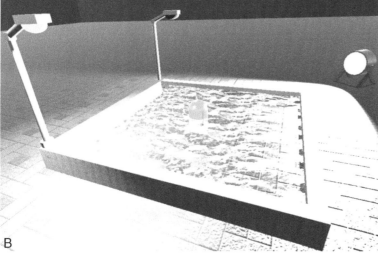

Fig. 11.25 Scene with exposure added. The (A) image is underexposed, and the (B) image is overexposed.

Ambient Occlusion

One major challenge with ambient light is that the light is evenly applied. That means using a single light value as a minimum, which will almost never look quite right. To give an example, the inside of a drawer has less light bouncing into it than under a table. Ambient occlusion estimates a fix for this by darkening the edges. Settings usually include intensity at the radius and thickness of the effect at a minimum. Examples of this are shown in Fig. 11.26.

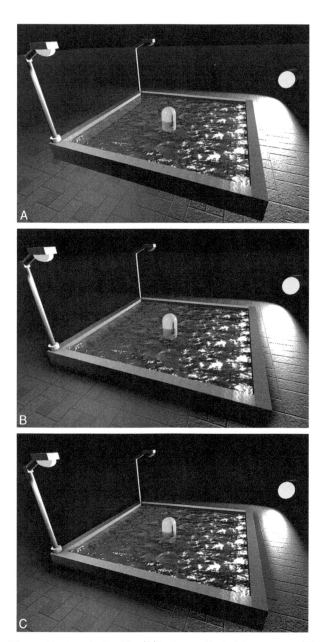

Fig. 11.26 Example of applying ambient occlusion. The (A) is the unaffected, base scene. (B) is the scene with ambient occlusion added. More shadows can be seen along the bottom edges of the boundary, where more light is blocked. (C) Scene with blue ambient occlusion added. Here the ambient occlusion is at maximum intensity with the shadow effects tinted blue to show the affected areas to emphasize the effect.

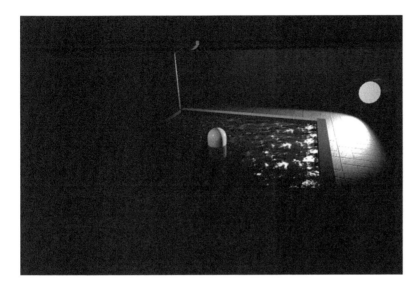

Fig. 11.27 Scene with vignette added.

Vignette

Vignette is essentially a cutout of the resulting image. This filter is important for offering a low-cybersickness mode as smaller fields of view dramatically decrease cybersickness [1]. Unlike most other options, there is only one common setting: intensity. Other potential options, such as location and blur, are all optional. This means creating a unique shader or approximating with an HUD may be needed in some cases. An example of this is shown in Fig. 11.27.

Shaders

There are postprocessing effects that are not built into either VR engine. Vignette is one such example in that the options are limited. Another example involves outlines to indicate selection. The solution to this is to make a custom shader.

Shader Basics

Overly simplified, a shader is a piece of code that performs the pixel summation math in Section Elements of Illumination plus more effects. The catch is that shaders constitute a huge field. An entire course (or two) can be on shaders. Plus, using them effectively requires a good understanding of what is going on behind the scenes in rendering graphics.

Shaders are typically written in either HLSL (High Level Shader Language) or GLSL (openGL Shading Language). These are specialized C-based languages. Both Unity and Unreal favor HLSL with some extra specifications. Both engines also have a graphical representation of the calculation to aid in development. Unfortunately, this largely only works with full shaders and not postprocessing. Regardless, this is useful when starting as the representation gives an idea of what is available in the shader. A shader can be a full lighting model or a specific point in the rendering pipeline.

A full lighting model shader is out of the scope of this course but would involve implementing the math given above in the three main steps of the rendering pipeline. However, postprocessing shaders can be very similar to image processing and only require an understanding of pixels to implement simpler options. The main differences are that

- Incoming values are often only pixel color and texture coordinates, so the vertex and geometric steps are largely completed at this stage. Fragment is another term for pixels in the shader world.
- The filter becomes percentage based due to using the texture coordinates rather than the pixel coordinates.
- Update changes are placed differently because the vertex and fragment (pixel) steps are two different functions.

The remainder of this section outlines building a custom postprocessing shader.

Elements of a Custom Shader

If the engine does not have the needed shader, the next option is to build a custom shader. Some of the major components needed to start are

- Member variables and parameter access
  - The access to the base component and member variables will look a bit different than usual.
  - The access is largely struct-based.
- Vertex shading
  - This is run when calculating anything with a vertex or a reference to a vertex.
  - This is run before pixel shading. In postprocessing, the vertices are only the corners of the screen.
- Fragment shading
  - This is also called pixel shading.
  - This is where the postprocessing effects are usually placed.

Many modern systems offer something similar to a macro for the base lighting model. This allows the developer to focus on the postprocessing stage.

The data types are based on the C-language data types but with unique names. Some also have a few specialized types:

- float: float
- int: int
- float3: three-value float
- float4: four-value float
- float4x4: 4×4 matrix
- Texture: 2D texture

Beyond these, different systems have different levels of prebuilt items. Unity offers a shader template that is useful for outlining the different parts of a shader in code. Adding a shader in Unreal is more involved because additional class declarations are needed. However, Unreal also uses HLSL, so there is some overlap.

Let's look at a simplified form of the Unity template:

```
Shader "name"
{
  Properties
  {
    _VariableName("Inspector Text", Range(0.0, 1.0)) = 0.5
  }

  HLSLINCLUDE
    # include "<shader library package>"
    TEXTURE2D_SAMPLER2D(_MainTex, sampler_MainTex);
    float3_VariableName;
    float4 Frag( VaryingsDefault I ): SV_Target
    {
      float4 color = SAMPLE_TEXTURE2D( _MainTex,
                                       sampler_MainTex,
                                       i.texcoord );
      return color;
    }
  ENDHLSL

  SubShader
  {
    //Settings
    Pass
    {
      HLSLPROGRAM
        #pragma vertex VertDefault
        #pragma fragment Frag
      ENDHLSL
    }
  }
}
```

There is a lot here already. Let's start by outlining the three major components:

```
Shader "name"
{
  Properties
  {
    _VariableName( "Inspector Text", Range( 0.0, 1.0 ) ) = 0.5
  }
  HLSLINCLUDE
    #    include "<shader library package>"
    TEXTURE2D_SAMPLER2D( _MainTex, sampler_MainTex );
    float3 _VariableName;
    float4 Frag( VaryingsDefault I ) : SV_Target
    {
        float4 color = SAMPLE_TEXTURE2D( _MainTex,
                                         sampler_MainTex,
                                         i.texcoord );

        return color;
    }
  ENDHLSL



  SubShader
  {
    //Settings

    Pass
    {
      HLSLPROGRAM
        #pragma vertex VertDefault
        #pragma fragment Frag
      ENDHLSL
    }
  }
}
```

The lines highlighted in yellow are the member variables. Properties{} are Unity-specific variables. In a postprocessing system, this mostly shows only what can be set and not much else. In a regular shader, this is where the user set elements are placed. The TEXTURE2D_SAMPLED2D line is a macro to find the correct texture datatype based on the hardware.

The boxed lines are the vertex components. Both Unity and Unreal offer some prebuilt fragment and vertex functions to load. Here, the standard illumination version is assumed.

The lines underlined in red are the fragment (pixel) components. In this case, the default is to be changed, though this code outputs the original pixel for now. One item to note is that because this is a post-process, the texture output is the entire frame, not an object in the scene.

The remainder of the code has various settings and markers for the shaders. The top line works like a class name. The HLSLINCLUDE, HLSLPROGRAM, and HLSLEND lines mark the sections of code that are run on the GPU. "SubShader" marks a section for a particular GPU and is Unity specific. The settings below that are optional flags for processing. Finally, the "Pass" is a single run of the vertex and fragment functions.

All this piece of code does is return the original color. In other words, it keeps the original frame rendering and does *nothing*. Pixel-by-pixel processing is fairly straightforward. The incoming color merely needs to be changed before being returned. Consider a simple grayscale transformation. The brightness can be found by this formula for luminance for contrast in web accessibility:

$$luminance = R \times 0.299 + G \times 0.567 + B \times 0.114$$

This means there are only two extra lines in the shader to make it convert the frame to grayscale:

```
float4 Frag( VaryingsDefault I ) : SV_Target
{
  float4 color = SAMPLE_TEXTURE2D( _MainTex,
                                   sampler_MainTex,
                                   i.texcoord);
  // luminance calculation (grayscale conversion)
  float luminance = dot( color.rgb,
                         float3( 0.299, 0.567, 0.114 ) );
  color.rgb = float3( luminance, luminance, luminance );

  return color;
}
```

Believe it or not, that's it for making a grayscale post-processing shader. It still needs to be connected in, but this is the Unity style HSLS code in one file. Basic pixel adjustments that do not care about other pixels are very close to the same effect with image processing. If elements like blurring, median, etc. are present that need to know nearby pixels, pixel lookup needs to be translated into the fragment framework. As noted at the beginning of the chapter, this starts to enter into topics deserving of a semester, or more, onto itself.

Acknowledgments

A thank you is needed for those working the VR Lab the semester this text was written. The exploration of postprocessing and eagerness to share what was found greatly enriched this chapter. A particular thanks is due to Christian Olson, who provided the example pool scene and tested out all the built-in shaders that Unity provided. Christian also provided the code for the grayscale shader.

Reference

[1] Rebenitsch L, Owen C. Estimating cybersickness from virtual reality applications, *Springer Nat*, 2020.

## 12

Three-Dimensional Sound

This chapter focuses on adding directional sound to an application. The materials begin with a refresher on loading and playing sounds in general before moving on to three-dimensional sounds and their unique settings. The remainder of the chapter focuses on sound management and some usability and safety recommendations. This chapter is meant to be an overview of the basics; advanced sound settings and effects could fill a full semester.

Sounds

Uploading sounds into either virtual reality (VR) engine is fairly straightforward, and many of the relevant settings for two-dimensional (2D) sounds are available in the game engine information panels. While there are a number of similarities, there are enough differences to warrant a comparison of importing a background sound. The steps are largely the same, but the terms vary.

To begin, individual sounds are called Audio Clips in Unity and Sound Waves in Unreal. The Audio Source component in the scene controls the sound in Unity, while Unreal uses an Ambient Sound actor. In Unreal, the sound is processed and forwarded to the speaker from the Sound Cue, and Unity uses the Audio Listener for sound forwarding. The takeaway here is that there are 3 main components even if the names change. 1) There is a sound, 2) there is a manager for multiple sounds, and 3) there are speakers that play the sound.

The steps for adding a background sound are then as follows:

- To add a background sound requires loading a sound into the Audio Clip in Unity and the Sound Wave or Ambient Sound in Unreal.
- To have a sound play continuously, both engines have a single check box to do so (Looping in the Ambient Sound in Unreal and Loop in the Audio Source in Unity). In Unreal, Looping can also be set in the Sound Wave asset.
- To start the sound on run, Unity requires checking the Play On Awake option. Unreal does not require this.

Adding three-dimensional (3D) sounds requires similar steps.

A Practical Introduction to Virtual Reality. https://doi.org/10.1016/B978-0-443-14036-5.00012-1

3D Sounds

The 3D sounds can be added in a similar manner as 2D sounds, because the same sound clip can be used. The main differences between 3D and 2D is that 3D sounds fade with distance from the source, while 2D sounds do not. As a result, 2D sound normally uses the sound clip for stereo effects, while 3D sound uses position to adjust the volume per ear.

In 3D, sound decibels (dB) follow an approximate logarithmic equation in real life. For those that just need a general feel, this means that sounds get quieter slower at greater distances rather than the linear drop off that is often expected. Otherwise, feel free to skip to the next page. For those that need to know the distance limits for detailed sound environments, a model of this decay uses the decay of the volume intensity of a point source spherical wave:

$$V(r) = \frac{P}{A(r)} = \frac{P}{4\pi r^2},$$

where P is the source's sound power, $A(r)$ is the surface area of the spherical wave at distance r from the source, and $V(r)$ is the volume or intensity of the sound at distance r from the source.

This can then be approximated into the inverse square law:

$$V \propto \left(\frac{1}{r}\right)^2,$$

where V is the volume setting and r is the distance from the sound source to the user's ear.

Decibels cannot be measured directly from the inverse square law, however, because the sound at the source is undefined ($r = 0$ results in a 0 in the denominator). As a result, sound intensity or volume is determined by comparing the measured volume to a *reference volume*. Using the inverse square law for two volumes gives

$$V_2 = V_1 \left(\frac{r_1}{r_2}\right)^2,$$

where V_1 is the volume at distance r_1, and V_2 is the volume at distance r_2. If V_1 is the reference volume set to the base threshold of undamaged human hearing in air, taking the log of $\frac{V_2}{V_1}$ gives the function to determine the decibel level, L:

$$L = 10 \log_{10} \frac{V_2}{V_1} dB.$$

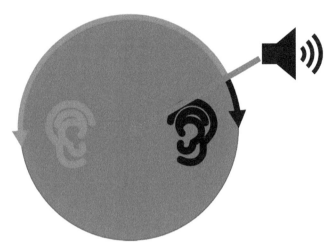

Fig. 12.1 A conceptual example of the distance sound travels from the sound source to a person's ears. Note that the sound directly impacts the right ear and indirectly impacts the left ear.

However, sound also bounces, so a sound that directly affects one ear will still indirectly affect the other ear as shown in Fig. 12.1.

Adjusting the sound positioning is a 3D sound setting. Adjusting a sound between 2D and 3D requires adjusting the Spatial Blend bar in Unity, while Unreal has an Enable Spatialization checkbox. After this, the main setting in Unity is the Spread bar under the 3D Sound Settings. In Unreal this is in the 3D Stereo Spread setting. This is the positional parameter for the range of hearing for a sound from both ears. Essentially these are settings for how much to balance a sound between ears when in the case shown in Fig. 12.1.

The volume fall of sounds is typically logarithmic based. This is because sound decibels follow a quadric-based equation in real life as shown earlier. As an example, Fig. 12.2 shows a logarithmic decay, or rolloff, of volume for a 3D sound. The red, vertical line is the distance from the Audio Listener (this is in Unity). However, there is an unintended effect. While this Max Distance was set to be 10 m, that is not what the graph is showing. A small volume remains at that position. The reason why this happens is that while the function is physics-based, the distance settings are not factored into the base equation. As a result, the distances are ignored. A fix for this is to drag the control points around the 10 m mark to zero, which changes the function to the Custom Rolloff shown in Fig. 12.3. This problem only increases at shorter distances.

Another option is to use Linear Rolloff. This does set the volume at 0 at 10 m as can be seen in Fig. 12.4. Unreal has a few more built-in settings: Inverse, Log Reverse, and Natural Sound. These settings all have different environmental uses, but in general, Logarithmic, Linear, and Natural Sound are more likely to be used.

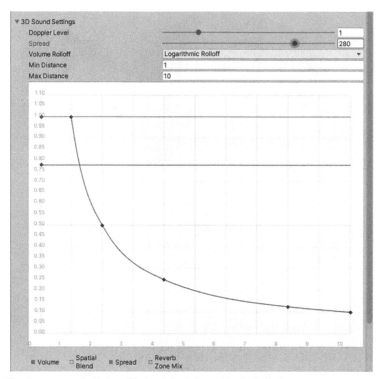

Fig. 12.2 Example 3D volume curve in Unity with the default Logarithmic Rolloff.

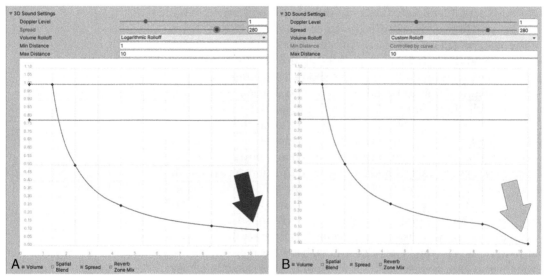

Fig. 12.3 Example of setting a custom volume rolloff. The (A) image is unchanged from the default. The (B) image has the volume change to 0 at 10 m.

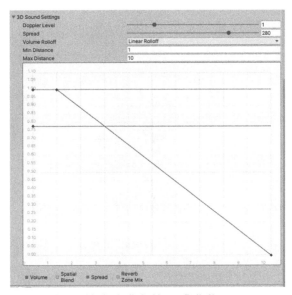

Fig. 12.4 Example 3D volume curve in Unity with the built-in Linear Rolloff.

That's about it for adding a 3D sound. The rest of this chapter focuses on adjusting the 3D sound settings.

Sound Settings

After setting up the sound clips, there are a large number of other settings to try tweaking. Let's go through the most common.

Volume, sometimes also called amplitude or gain, is fairly self-explanatory, except for normalization. In some applications, one sound may be much louder than another and should be quieter. Normalization basically averages the volume so that all sounds have a similar decibel level if the application is played at the same volume. There are a number of software packages available for this.

Pitch refers to how high the sound is. Mathematically, this refers to the wavelength shift in Hertz. In music, this means a shift in notes (e.g., C4 to G4). Pitch shifts are useful for adjusting a sound clip to be higher or lower. One note on pitch limits, however; many speakers cannot handle pitches below about 200 Hz or G3 (Fig. 12.5).

Pan is only used for stereo sounds. This refers to how much of the sound is directed into the left or right ears. Other than a sounds test, this is often left to the system to mimic 3D sounds.

Reverberation, often shortened to reverb, refers to sound bounces. This is similar to a tiny echo. The reverb sound setting sets the

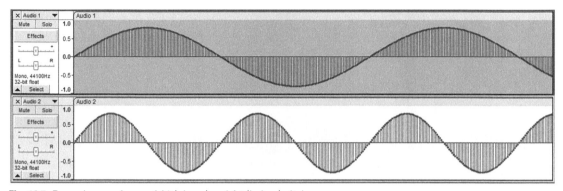

Fig. 12.5 Example waveforms of A3 (above) and A4 (below) pitches.

amount of reverberation. In general, there is more reverb inside than outside in real life.

Doppler refers to how oncoming sound objects have a higher pitch and receding sound objects have lower pitches. This can often be observed as a car with a siren approaches, passes, and leaves.

Spatial, also called spatialization or attenuation, refers to how sounds become quieter the farther the sound source is placed. The environment and the wavelength of the sound can also affect the spatial distribution due to sound absorption. In 3D applications, this can be the distance setting from the user where the sound is no longer produced. Unreal has an Air Absorption option in the Attenuation settings.

Both engines have all of these settings and more.

Usability Tips

A handful of tips are recommended for sounds. These are recommended as both realistic volume ranges and to prevent hearing damage:

- Sound should never go above 100 dB at any time.
- Sound should not exceed 80 dB for extended (>15 seconds) periods of time.
- Rustling leaves are at about 30 dB.
- Speech is about 50 to 70 dB.

Sound can and should be normalized to meet these recommendations. These recommendations are approximations from the Occupational Safety and Health Administration [1] and the National Institute for Occupational Safety and Health [2].

References

[1] Occupational Noise Exposure. Occupational Safety and Health Administration. Retrieved 2023. https://www.osha.gov/noise

[2] Noise and Occupational Hearing Loss. National Institute for Occupational Safety and Health. Retrieved 2023. https://www.cdc.gov/niosh/topics/noise/

## 13

Particle Systems

This chapter gives an overview of particle systems, their main components, and where and how they are used. The main topics are: particles and their types, main components, two-dimensional versus three-dimensional, vector fields and physics, effects, and an example application with campfire.

The last main topic gives a conceptual example of applying particle systems to create a basic firework and then expanding upon that to create a campfire with smoke and sparks. The example is interwoven throughout the chapter. Particle systems and vector fields also use physics to create the effects. Therefore, a short survey of the physics requirements is outlined for the conceptual example.

Particles and Their Types

Particles systems were first introduced by William Reeves for the Genesis Demo sequence in Star Trek II: The Wrath of Khan [1]. Since then, these systems have been greatly expanded and refined for a wide variety of graphical applications. The minimum characteristics of a particle are its position and velocity, as these allow physics to be applied to the particles. Euler Steps are applied to update the particle each time step as described in Chapter 3 Basic Physics. Both characteristics are in vectors with the position referring to the position of the particle and velocity in either pixel or world units. The appearance of a particle is, ironically, secondary. No particle can be shown if its location and movement are not known.

In general, there are two categories of particles: big and small. Big particles have an area greater than a pixel or voxel, while small particles have an area less than a pixel or voxel. A voxel (volumetric pixel) is similar to a pixel, but is the 3D dimensionally equivalent, which can be used in water or smoke systems. Small particles also have no geometry; the engine uses their density to render effects. Consider the images in Fig. 13.1. The smoke particle is rather large and will cover possibly a few hundred pixels in the application. The sand particle decides its alpha level based on the density of the particles at

A Practical Introduction to Virtual Reality. https://doi.org/10.1016/B978-0-443-14036-5.00013-3

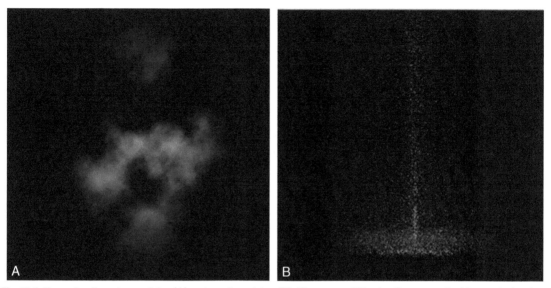

Fig. 13.1 Example of smoke particles (A) and sand particles (B). (Courtesy of Charles Owen, used with permission.)

that pixel location. For cost reasons, games usually use big particles in smaller quantities rather than a mix of big and small.

Particles are commonly included in game systems now, including Unity and Unreal. However, what support is included and how the particle systems are organized may vary. For example, Unity's built-in particle system includes the particle components, the particle force field component, and the visual effects graph. However, small particles are not readily built in. Conversely, Unreal has a complete built-in particle system in one asset, which can be edited in its Cascade Particles editor, with more vector fields options and small particles already built-in.

More advanced particles still require knowing how a particle system works and understanding their underlying needs, which aids in understanding the copious parameters given in game engine implementation. Therefore, the remainder of the section outlines the other basic characteristics and components of particles needed to make your own particle system.

Two- and Three-Dimensional Particles

Just as there are big and small particles, the particles can also be generated in 2D or 3D. Both have their uses. 2D particles are simpler to create by overlaying on the screen but can conversely have visual artifacts, particularly with occlusion. 3D particles are placed in 3D space and may use billboarded textures so that the particles always face the viewer or 3D meshes. While these particles do not have the same level of risk of visual artifacts, they are more involved to implement.

The 2D particles are usually implemented by using small images put together to general a larger effect. These are usually overlayed on the screen, such as rain. For smoke and fire, many 2D particles can be generated and then blended together.

The 3D particles start with the same concepts as 2D particles except that the position, velocity, and acceleration are in 3D space. The 3D particles are then maintained at the correct world position as the camera rotates and are sensitive to occlusion.

Particle Components

While a minimum particle only contains position and velocity, most involve far more with more components to affect their appearance over time, not just to move at a constant velocity. More complete particles have a lifetime. They exist for a specific period of time and then disappear. With this additional behavior, a more complete particle may have the following information:

- Vector position
- Vector velocity
- Vector acceleration
- Float lifetime
- Float age
- Float scale
- Float orientation
- Float angularVelocity
- Float alpha
- Color tint
- And possibly more!

The age and lifetime are both usually in seconds. Scale refers to the size of a particle. Orientation refers to the angle to draw the particle, and the angular velocity refers to the spinning speed the particle if relevant. Alpha and tint are color adjustments over time. Particle systems may have numerous other parameters to affect the appearance. Many of those appearance parameters may instead become curves over time rather than a constant value. For example, a particle may pulse between two colors.

The physics portion of the system will be using position, velocity, and various forces using similar mathematics as physics engine. The main differences are the extent of forces allowed are typically diminished and there is often a time limit forces are applied due to a particle's limited lifetime. The appearance portion uses the remainder and basic technique in which these affect the appearance to stay the same.

Another element of particle systems is the ability for a particle to release more particles. These are usually called "**events**" in particle systems. As an example, when a particle dies, it may produce another particle. Consider a firework that changes its color and shape over time. When one particle dies, a new one is released in the position the first died, only with new colors and shapes. This doesn't change the base set of parameters of a particle; it simply adds more particles. This is a common theme of particles. Every new appearance adjustment is simply more variables.

Initializing a Particle System

A particle system object consists of a list of active particles. More particles are added to the list as new particles are generated and the system iterates over them to update and draw. This means that many particles are created and destroyed at a rapid rate. C# of Unity uses garbage collection, which struggles with allocating and deallocating at high rates of speed. This can cause pauses as the garbage collector churns. C++ of Unreal leaves the garbage collection to the developer, so the high allocation/deallocation speed is less of an issue, but care is still desirable for efficiency.

For our purposes, the number of particles is fixed and reused instead of creating new particles which lessen the memory issues. A *living* particle is one whose age is less than its lifetime and is currently displaying. A *dead* particle is one whose age is over its lifetime and should be hidden or deleted. To do so, the different particles are designated as live and available. Consider the following code. The Particle class simply stores the parameters needed to place the particle, such as its speed and age. There are two lists of Particles: those who are showing and those that are hidden but are preallocated to later use for memory efficiency. On start, the particles are simply created for later use, but do not show yet.

```
class Particle
  Vector position
  Vector velocity
  Vector acceleration
  float lifetime
  float age
  float orientation
  float angularVelocity
  // any more parameters the particle allows

// The list of live particles
List<Particle> liveParticles

// A list of available particles
List<Particle> availableParticles
```

```
function Initialize()
  for i = 0 to howManyEffects * maxNumParticles
    availableParticles.AddLast( Particle() )
```

how Many Effects refers to the number of active particle production areas at any given time. *maxNumParticles* refers to the maximum number of particles to use for an effect.

Adding new live particles simply means removing the particle from the available list, reinitializing the available particle's variables in its starting point as a new live particle, and adding it to the live list as shown in the code below.

```
function AddParticles( Vector where )

  // create this many particles, if you can.
  for i = 0 to i < numParticles && availableParticles.Count > 0

    // Remove the particle from the list of available particles
    particle = availableParticles.PopFirst()
    availableParticles.RemoveFirst()

    // Reinitialize the particle
    node = MakeParticle( particle, where )

    // Add to the list of live particles
    liveParticles.Add( node )
```

The function above is called an *emitter* since it emits particles into the system. When the available particle is reinitialized, it's given a randomized range of characteristics in the MakeParticle() function implemented below:

```
function MakeParticle( Particle p, Vector where )

  // Pick some random values for our particle
  velocity = RandomBetween( minInitialSpeed, maxInitialSpeed )
  acceleration = RandomBetween( minAcceleration, maxAcceleration )
  lifetime = RandomBetween( minLifetime, maxLifetime )
  scale = RandomBetween( minScale, maxScale )
  rotationSpeed = RandomBetween( minRotationSpeed, maxRotationSpeed )
  orientation = RandomBetween( 0, (float)π * 2 )

  // Then initialize it with those random values,
  // and make sure it is marked as active.
  Create( p, where, velocity, acceleration, lifetime, scale,
          rotationSpeed, orientation )
```

Particle Physics

After the particles are ready, and alive, they are ready to be moved. Particles are moved using Euler steps. Euler steps were previously covered in Chapter 3. Updating the steps for a particle is straightforward in pseudocode:

```
function Update()
  node = liveParticles.First()
  while node! = null
    // Update velocity
    node.velocity += node.acceleration * deltaTime

    // Update position
    node.position += node.velocity * deltaTime

    // Update orientation
    node.orientation += node.angularVelocity * deltaTime

    // Update age
    node.age += deltaTime

  // Node died, remove from living list and add to available list
  if !node.Active
    liveParticles.Remove( node )
    availableParticles.AddLast( node )
    node.NextNode()

  // Advance to next node
  if( node.HasNext() )
      node = node.NextNode()
```

The above only applies to linear forces. If other forces are needed, they are simply added to the Euler steps above. This is all that is needed to apply motion to the particles.

Particle Appearance

After the particles are moved, the appearance effects can be applied. How to apply these effects tend to be almost identical. Therefore, only adjustment of size over time is presented here. To start, each new appearance option simply adds its control parameters to the Particle class. In this case, the particle needs its presenting size, the size at the state of its life, and the size at its death.

```
class Particle
  Vector position
  Vector velocity
  Vector acceleration
  float lifetime
  float age
  float orientation
  float angularVelocity
  float size
  float startScale
  float endScale
```

With this, updating the appearance can be done after the physics update with a simple function call to determine its appearance at this point in time. This is usually based on the percentage of the life left of the particle. Here, this is just a linear interpolation between the start and end sizes shown below in UpdateAppearance().

```
class Particle
  // prior parameters

  function UpdateAppearance()
    percentDone = age / lifetime
    size = LERP( startScale, endScale, percentDone )
```

Updating can be as simple or as complex as the system allows. Most modern system offer curves rather than simple linear interpolations. As an example, if the size pulsed in a sine wave fashion, the function could be updated to

```
class Particle
  // … prior parameters
  float minSize
  float maxScale
  float pulseRate

  function UpdateAppearance()
    percentDone = age / lifetime
    amplitude = maxSize - minSize
    size = amplitude * sin( pulseRate * percentDone ) + minSize
```

Particle Effects

Particles have a lot of uses. An inexhaustive list includes:
- Smoke
- Explosions

- Fog
- Fountains
- Rain
- Snow
- Dust
- Clouds
- Falling leaves
- Selection indication
- Volcanic eruptions
- Exhaust
- Fantasy effects

To demonstrate the results of the code above, consider a basic firework where two basic particle effects are needed: explosions and smoke. For both effects, transparent textures and enabled transparency are needed. However, the particles for these effects are also influenced by other factors, such as wind, color change, shape, gravity, and bounce.

These requirements do not change the basic requirements of the particle system. There are simply more variables for each particle. In some cases, there may be additional lists if only some of the particles are affected and not others. Particles can also be emitted in a shape. At this point, though, only the placement of the particle is known, not how to present it.

Firework Variables

To get an idea of the variables needed, here are some sample uses for explosion, smoke puff, and smoke plume particles:

Variable	Explosion	Smoke Puff	Smoke Plume
Texture	**explosion**	**smoke**	**smoke**
minInitialSpeed	40	20	20
maxInitialSpeed	500	200	100
minAcceleration	*	−10	**
maxAcceleration	*	−50	**
minScale	0.3	1.0	5.0
maxScale	1.0	2.5	7.0
minNumParticles	20	10	10
maxNumParticles	25	20	100
minRotationSpeed	$-\pi/4$	$-\pi/4$	$-\pi/2$
maxRotationSpeed	$\pi/4$	$\pi/4$	$\pi/2$

*The explosion acceleration is computed to decelerate to zero during the lifetime.
**The smoke plume acceleration is set to go up with some additional wind effects to the right.

Requirements for a Firework

Let's look at creating a fireworks effect to start building up to a campfire. The fireworks use the same variable values as above, to which the later campfire will add some shape and behavior tweaking. When thinking about a fireworks particle system the following items are needed:

- Texture or mesh
- Shape of the flame
- Fire die off
- Smoke dissipation
- Wind, if any
- Strength of fire

The texture here is the texture for the particle. Because both fire and smoke particles are to be generated, two textures are needed, shown in Fig. 13.2. For both effects, transparency is needed. The particles are typically more transparent than one would expect. The strength of the fire in this instance refers to how far and high the flame reaches before dying off, plus the thickness of the flames and smoke. In short, strength here refers to the number of particles to be used for the effects.

After creating one particle system object, the explosion variables and the fire can be added to that particle system. What will take more tweaking are the die-off behaviors of the particles, wind and strength.

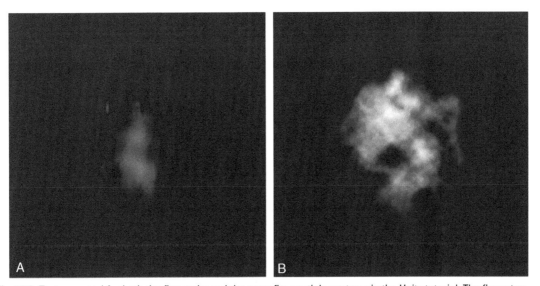

Fig. 13.2 Textures used for both the fireworks and the campfire particle systems in the Unity tutorial. The flame texture is (A) and the smoke texture is (B).

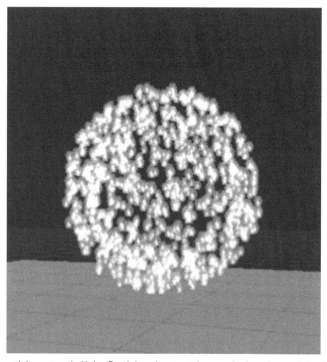

Fig. 13.3 Initial firework particle system in Unity. Particles shoot out from a single point, emitting light.

Let's address the initial emission first. A firework will have an emission starting from a single point and then expand outward in all directions. The MakeParticle() function can be used directly here since the velocity is random and will point in any direction. There are no other adjustments needed. Assuming the flame particle is used at every particle point, this will result in an outward expanded ball of particles with constant particle appearance as shown in Fig. 13.3.

Let's address the flame die-off next.

Fire Die-Off

To improve this example, flame particles are emitted, and then change color and eventually fizzle out. Smoke is also emitted from the fire and dies off/dissipates as well. That means that there are three main die-off items to implement: speed, color, and size. Speed should slow over time due to wind resistance. The color should dim over time, and the size should shrink over time. These items can be implemented in the built-in particle systems. To keep things simple, assume each of these is updated according to the function template given in the

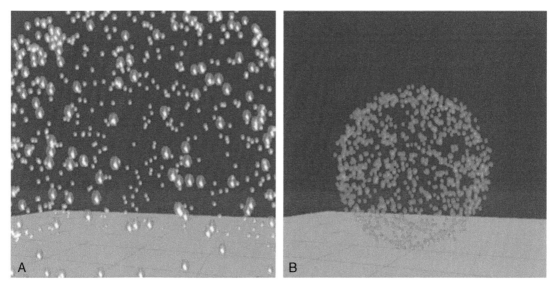

Fig. 13.4 The fireworks particle system with no die-off in (A) and with die-off in (B) in Unity at the same time stamp.

section Particle Appearance. In other words, assume a linear die-off. Both Unreal and Unity support this update method.

With the initial particle system values and linear die-off setting for speed, color, and size implemented, the particle system already looks similar to fireworks, as can be seen in Fig. 13.4. The original left firework is brighter and larger and has bigger particles at the same time stamp as the firework with the die-off implemented.

Smoke Event Particle

To add more realism, smoke can be added. A firework produces some smoke but mostly after the main flame has died. Secondary emitters can be added to an emitter to allow for more particles to be generated after a state event. In this case, smoke particles can be added after the state event of a flame dying off. Both Unity and Unreal support death, birth, and collision events. Both have a few other events as well. For this, a new particle system is created based on the particle events from the main emitter on the death of the main particle. The new particle system will be the smoke, so the variables and texture for the smoke are applied here.

Like fire, smoke also dissipates or dies off, so the speed, color, and size should change over the lifetime. Speed should be affected by the wind and float upward, color should fade to transparent, and size should expand. This can also be input into the function template given in the section Particle Appearance in the Update()

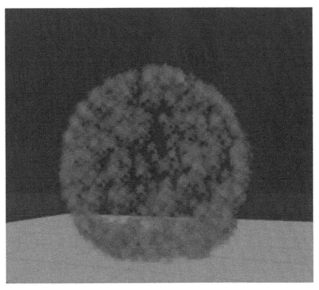

Fig. 13.5 The smoke particle system after the fireworks particle system has died-off in Unity.

function by activating a smoke particle right after the availableParticles.AddLast(node) line at the same position of the newly dead spark. Then the smoke effect can be shown after the firework dies off, as shown in Fig. 13.5. Both Unreal and Unity support this update method.

External Forces of Wind and Gravity

Wind and gravity are external forces acting on the particles. In both Unity and Unreal, these effects can be added in the built-in particle system. In the case of our fireworks example, gravity is applied to the fireworks and wind to the smoke whose physics are already implemented in the Update() function! The coder simply needs to set the force strength.

That's it. While tweaking the example may increase the realism, all the needed components are present and working for a fireworks display.

Converting to a Campfire

It is possible to convert the fireworks example into a campfire. The changes to do so are as follows:

- Change the initial position and velocity vectors: The fire moves mostly up as does the smoke.

- Change the shape: The fire and smoke are no longer an expanding sphere. Instead, the fire is closer to a condensed hemisphere and the smoke to a cylinder.
- Add looping: A firework lasts for one round, while a fire lasts longer. Looping allows for that longer effect.

Reshaping the emitter takes the most work, but it largely comes down to adjusting the velocity calculation in the MakeParticle() function. Rather than a random direction velocity, this calculation is split into direction and magnitude, similar to following which emits in a cone:

```
theta = RandomBetween( 0, 120 ) // restrict to upper cone
phi = RandomBetween( 0, 360 )
direction = UnitVectorOnSphere( theta, phi )
magnitude = RandomBetween( minInitialSpeed,
                           maxInitialSpeed )
velocity = direction * magnitude
```

The textures do not need to be changed. One factor that requires more tweaking, however, is the required amount of noise or randomization. Far more noise is needed for the campfire. The tutorial associated with this chapter walks through the details.

Vector Fields

Particles can be affected by more complex forces. This can be thought of as similar to wind or gravitational modeling. As can be seen in the fireworks example, most systems have some forces built-in, but others require specialized software.

In Unity, these are called Particle System Force Fields. In Unreal, there are different tools, but here, the Physics Fields or Vector Fields depend on the exact particle system used.

For the most part, needed vector fields are available as built-ins of external forces, such as gravity, collisions, attraction, and shape. At a minimum, linear forces and rotations within a defined area are usually supported. Consider the example from Unity in Fig. 13.6. The top hemisphere rotates the particles. The middle cylinder

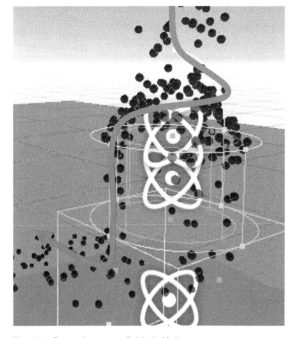

Fig **13.6** Example vector fields in Unity.

pulls the particles to align to the cylinder, and the bottom box pushes them out the back. Fancier vector fields involve 3D textures, which define the forces at that exact point within the field.

Vector fields tend to be finicky and require a fair bit of time to get right since the forces need to match the particles. However, they can result in much nicer animations.

Reference

[1] Reeves W. Particle systems—a technique for modeling a class of fuzzy objects, *ACM Trans Graphics* 2(2):91–108, 1983. CiteSeerX 10.1.1.517.4835. doi:10.1145/357318. 357320. S2CID 181508.

## 14

Artificial Intelligence

This chapter focuses on artificial intelligence (AI) and its uses in applications and games only. The contents outline what AI is, what AI is not, and its operational basis. After that, the application of AI to virtual reality is discussed. This includes game AI restrictions, decision trees, navigation meshes, and behaviors. Reviewing the Model-View-Controller (MVC) and visitor patterns is recommended.

Definition of AI

The definition of "intelligence," according to the *Merriam-Webster's Dictionary* [1], is

1. The ability to learn or understand or to deal with new or trying situations and
2. The ability to apply knowledge to manipulate one's environment or to think abstractly as measured by objective criteria (such as tests).

The definition of AI, on the other hand, using the same reference, is

1. A branch of computer science dealing with the simulation of intelligent behavior in computers and
2. The capability of a machine to imitate intelligent human behavior.

AI is a large, rapidly developing field. For our purposes, only the areas of AI applied to game mechanics are discussed here. Restricting to game AI merely means that the only aspects of AI to be used are shippable. That means that solutions must

- use what works,
- be reasonable to implement,
- be robust, and
- have reasonable performance.

On the other hand, academic AI researchers tend to be more focused on

- theoretical performance,
- what can be proven,
- proving what cannot work, and
- future or far-future solutions.

A Practical Introduction to Virtual Reality. https://doi.org/10.1016/B978-0-443-14036-5.00014-5

The differences are important to know when browsing AI literature for a game AI solution. In general, it helps to be restricted to sources that are focused on attempts to simulate intelligence in nonplayer characters and the environment. There are different approaches, and this chapter gives an introduction for four such approaches: state machines, decision trees, path finding, and heuristics. There is more recent push for other AI types in games, but as of yet the computational needs make these options less feasible.

State Machines

Game AI can be viewed as a three-step process (Fig. 14.1):
1. Sense the environment to get the current state.
2. Make a decision based on the environment.
3. Perform the action based on that decision.
Let's walk through how to apply each of these steps.

Sense the Environment

Sensing the environment essentially asks
- What does the entity know?
- What can the entity find out or sense?

As an example, let us take a vampire bat and ask these same questions.

What does a vampire bat know?
- Its energy needs, which is enough for flying, walking, etc.
- Its hunger, which is when the bat eats enough or sometimes more than enough.
- Its nurturing responsibilities, which occurs, if and when, a bat is responsible for feeding other bats.

What can a vampire bat find out or sense?
- The vampire bat can sense the *time* because bats hunt at night and return home for the day.
- The bat can sense its *location*.
- The bat can sense its surroundings using *echolocation*, which is what the bat sees audibly.
- The bat can *hear* well enough to sense breathing.
- The bat can sense heat in its surroundings using *thermoception*, which is what the bat sees as heat.

Fig. 14.1 Initial three-step process for a game AI.

There is a caveat to this, however. It's very easy to let the AI cheat and know more than what is reasonable. In the case of a cheating vampire bat, the bat could already know where the victim lies sleeping in an AI model.

With both lists drawn up, the different actions can be placed in code. The MVC pattern is helpful for this. Each item in the "know" list goes into a model or class. Each item in "the sense" list are functions run during the update and are called to model in the MVC pattern. In a more involved system, swapping out the sensing could use the strategy pattern or inheritance. This is still the model, though, because returning a location is a call on the model. Returning a list of items of interest would need the model's parameters and possibly the visitor pattern. The information returned is still pure data. The view in this case is the three-dimensional (3D) model of the bat. The controller, on the other hand, takes more deliberation and veers into making decisions based on the data returned by the model. This separation follows the built-in support that is often provided in game engines.

In the context of game engines and what goes where, the character has its parameters or model that is a component of this game object entity and can return information based on those parameters. The appearance of the character can be any mesh(es) that are components attached to this game object entity. How to respond is yet another component and uses the model and meshes as needed to make decisions.

Reason Based on Environment and Decision Trees

Keeping the bat example, there are two main questions to answer for this step:

- How does the vampire bat make decisions?
- How does that bat act on those decisions?

Answering these questions gives the controller requirements.

There is one item to keep in mind when designing solutions for the decisions. At first glance, there is a temptation to code up the decision process using if/else statements.

```
if IsCloseToDawn()
  if energy > MinEnergy
    ReturnHome()
  else
    CollapseAndDie()
else
...
```

However, hard-coding decisions makes it hard to design behaviors, adapt behaviors, visualize possible behaviors, etc. A more flexible approach is to use decision trees.

Decision trees have three types of nodes:

- Decision
- Chance
- End

The representations of the three nodes are in Fig. 14.2. An example drawing of a decision tree is shown in Fig. 14.3.

There are a couple of options for drawing up a decision tree. While the decision trees are not needed if all instances are already hard-coded, this is a tedious and more error-prone process. Conversely, setting up a decision tree can require implementing graphical editors and saving using the editor's underlying file format. This allows noncoders to build the decision tree. However, after drawing up the tree, it still needs to be implemention in code. Again, converting to if/else code is tedious. As a result, a common option is to compile to if/else code using custom code generation based on the save file generated by the editor. There are several third-party add-ins for decision trees.

 Decision Nodes

 Chance Nodes

 End Nodes

Fig. 14.2 Representation of decision tree nodes.

Perform the Action

After the decision has been made, the last step of the state machine comes into play which performs the action noted at the end node in the decision tree. At its simplest, this is a one-time event, like "continue to sleep." However, many actions take place over time. Take the Return to Cave end node from above. The bat does not teleport. It takes time to reach the cave, but the action may disallow any other

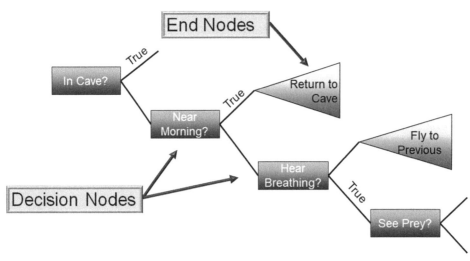

Fig. 14.3 Example decision tree.

action until the cave is reached. Requiring completing an action before a new action is typical in many applications.

That is not to say that the action itself cannot be adjusted during its process. Let's say that the vampire bat needs to know about nearby predators to perform this action correctly. While it is possible to make a node for every predator, it is also possible to retrieve the avoidance level instead and adjust the direction during the bat's return home. This veers into needing the visitor pattern for the action or having a decision tree within a decision tree!

The major area where the visitor pattern in AI is heavily used is for path finding and interaction effects between objects. In fact, most built-in AI support is focused on path finding and obstacle avoidance, where the obstacles can change during the trip to the target location.

Path Finding

Given path finding is possibly the most common AI problem in games, how it works at a high level can aid in the effective use of the AI packages. The base question is how to find a path from point A to point B, but there are variations to the path. In the vampire bat example, there are two variations for path finding:

- Hunt/stalk
- Escape/retreat

Unity and Unreal both have a built-in package for this, called Nav(igation) meshes. The meshes are limited, however, in that the meshes address only where the character or object can go. The decision aspect is still the developer's responsibility.

To best use this, let us look at how these navigation meshes work at a high level.

Let's start with an example without the changing nature of a game-like application. Assume a manually created graph with vertex locations that the user can walk to and from with edges between some but not all the locations, such as the one shown in Fig. 14.4. In this case, the shortest path can be found using Dijkstra's algorithm, or just as frequently the A* algorithm.

The situation changes drastically if the paths are automatically generated. This is even more apparent if the path is changed every time, such as a changing maze game. This is where navigation meshes come in.

Think of the vertices as nodes and what other vertices are reachable from those nodes. Repeating this process for every vertex pair gives the graph. To help with this process, there are sweep and prune algorithms for this. Next, paths are created from the start and end point to all the other visible vertices. Finally, Dijkstra's or the A*

Fig. 14.4 Example of a simple navigation mesh with paths.

algorithm can be applied to find the shortest path. These four steps are illustrated in Fig. 14.5.

There are additional factors to consider other than simply finding the shortest path. Animation-wise, the path in Fig. 14.5 is jarring and noncharacteristic of a flying bat. Applying curve methods will smooth the path. Different paths can have additional characteristics. Static "threat" level avoidances also may use the A* algorithm, which is much like Dijkstra's but does not backtrack for speed, which is less affected by the decreased accuracy. This will add the buffer around corners. For nonstatic threat levels, such as the prey observing the bat and running away or a predator observing the bat and then hunting the bat, the visitor pattern may be needed. The packages typically can handle the A* static threats, but nonstatic threats are typically on the coder (Fig. 14.6).

Navigation Meshes

Both Unity and Unreal have navigation mesh systems, which are largely for path finding and travel logic. These are the next steps in path finding. Conditions for travel are left to the developer to create a decision tree. Unreal has a few more advanced features, but the basics are largely the same.

At a high level, a navigation mesh takes the character and the movement options and then determines where the character can travel.

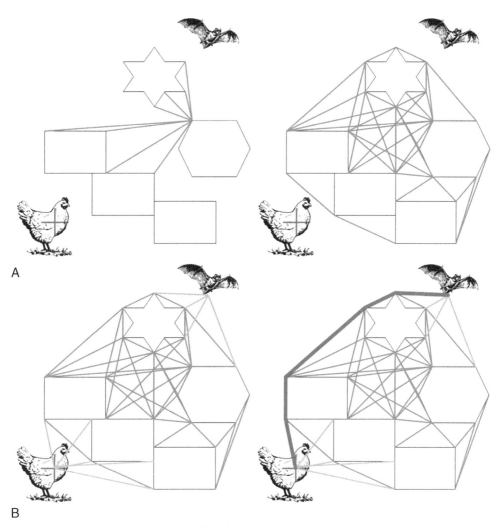

Fig. 14.5 Steps to developing a navigation mesh. (A left) Connect one vertex to other reachable vertices. (A right) Apply this process to all available vertices. (B left) Create paths from the start and end points to all visible vertices, creating the navigation mesh. (B right) Apply Dijkstra's algorithm to find the shortest path in the navigation mesh, which is shown in red here.

This is like automatically making the path graph in the prior section based on the geometry of the meshes. In Fig. 14.7, a navigation mesh was baked into the environment but with a slope threshold that disallows movement in areas where the slope is considered too steep. Once the mesh is applied, an object specified to use the mesh can be dropped into the environment. Often the decision tree determines the placement of the object.

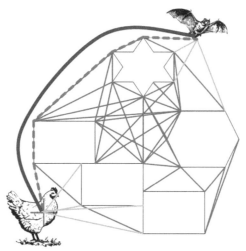

Fig. 14.6 Shorted path with smoothing added.

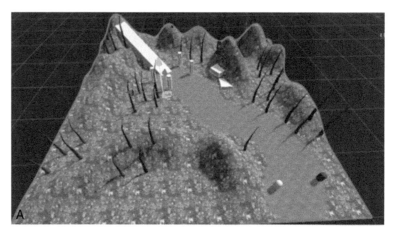

Fig. 14.7 Example of a navigation mesh in Unity. (A) shows the original environment, and the (B) shows the allowed movement areas highlighted in blue. The blue is the baked navigation mesh.

Fig. 14.8 Zoomed in image of the two ledges in the environment shown in Fig. 14.7.

There are some missing instances in the current mesh.

1. There is no way to reach the second ledge near the top right, even though the area is legal. This can be seen as the selected ledge in Fig. 14.7B and 14.8.
2. Movement is limited in areas less preferred, such as if the environment has a temporary fire.

The extra instances can be addressed by adding off mesh links. For the first instance, if automatically generated, the distance and allowable drop height can be set. Then mesh links can be manually added by choosing the areas of exception. (Fig. 14.9).

Areas can also be marked as having higher costs. In Unity, this is an enum with a cost. In Unreal, this is a Nav modifier component, but both use these off-links, which is just a fancy name for a link "off" the mesh onto another one. This can be used for the second instance by designating an area with a fire cost (Fig. 14.10).

After creation, using the meshes tends to be very straightforward. In both Unity and Unreal, this largely comes down to one line with the following meaning:

```
character.NavMesh.target = newTarget
```

That simply says "character, move to the new target along the nav mesh based on your speed while considering avoidances." The character will keep trying to move to that area until it is reached or if the nav mesh decides it is impossible to reach. There are usually far more options than this, but this is the simplest version.

There are a few more options for navigation meshes. For example, consider an application that has two types of characters, and one type

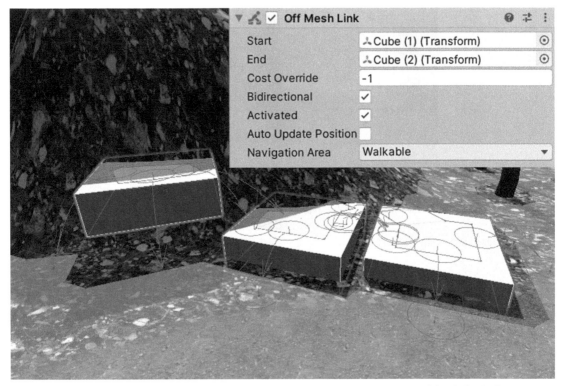

Fig. 14.9 Example of adding an off-mesh link to allow for jumping from a lower ledge to a higher ledge in Unity.

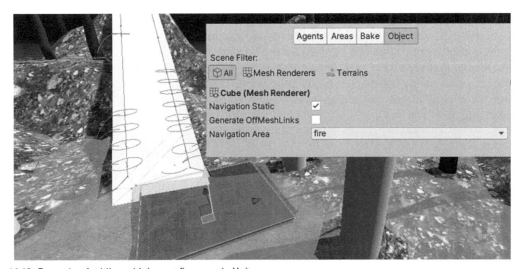

Fig. 14.10 Example of adding a high-cost fire zone in Unity.

is unaffected by fire. Handling this varies according to the engine. In Unreal, this usually takes creating a second navigation mesh. For Unity, there are more options: using different groups of sizes; using a navigation mesh agent with an area mask, which contains the list of areas a character *can* walk; and setting the cost per character per area in code. For non-static geometry, such as an automatically generated maze, both Unreal and Unity use special components for handling the navigation. Unity uses a Nav Mesh Obstacle component and Unreal uses a Nav Modifier component.

Reference

[1] *Merriam-Webster Dictionary*. Retrieved 2023. https://www.merriam-webster.com/dictionary/intelligence

## 15

Advanced Physics

Sometimes more advanced physics is required to prevent tunneling or to create the correct effect in an application. This chapter covers some of the more advanced techniques: tunneling, collision detection (two- [2D] and three-dimensional [3D]), collision response, and rays. Pseudocode examples are included in all the topics.

Refresher on When to Use Custom Physics

The main instance for requiring custom physics is tunneling, especially at high speeds.

While VR engines provide means and shortcuts to handle some tunneling, sometimes the physics shortcuts in an engine as described in Chapter 3 are just too short. Such an example comes from Chapter 3: the golf ball swing. Swinging a club to hit a golf ball is too fast for the default physics. When this happens, it is up to the developer to add the necessary physics. Modern physics engines in many game engines send the computational load to the GPU. Hacking the physics engine and doing it yourself tends to offload the physics to the CPU. Using the CPU is far slower than using the GPU. This means bypassing the engine should be done on only as few objects as possible.

Going back to the golf example from Chapter 3, recall that the maximum time step to avoid tunneling is about 0.0008 s. Not only do physics engines usually have 0.01 to 0.02 s time steps, but a 0.0008 s time step would typically stall the engine.

When this happens, custom physics beyond the default engine is required for high-speed collisions.

Collisions are a complex topic with many subtopics. Here, the topics are restricted to

- Detecting collisions
- Determining what happens when hitting a wall
- Correcting an incorrect collision

This covers the bare minimum to catch and respond to tunneling. First, the problem of detecting collisions will be outlined in 2D

A Practical Introduction to Virtual Reality. https://doi.org/10.1016/B978-0-443-14036-5.00015-7

because that provides all of the needed information but is a bit simpler than the 3D version. The extension into 3D is afterward. The corrections to the tunneling are covered next.

Two-Dimensional Collisions

In graphics, a collision is the penetration of one polygon into another polygon. This is indicated by a point of one polygon placed inside another polygon, such as in Fig. 15.1.

Determining when a collision occurs then requires determining when one polygon is inside of another, which at a high level is checking all polygons, against all other polygons, with the space case of one polygon completely inside another:

```
for polygon p1 in objects // for each pair
  for polygon p2 in objects
    if p1 != p2
      if !Test( p1, p2 ) // check pair in both
        Test( p2, p1 )
```

While it may be tempting to test if any vertex in the first polygon (p1) is contained in the second polygon (p2), this does not always work in an overlap such as in Fig. 15.2.

The solution for testing for overlap is to use separator lines. A *separator line* is a line in space such that all vertices in p1 are on one side and all vertices in p2 are on the other side. If a separator line exists, the line will be placed parallel to or on an edge of one of the polygons (Fig. 15.3).

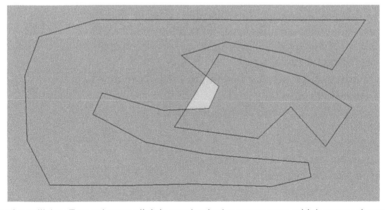

Fig. 15.1 Example of a collision. Two polygons slightly overlap in the green area, which means that a collision has occurred. (Courtesy of Charles Owen, used with permission.)

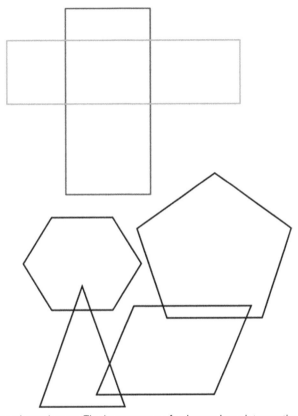

Fig. 15.2 Examples of intersecting polygons. The lower group of polygons have intersecting vertices; the top group does not. (Courtesy of Charles Owen, used with permission.)

Fig. 15.3 Two polygons with a red separator line in-between. (Courtesy of Charles Owen, used with permission.)

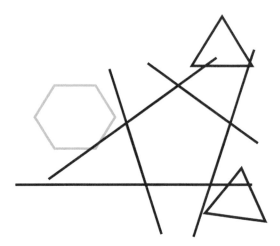

Fig. 15.4 Pentagon with separator lines placed on all edges.
(Courtesy of Charles Owen, used with permission.)

The Separator Equation

Let's consider a pentagon with separator lines placed on its edges, as shown in Fig. 15.4.

The line endpoints of the pentagon can be used to create the separator lines, which means that at least one of the line equations can be used:

$$y = mx + b$$

$$Ax + By = C$$

$$y_2 - y_1 = m(x_2 - x_1)$$

In this case, the second option works the best. Let (x_1, y_1) and (x_2, y_2) be line endpoints for a separator line. The line equation for the separator line can be found by using

- $A = y_1 - y_2$
- $B = x_2 - x_1$
- $C = -Ax_1 - By_1$

The last item is to switch C's sign so that any point on the line can be represented as follows:

$$Ax + By + C = 0$$

Each separator line can then be determined using the same steps. Here, the lines are determined clockwise around the polygon.

With the lines determined, a condition can be used to determine if a collision occurred. If the second polygon is outside of the pentagon's separator line, then

$$Ax + By + C > 0.$$

If the second polygon is inside of the pentagon's separator line, then

$$Ax + By + C < 0.$$

This can be represented in pseudocode as follows:

```
for each edge e in p2     // Try each edge
  compute line equation a, b, c
  possible = true         // Could be a separator

  // Try each vertex against edge
  for each vertex v in p1
    r = av_x + bv_y + c    // Line equation

    // If true, not a separator line
    if r ≤ 0
      possible = false
      break
  if possible == true
    return false     // No collision

return true          // Collision possible
```

Test your Understanding 15.1

Consider the collision in Fig. 15.5. What is the value of the test with points (3,3) and (12,5) in the line from (5,5) to (10,0)? Which point has the collision, and which is outside of the collision?

The problem requires finding the separator line equation for one edge of the triangle and then computing the result of the conditional test for both (3,3) and (12,5).

First, the separator line can be determined using the line functions above:

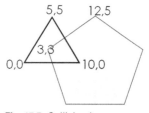

Fig. 15.5 Collision between a pentagon and a triangle with vertex positions included.

$$A = y_1 - y_2 = 5 - 0 = 5$$

$$B = x_2 - x_1 = 10 - 5 = 5$$

$$C = -Ax_1 - By_1 = -5 \times 5 - 5 \times 5 = -50$$

This gives a separator line of

$$5x + 5y - 50 = 0.$$

Next, the points in question can be inputted into the separator line.
For point (3,3),

$$5(3) + 5(3) - 50 = -20.$$

For point (12,5),

$$5(12) + 5(5) - 50 = 35.$$

Point (3,3) gives a negative number, while point (12,5) gives a positive number. Therefore, point (3,3) is inside the collision, and point (12,5) is outside of the collision.

To test for collisions then, all the edges for both polygons need to be checked, and just like the high level version, both directions need to be checked:

```
function TestForOverlap( CollisionItem c1, CollisionItem c2 )
  // Symmetrical search for an edge that segments the two...
  if !TestLeftRight( c1, c2 )
    return false

  if !TestLeftRight( c2, c1 )
    return false

  // We know we have a collision if we get to here.
  // Create some list of collision items to resolve...
  return true
```

Here CollisionItem holds the data describing an object that can collide and its collision state. CollisionItem will be further discussed later. For now, let's outline the pseudocode to test for collisions. Using line separators, every edge needs to be checked relative to each polygon. Here, the edges are tested in a clockwise, left-to-right order.

```
function bool TestLeftRight( CollisionItem c1, CollisionItem c2 )
  vertexList1 = c1.GetPerimeterList()
  vertexList2 = c2.GetPerimeterList()

  // Last vertex in v2
  priorVertex = vertexList2.last
  for currentVertex in vertexList2
    // Compute the edge line function
    compute a, b, c with priorVertex and currentVertex
    possible = true

      for testPoint in vertexList1
        r = a testPoint_x + b testPoint_y + c
        // If r <= zero, we're on the wrong side of the line.
        // This can't be a separator line.
        if r <= 0
          possible = false
            break

      // If the possibility that this is a separator line
      // never got cleared,
      // it just became one.
      if possible
        return false
      // Make this the end point for the next pass
      priorVertex = currentVertex
  // If no separating edges have been found,
  // we potentially have an overlap.
  return true
```

While this does effectively check for a collision, if checking all polygons with TestLeftRight(), there is a caveat: the runtime. This method has a runtime of $O(n^2)$, which is computationally very expensive. The running time worsens if all of the polygons are touching each other.

This is why so many physics engines use shortcuts for collisions. Two such options are bounding box tests and witness tests, which are helpful for situations using acceleration.

Bounding Boxes Test

Bounding boxes are essentially a strong simplification of the separator line method. A bounding box is fitted around the polygon on all sides, so that each object's minimum and maximum positions are computed in each dimension. This way, the simpler bounding boxes are tested for collisions instead of more complicated polygons.

This can be illustrated by taking intervals in one dimension,

- $i_1 = [2, 7]$
- $i_2 = [6, 9]$
- $i_3 = [4, 8]$
- $i_4 = [11, 14]$
- $i_5 = [15, 16]$
- $i_6 = [17, 21]$

and determining the overlaps in the intervals (Fig. 15.6). This requires scanning or sweeping forward and keeping track of which interval is currently active.

This gives a runtime of $O(n \log n + k)$, which is better but not at all times. If all the boxes are in the same area, then the runtime turns right back to $O(n^2)$.

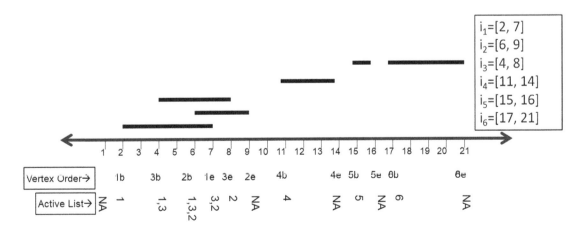

Fig. 15.6 Comparison of intervals and overlaps along the number line.

In 2D, this means that collisions occur when two bounding boxes overlap in both dimensions. Then a hash table of all objects overlapped by this object can be created.

All of this information will need to be kept in a data structure:

```
// All of the items we know about to test for collisions.
class CollisionItem
  // Bounding box overlaps
  // (hashes CollisionItem to integer count)
  Hashtable overlap

  // The polygon
  Polygon poly

// We also keep an array of beginning and end points.
class EndItem
  bool begin                      // Is this a beginning?
  CollisionItem item              // Back reference to the item
                                  // we are referring to

// A list of collisions
class Collide
  Polygon p1                      // First polygon
  Polygon p2                      // Second polygon
  Vector v1                       // Intersection point
  Vector N2                       // Normal to polygon 2
  float r                         // Amount of penetration

boxSortedX = EndItem[]   // Bounding box items in X axis (EndItem)
boxSortedY = EndItem[]   // Bounding box items in Y axis (EndItem)
items = CollisionItem[]  // All of our items (CollisionItem)
```

A polygon can then be added to the system for a collision check:

```
// Adds a polygon to the collision system
function Add( Polygon p )
  // Create an object for the item
  CollisionItem c
  c.poly = p
  items.Add( c )

  // Create two bounding box items for this polygon
  EndItem beg
  beg.begin = true
  beg.item = c
  EndItem end
  end.begin = false
  end.item = c
```

```
// Add to the two array lists
boxSortedX.Add( beg )
boxSortedX.Add( end )
boxSortedY.Add( beg )
boxSortedY.Add( end )
```

The list of polygons can then be tested for collisions. First, the polygons are added to the lists. Then, the lists for both dimensions are sorted and swept for collisions. The potential collisions are then placed in their own list and compared to see which polygons overlap in both dimensions. If any entries in the lists meet these criteria, then a collision has occurred.

```
function Test()
  anyCollide = false
  collides.Clear()

  // Set all of the begin EndItems to an empty overlap set
  for CollisionItem c in items
    c.overlap.Clear()

  // Insertion sort the two lists
  SortOnX( boxSortedX )
  SortOnY( boxSortedY )

  // Sweep the lists
  Sweep( boxSortedX )
  Sweep( boxSortedY )

  // At this point we know all bounding boxes overlap
  // from the fact that they have entries in their overlap list
  // that overlap in two dimensions
  for CollisionItem c1 in items
    for CollisionItem c2 in c1.overlap.Keys
      if c1.overlap[ c2 ] < 2
        continue

      // We have an overlap between items c1 and c2
      // Test them for overlap
      if TestForOverlap( c1, c2 )
        anyCollide = true

  return anyCollide

function Sweep( EndItem[] box )
  // Set of all active items.
  active = Hashtable()
```

```
// Scan a dimension
for EndItem b1 in box
  if b1.begin
    // We're adding a polygon.
    // We have an overlap with
    // every item in the active list
    for CollisionItem b2 in active.Keys
      // Overlap is symmetrical.
      // To prevent two entries, we
      // keep track of overlaps with
      // increasing id values.
      CollisionItem c1, c2
      if b1.item.poly.Id < b2.poly.Id
        c1 = b1.item
        c2 = b2
      else
        c2 = b1.item
        c1 = b2

      if c1.overlap[ c2 ] exists
        c1.overlap[c2]++
      else
        c1.overlap[c2] = 1

    // Add to the active items
    active.Add( b1.item, b1 )

  else
    // Remove from list of actives
    active.Remove( b1.item )
```

There may be some aspects to the Test() function that seem odd, such as using insertion sort. Initially, the default sort to use for large lists is quick sort. However, there are times when using insertion sort is faster and that is when the items are already sorted.

Graphics and simulations often have the property of *coherence*. Coherence, here, informally means that there is little to no change at small distances. In particular, objects do not move very far. Due to this coherence, lists in graphics and simulations tend to have near-sorted lists. If an item is out of order, the corrected placement in the list is nearby. As a result, using insertion sort here gives a run time of about $O(n)$ instead of longer.

Witness Test

With the property of coherence, collision detection can be sped up even further using witness tests. Witness tests use a comparison of prior and current updates to see which currently overlapping polygons were not previously overlapping.

Witness tests work in three steps:

1. For every object, keep a list of witnesses: this usually means keeping a hash on the other object.
2. A witness records that it "witnessed" a separator line in the last update.
3. If there is a witness, check the associated separator line first.
   a. If the line condition works, finish. There was no collision.
   b. If the line condition does not work, perform the full collision test.

Following this procedure reduces the number of polygons to check. This can be added before testing for any collisions:

```
function TestForOverlap( CollisionItem c1, CollisionItem c2 )
  // Symmetrical witness tests
  if !TestWitnessLeftRight( c1, c2 )
    return false
  if !TestWitnessLeftRight( c2, c1 )
    return false

  // Symmetrical search for an edge that segments the two...
  if !TestLeftRight( c1, c2 )
    return false
  if !TestLeftRight( c2, c1 )
    return false
  // We know we have a collision if we get to here.
  // Create some list of collision items to resolve...
  return true
```

The first part of a witness test is to check if there is a witness and, if so, to pull the associated separator line. The second part uses the separator test from before to determine a potential collision but does not require the nested loop, which brings the expected runtime from $O(n^2)$ to $O(n)$.

```
function TestWitnessLeftRight ( CollisionItem c1,
                                CollisionItem c2 )

  // See if a witness exists
  if (!c2.witness.Has( c1 ))
    return true

  // It does. Let's try it...
  witnessLineIndex = c2.witness[ c1 ]
  vertexList1 = c1.GetPerimeterList()
  vertexList2 = c2.GetPerimeterList()
```

```
// get the exact line that was the separator
endSeparator = vertexList2[ witnessLineIndex ]
if (witnessLineIndex == 0)
    beginSeparator = vertexList2[ vertexList2.Count - 1 ]
else
    beginSeparator = vertexList2[ witnessLineIndex - 1 ]

compute a, b, c with beginSeparator and endSeparator

// same test as before, but only one line needs to be checked!
possible = true
for each testPoint in vertexList1
  r = a testPoint_x + b testPoint_y + c
  if r <= 0
     possible = false
     break

     // We have a separator line. This is our witness, save it
  if possible
     return false

// Witness is invalidated
c2.witness.Remove( c1 )
return true
```

Any witnesses can then be used to reduce the number of collisions to check:

```
function TestLeftRight(CollisionItem c1, CollisionItem c2)
  vertexList1 = c1.GetPerimeterList()
  vertexList2 = c2.GetPerimeterList()
  // Last vertex in v2
  priorVertex = vertexList2.last
  witnessEdgeIndex = 0          // Edge counter
  for currentVertex in vertexList2
    // Compute the edge line function
    compute a, b, c with priorVertex and currentVertex
    possible = true
      for testPoint in vertexList1
      r = a testPoint_x + b testPoint_y + c
        // If r <= zero, we're on the wrong side of the line.
        // This can't be a separator line.
        if r <= 0
          possible = false
          break
```

```
    // If the possibility that this is a separator
    // line never got cleared, it just became one.
    if possible
      // We have a separator line.
      // This is our witness, save it
      c2.witness[c1] = witnessEdgeIndex
      return false

    // Make this the end point for the next pass
    priorVertex = currentVertex
    witnessEdgeIndex++


// If no separating edges have been found,
// we potentially have an overlap.
return true
```

Tunneling and the Bisection Search

While the above helps to improve the computational cost of determining a collision, nothing thus far has addressed the potential for tunneling.

Tunneling is particularly problematic if the time step is large, such as after a system pause. Before going into methods to address tunneling, however, it is helpful to better understand how to update the position first.

Take the following update pseudocode:

```
function PhysicsUpdate()
  timeLeft = deltaTime
  // 1) split up time update, if too big
  while  timeLeft > 0
    step = timeLeft
    // 2) maximum allowable step
    if step > 0.05f
      step = 0.05f

    // 3) update this time step according to physics
    for obj in canCollideList
        obj.SaveState()  // Save state, to revert if needed
        obj.DoEulerStep( step )

    // check for collisions, and if this step was too much
    state = collisionSystem.Test()
```

```
// 4) for right now, on any collision STOP
if state == true
  // undo update state
  for obj in canCollideList
      obj.RestoreState()

timeLeft -= step
```

The outermost loop marked with 1) allows for multiple steps if the frame update is slow. Here the step size is set to the largest allowable value of 0.05 s as shown in the lines marked with 2). The progress over the time step is checked at the lines marked with 3), and stopped at 4) where the collision occurs. But, tunneling can still occur if the collision is smaller than the time step. The time step could be set to the maximum legal distance, which would prevent the tunneling. Unfortunately, that method can be slow, such as with the golf swing time limit example.

One solution to this is to perform a *bisection search*.

A bisection search asks, "If the current step is too deep, what about step 2?"

To answer this question, additional collision data is needed:

- The ability to try a step and back up if needed. This is why the state was placed in a class in the data structure pseudocode.
- The ability to compute the penetration of the vertex into the polygon when a collision occurs. Here a valid collision is considered to be $0 < p < \varepsilon$ for some small ε, where p is the penetration. Units will be whatever the distance unit is for the engine.
  - A collision greater than ε is too deep.
  - ε can be as small as 0.0001.

Penetration, p, can be found as

$$p = - (ax + by + C)$$

where a and b are the normalized coefficients from the 2D line equation. The coefficients can be normalized by

$$length = \sqrt{A^2 + B^2}$$

$$a = \frac{A}{length}$$

$$b = \frac{B}{length}$$

The algorithm used to determine the penetration should be familiar since a version was used for collision detection:

```
for Vertex v in p1
  possible = true    // Until we know otherwise
  bestR = ∞          // Candidate for best R for this vertex
  for Edge e in p2
    compute a, b, c
    r = ax + by + c

    // check which side the vertex is
    if r > 0
      possible = false
      break
    else if -r < bestR // So far…
      bestR = -r

  if possible
    return bestR
```

While this method can be readily integrated with the prior TestForOverlap code, it's important to note that this method has the possibility of missing a second vertex penetration. Regardless, since this offers more control on catching incorrect collisions and partial updates, updates can be corrected at the collision correction section marked with 4).

```
function PhysicsUpdate()
  timeLeft = deltaTime

  // 1) split up time update, if too big
  while timeLeft > 0
    step = timeLeft

    // 2) maximum allowable step
    if step > 0.05
      step = 0.05
      badCollision = false

    // 3) update this time step according to physics
    for obj in canCollideList
      obj.SaveState() // Save state, to revert if needed
      obj.DoEulerStep( step )

    // check for collisions, and if this step was too much
    state = collisionSystem.Test()
```

```
// 4) there was a collision!
if (state == true)
  // if it was too much... do a half step
    if collisionSystem.BestR > deepestAllowable
      badCollision = true  // We can't go this far, backtrack
      step = step/2        // Halve our step size

        // undo update state
        for (obj in canCollideList)
          obj.RestoreState()

    if !badCollision
      timeLeft -= step
```

Unfortunately, this still has a risk of tunneling. Plus, while the minimum step can be calculated, doing so is wasteful in most cases. One way of improving tunneling detection is to factor in acceleration or the before/after positions.

This means detecting when the time step may be too long and only running the rapid update when tunneling could be found.

Detecting when a time step may be too long is something of a shortcut; one way to do this is to create a bounding box of the before and after positions. If there is an intersection with the bounding box, a collision detection was found. While Unity and Unreal already do this to some extent, there is a notable issue with this technique.

Let's go back to the golfing example and place a tracking bounding box on the club head. If the club is moving fast enough, the before/after bounding box misses the ball, similar to Fig. 15.7.

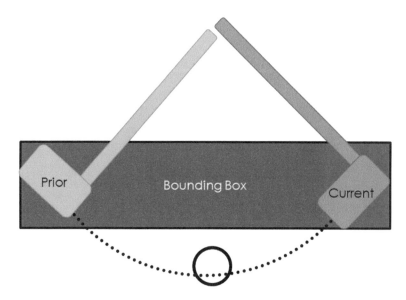

Fig. 15.7 Example of tunneling despite the bisection intersection detection. A golf club swings through a gold ball, but the golf ball is still outside of the detection bounding box of the club head.

While this could potentially be fixed by changing the detection bounding box into a rotational reference frame, virtual reality (VR) engines do not yet readily support this setting. A rotating reference frame is a nonstable (or noninertial) reference frame, where the point of view of the observer is in rotation relative to a stable reference frame. The concept can cause some dizziness but is also very common in more advanced simulations. An example is where anyone placed on a rotating earth is in a rotational reference frame relative to a rocket moving in a straight line in space. Adding a rotational reference frame would potentially require defining the new rotational frame, the associated fictitious forces, and the conversion between the rotational frame and the stable frame of the VR environment.

Fortunately, there are other options:

- Check if the separator line switched signs to indicate a potential incorrect collision. This increases memory use but can still fail with concave objects.
- Add a context-specific plane. In the golf setting, this means possibly setting a plane in the golf swing and then checking for an intersection in the estimated arc. Adding context-specific options can be more effective but can also require a bit more creativity to develop.

Both options are valid in certain circumstances. Adding context-specific options can be more effective but also require a bit more creativity to develop.

Extending to 3D

All that has been discussed so far works when extended into 3D. The main changes are that the edge normal is now in 3D rather than 2D and the separator line is now a plane. A minor change is that the box sort is now run three times for three directions: x, y, and z. As before, 3D space is represented in left-hand notation (Fig. 15.8).

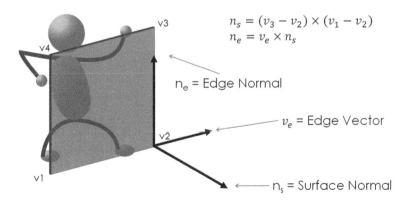

$$n_s = (v_3 - v_2) \times (v_1 - v_2)$$
$$n_e = v_e \times n_s$$

n_e = Edge Normal

v_e = Edge Vector

n_s = Surface Normal

Fig. 15.8 Model with separator plane, labeled points in the plane and derived axes.

There are a couple of items to note about separator planes.

First, a *separator plane* is a plane in space such that all vertices in one polygon are on one side of the plane and all vertices of another polygon are on the other side. One of the characteristics of any plane is a face. To find the axes relative to the plane, and thus the face, lines and cross products can be used. Using Fig. 15.8 as an example,

- Edge vectors can be found by using a combination of two vertex points in the surface: $v_2 - v_1 = v_3 - v_4 = v_e$.
- The surface normal to the plane can be found using the cross product of two lines in the plane, such as $(v_3 - v_2) \times (v_1 - v_2) = n_s$.
- The edge normal to the surface normal can be found by crossing the surface normal with the edge vector: $v_e \times n_s = n_e$.

Edges and lines may be used interchangeably here because the application is so similar. In general, lines do not have endpoints, but edges do have endpoints at the polygon vertex points.

Second, the separator equation can be extended to planes by adding another dimension:

$$Ax + Bx + Cz + D = 0.$$

This gives the plane equation for the face of a convex polyhedron. The conditional statements for determining a collision also apply when extending to 3D. If the second polyhedron is outside of the convex polyhedron's separator plane, then

$$Ax + By + Cz + D > 0.$$

If the second polyhedron is inside of the convex polyhedron's separator plane, then

$$Ax + By + Cz + D < 0.$$

As a result, the algorithm used for testing for 2D collisions can be extended to 3D by changing the line equations into plane equations:

```
for Vertex v in p1
  possible = true      // Until we know otherwise
  bestR = ∞    // Candidate for best R for this vertex

  for face in p2
    compute face's a, b, c, d
    normalize a, b, c, d
    compute d
    r = ax + by + cz + d
```

```
    //check which side the vertex is
    if r > 0
      possible = false
      break
    else if -r < bestR    // So far…
      bestR = -r

  if possible
    return bestR
```

Like before, this algorithm might miss a second vertex penetration, but the methods in the previous section also apply as solutions.

Collision Response

After the collision has been detected, the collision response comes next. When the collision detection is removed from the control of the physics engine, handling the response is also diverted to the developer.

Some responses to collisions are to

- Bounce back a bit.
- Apply missing forces.
- Remove colliding object.
- Stop.

The last option is the simplest as the first polyhedron only needs to be moved back by the overlap distance. The first and third options are slightly more complex than the first but have similar solutions. The second option requires far more complex solutions.

Dragging Force and Intersecting Lines

Let's start with a situation of applying a dragging force. This is a common force used for sliding across surfaces, such as a wall or floor. In this case, neither bounce nor rotation is present, so only the dragging force needs to be addressed. This will also be limited to 2D to limit the complexity.

Calculating the force first requires finding the intersection between two lines. For now, let's assume two lines with each line expressed by two points. There is a way to express any point on each line as a single value, let's say t_n.

- For line a: $p_a = v_1 + t_a(v_2 - v_1)$.
- For line b: $p_b = v_3 + t_b(v_4 - v_3)$.

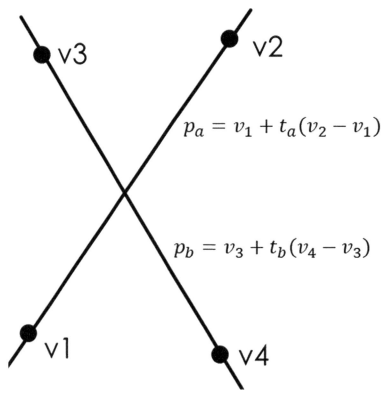

Fig. 15.9 Two intersecting lines.

This form may look somewhat familiar to the point-slope form of the line equation, but please keep in mind that this is using vertex points. This is a linear Bézier curve for each line segment. At the intersection point, $p_a = p_b$. Using this relation, the formulas for t_n can be found:

- For line a: $t_a = \dfrac{(x_4 - x_3)(y_1 - y_3) - (y_4 - y_3)(x_1 - x_3)}{(y_4 - y_3)(x_2 - x_1) - (x_4 - x_3)(y_2 - y_1)}$

- For line b: $t_b = \dfrac{(x_2 - x_1)(y_1 - y_3) - (y_2 - y_1)(x_1 - x_3)}{(y_4 - y_3)(x_2 - x_1) - (x_4 - x_3)(y_2 - y_1)}$

Note how the denominator is the same for both lines. While this was derived under the assumption that the lines intersect, this can be used to check for parallel lines (Fig. 15.9). If the denominator is 0, the lines are parallel. Otherwise, the lines intersect.

The t values can then be determined by plugging in the line or vertex values, and then the intersection point can be found by plugging in the t_n values into the point equations.

Test Your Understanding 15.2

To illustrate this, let's take the following lines:

- Line a has vertex points (0,0) to (10,10).
- Line b has vertex points (0,10) to (20,10).

For these lines,

a. What is the value of t_a?

b. Where is the intersection point?

a) For the first question, the vertex points need to be defined first:

$$v_1 = (x_1, y_1) = (0, 0)$$

$$v_2 = (x_2, y_2) = (10, 10)$$

$$v_3 = (x_3, y_3) = (0, 10)$$

$$v_4 = (x_4, y_4) = (20, 10)$$

Then, the vertex points are plugged into the formula for t_a:

$$
\begin{aligned}
t_a &= \frac{(x_4 - x_3)(y_1 - y_3) - (y_4 - y_3)(x_1 - x_3)}{(y_4 - y_3)(x_2 - x_1) - (x_4 - x_3)(y_2 - y_1)} \\
&= \frac{(20 - 0)(0 - 10) - (10 - 10)(0 - 0)}{(10 - 10)(10 - 0) - (20 - 0)(10 - 0)} = 1
\end{aligned}
$$

b) For the second question, the value for t_a is plugged into the intersection point formula for p_a.

$$p_a = v_1 + t_a(v_2 - v_1) = (0, 0) + 1((10, 10) - (0, 0)) = (10, 10)$$

The reason for using this method is that the line intersection can also be determined to be within the line segments or outside the line segments. If the line segments intersect, then $0 \le t_n \le 1$ for both lines.

This method can then be used to determine if a moving object collides with a wall. Let's assume the situation in Fig. 15.10. The edges of the object's motion can include the current position and the attempted step, which gives a line segment. This can be tested against the line segment representing a wall. If $0 \le t_n \le 1$ for both lines, then both the edge and the collision point on the wall have been found.

There is a minor caveat to this. The intersection point may be computed to be outside of the wall due to potential round-off errors. This can be prevented by adding the edge normal times some small value to bump the intersection point in a bit.

Once the intersection is found, a potential choice arises: either to keep the user at position v_1 or move the user to position v.

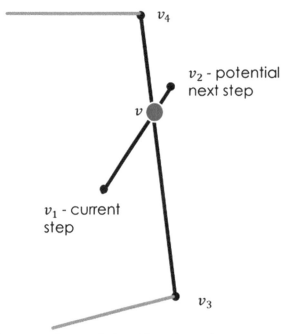

Fig. 15.10 Approximation of a user step into a wall, viewed from above. v_1 is the current position of the user and v_2 is the attempted next step, which gives one line segment. v_3 and v_4 are the end points of a wall, which gives the other line segment. v is the point of intersection.

Keeping the user at position v_1 is straightforward but does not let the user move. Moving the user to position v does let the user progress, but a potential error can occur depending on the direction the wall edge is defined. The dot product may be negative or positive depending on whether the wall edge is defined in clockwise or counterclockwise direction. This is corrected by adding π to the target direction when needed.

There are a few more notes to mention about dragging. As mentioned above, it is helpful to add a small amount times the wall's surface normal to the turn to prevent dragging on the wall due to roundoff errors. Also, due to the chances of the user becoming stuck after getting too close to a wall, many systems have a collision model that is a simplified version of the active area. As an example, Fig. 15.11 shows an environment and added collision walls to contain the player's movement.

The last item to note is friction. Friction can be applied similarly to the added wind resistance as shown in Chapter 3. The main difference is that the frictional force adjusts the total force on the system. This means applying other forces. Recall from Chapter 3 that

$$f_n = \mu_n N,$$

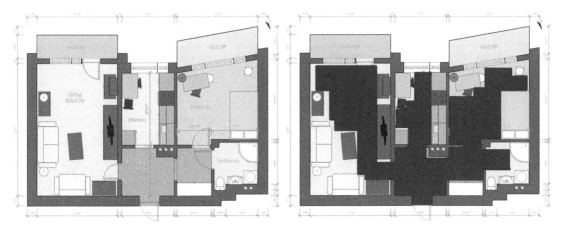

Fig. 15.11 Example of an environment with colliders. The layout the user sees is on the left, while the accepted areas for the user to move are shown in blue on the right. (https://openclipart.org/detail/308187/house-plan.)

where f_n is the force of friction, N is the force normal to the surface, and μ_n is the coefficient of friction. Friction can be either static (no movement) or dynamic (force opposite of movement).

Extending this to 3D requires changing the line equations into place equations or projecting lines onto the plane. Sliding and dragging are largely 2D movements, so not much else is required.

Bounce and Newton's Law of Restitution

Let's add bounce next. Similar to friction, bounce involves adding missing forces to a collision. Consider the collision shown in Fig. 15.12. The point of collision is centered on box B's lower edge.

This collision can be described using Newton's law of restitution for instantaneous collisions. The velocities before and after the collision for one object can then be represented as

$$v_{fk} \cdot N = -\,\varepsilon v_{ik} \cdot N, \; k = A \; or \; B,$$

where ε is the coefficient of restitution, v_{ik} and v_{fk} are the velocities of each object before and after the collision, and N is the normal of the contact point. For our purposes, the coefficient of restitution has a range of $0 \leq \varepsilon \leq 1$, where 0 represents a total inelastic collision and 1 represents a total elastic collision. Other values are possible but beyond the scope of the topic.

For simplicity, the collision is assumed to be without friction. The velocity of the bouncing object can be represented at a point as

$$v_p = v_k + \omega_k r_\perp,$$

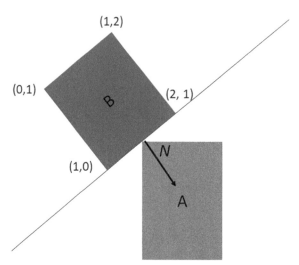

Fig. 15.12 Collision between two boxes, where box B is dropped onto box A. The line between is the separator line aligned with box B's edge and the force exerted by box B is exerted normal to the separator line.

where v_p is the instantaneous velocity at a point in space, v_n is the linear velocity of the boxes, ω_n is the angular velocity of the boxes, and $r_\perp$ is the vector from the center of mass to the point.

Newton's Third Law (for every action, there is an equal opposite reaction) can then be applied to find the impulse. The rebounding of the objects gives an exchange in momentum before and after the collision. Then, using the conservation of momentum as an application of Newton's Third Law,

$$m_k v_{fk} = m_k v_{ik} \pm JN,$$

where m_k is the mass of the box and J is the impulse. Whether to have the last term as positive or negative depends on the direction of the force on the object. For box A, the force is positive and aligned with N; for box B, the force is negative and the opposite of N.

These formulas combine to compute the bouncing response immediately after collision. Simple physics engines tend to keep the impulse constant, but for more complicated responses, J will need to be computed.

Adding Rotation and Moment of Inertia

The final collision response to add is rotation forces and motion. These motions are very common in real life, such as turning, swinging pendulums, or swinging a golf club. However, in-depth discussions of adding 3D rotation require a higher level of calculus than what is assumed for this text. Therefore, the discussion is kept at a high level for this topic.

Adding rotational forces is very similar to adding linear forces. Just as there are linear kinematic equations, there are rotational kinematic equations. The rotational kinematic equations take on the same form as the linear equations, but the variables are changed to rotational variables:

1. $\omega_f = \omega_i + \alpha t$
2. $\theta = \omega_i t + \frac{1}{2}\alpha t$
3. $\omega_f^2 = \omega_i^2 + 2\alpha\theta$
4. $\theta = \frac{1}{2}(\omega_f + \omega_i)t$

The relations between the variables are

1. $d = r\theta$
2. $v = r\omega$
3. $a = r\alpha$

where r is the radius of rotation.

For similar reasons, torque is rotationally related to force as

$$\tau = F \times r.$$

in left-handed notation, but can be summed like force:

- Total force: $F(t) = \sum F_i(t)$
- Total torque: $\tau(t) = \sum \tau_i(t)$

The relationship between r, F, rotation direction, and torque is shown visually in Fig. 15.13. For our purposes, let's consider the

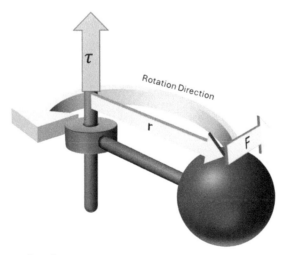

Fig. 15.13 The relation between r, F, and τ.

torque at point i. For this position, the vector distance from the rotation point, or radius of rotation, becomes

$$r_i(t) = p_i(t) - p(t),$$

where $p_i(t)$ is the position of the point and $p(t)$ is the rotation point. The torque then becomes

$$\tau_i(t) = F_i(t) \times r_i(t) = F_i(t) \times \left(p_i(t) - p(t)\right).$$

Oriented onto a 2D plane, torque can be represented as

$$\tau_i(t) = |F_i(t)| \left|\left(p_i(t) - p(t)\right)\right| \sin\theta,$$

which is the perpendicular complement to the dot product. This can be used to slightly simplify the torque at point i:

$$\tau_i(t) = F_i(t) \cdot \left(p_i(t) - p(t)\right)_\perp.$$

Here the perpendicular complement, $\perp$, or perp for short, performs a 90° counterclockwise rotation of the vector, so that

$$(x, y)_\perp = (-y, x).$$

A number of systems use a perp, or perp dot product, operator as a computational short cut. It's faster to rotate 90° and perform a dot product than to perform a full cross-product computation. While this does give a scalar result, keep in mind that torque is a pseudovector (in this case, a vector that changes with position). The 2D angle is included in the result, so the result can be converted back into a pseudovector.

The total torque at all points in space is then summed:

$$\tau(t) = \sum\nolimits_{\tau_i}(t) = \sum\nolimits_{F_i}(t) \cdot \left(p_i(t) - p(t)\right)_\perp.$$

Finally, just as the linear acceleration can be found from the summed force,

$$a_{tot} = \frac{F_{tot}}{m},$$

the angular acceleration can also be found from the summed torque:

$$\alpha_{tot} = \frac{\tau_{tot}}{I},$$

where I is the moment of inertia, the rotational analogue to mass.

Calculating the moment of inertia requires integrating the distribution of the mass over the object:

$$I = \int m_p \left| r_p \right|^2 dp,$$

where m_p is the mass at point p and r_p is the vector from the center of mass to point p.

This can quickly become difficult to compute. As a result, moment of inertia primitives, where the algebraic version of the formulas are known, are often used to reduce calculation difficulties. Some of these were provided in Chapter 3 Basic Physics, Fig. 3.1.

With this, all the needed materials are available to add rotational motion. To apply

- Calculate the defined center of mass and the moment of inertia.
- Set the initial position, orientation, and linear and angular velocities.
- Determine all the forces on the object.
  - Linear acceleration is $a_{tot} = \frac{F_{tot}}{m}$
  - Angular acceleration is $\alpha_{tot} = \frac{\tau_{tot}}{I}$
- Numerically integrate using Euler steps to update position, orientation, and the velocities.

## 16

Joints

This chapter focuses on movement constraints in models, or joints for short. The topics focus on components of movement constraints/joints, uses for joints, forward kinematics, poses, and joint categories (hinge, ball in socket, spring, complex). Some of these topics may appear familiar to those with a prior graphics course, and many of these topics do overlap in graphics, depending on the graphics course. Joints are required on both the graphics and the developer's side and thus are included here. Moreover, VR tends to need them sooner due to user hands and bodies being mapped into the virtual environment. If needed, reviewing the model chapter is recommended.

Defining Joints and Poses

Models often contain more than one component. Connected components are often given a restricted range of motion. As a real-life example, take a human skeleton. The elbows do not bend backward (Fig. 16.1). The restricted range of motion of the elbows is called a *movement constrain*, or *joint*.

Let's go into the components that make up the joints. Models are given underlying *bones* to form a *skeleton*. A skeleton is a poseable framework of joints arranged in a tree structure. This does not render in the scene but provides an armature to manipulate the surface, or skin, and other geometric data. The joints are then applied to the bones of the skeleton, making up an underlying physical movement model. The joints and skeletons can then be used for defining physics-based responses or even ragdoll-type effects. Once defined, the underlying model can also be used in inverse kinematics to improve animation, such as placing a hand on the rocket launcher such as in Fig. 16.2.

The restricted range is defined by the degrees of freedom (DOF). Here, a variable, ϕ, describes a particular axis or dimension of movement within a joint. Joints typically have between one and six DOF ($\phi_1 \cdots \phi_n$), but they can have more. For example, affine transformations (translation, rotation, skew, and scale) can have up to nine DOF. Changing the DOF values over time results in the animation of the skeleton.

DOF have many uses. Let's start with forward kinematics, or the placement of a bone starting at a source bone, and adjusting along the way to the tip. Consider the left arm in Fig. 16.2. Let's say the

A Practical Introduction to Virtual Reality. https://doi.org/10.1016/B978-0-443-14036-5.00016-9

Fig. 16.1 Model with elbow range of motion defined.

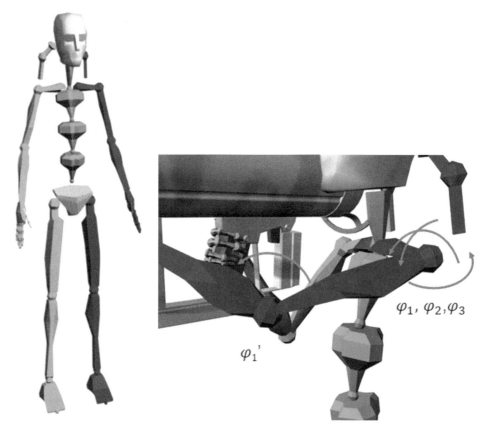

Fig. 16.2 Skeleton model with joints on the right. On the left, the model is used to hold up a rocket launcher. The degrees of freedom are shown for the left arm's elbow and shoulder. (Courtesy of Charles Owen, used with permission.)

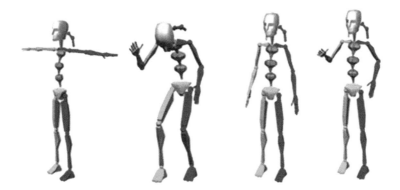

Fig. 16.3 Different poses of a skeleton. (Courtesy of Charles Owen, used with permission.)

angles of the joints are needed to place a location. One may start by rotating the shoulder, forward the next rotation to the elbow, forward the next rotation to the hand, etc. This is forward kinematics.

More formally, *forward kinematics* comprises the following: Each joint computes a local matrix, M, based on the DOF and some formula representative of the joint type:

$$Local\ matrix\ \mathbf{M} = \mathbf{M}_{\text{joint}}\left(\phi_1, \phi_2, \dots, \phi_N\right).$$

Then the world matrix, W, is computed by concatenating M with the world matrix of the parent joint:

$$World\ matrix\ W = M\mathbf{W}_{parent}.$$

Forward kinematics can then be used to adjust the DOF to specify the *pose* of the skeleton. Animations are essentially changing poses over time (Fig. 16.3).

A pose can be defined more formally as a vector of n numbers that maps to a set of DOF in the skeleton:

$$\Phi = [\phi_1 \quad \phi_2 \quad \dots \quad \phi_n]$$

In essence, the constraints ensure that the final pose is reasonable, unlike in Fig. 16.4.

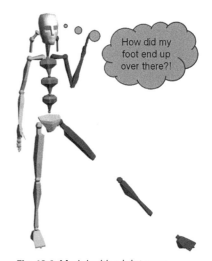

Fig. 16.4 Model with a joint error.

Joint Characteristics

While varying, most systems support joints with 0–3 DOF rotation, 0–3 DOF translation with limitations, and some form of harmonic motion and driving force. Harmonic motion includes springs, basic rotating, dampening spring motion, and other forms of cyclical motion. Driving force includes motors or applied force. Systems are less likely to have, but still may support, other options, such as scaling or shear (Fig. 16.5).

Several terms are worth mentioning at this point about the states of joints and the DOF:

- Locked: A DOF cannot change and is thus *locked*.
- Free: A DOF has an unlimited range of values.
- Limited: A DOF has a limited range of values.
- Breaking force: The minimum amount of force required to break a joint if enabled. The two components are no longer affected by their movement constraints.
- Motor: An engine applying a force along a DOF.
- Spring or Soft Constraint in Unreal: Rubber band–like forces, which cause a type of harmonic motion, where the more push or pull applied to the object results in a stronger reverse force.
- Projection: Children are shifted to fix any remaining errors in the constraints.
- Restitution or bounce: Bounce reaction after hitting a limit.

These terms hold across Unity and Unreal. Most of those terms are familiar from real life in various toys. However, projection is a result of code finite limitations and round off errors. Let's go into projection in more detail, before looking at different types of joints.

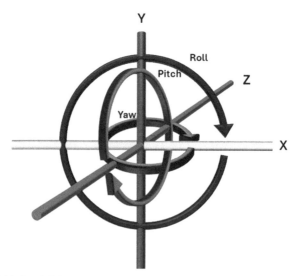

Fig. 16.5 Typical DOF available to a joint.

Projection

When working with poses and joints, the term *projection* often arises. A projection is used to fix up final calculated results by tweaking the joints to be more solid. This usually means that the last child in a skeleton chain is adjusted to remove remaining errors if possible. Projection only shows up in joints with multiple DOF.

Let's illustrate how this works in an example. Consider the highly conceptualized snake object in Fig. 16.6, which is composed of blocks with yellow joints.

The joints are placed between blocks that will permit up to a 45° rotation and will pull the blocks back together if stretched too far. Pulling the snake around an oblong column could initially result in Fig. 16.7 from the physics solver, which has errors.

Projection then attempts to project back to the closest legal position. If enabled, the snake object is to be corrected to something like Fig. 16.8.

Projection is especially important for joints with locked DOF. However, projection is usually only a partial fix. It tends to fail in complex collisions and will not repair joints that fail a "sanity" check of being well outside its limits.

Fig. 16.6 Snake object with the joint positions in yellow.

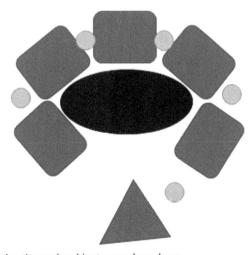

Fig. 16.7 Initial attempt at wrapping the snake object around a column.

Fig. 16.8 Projecting back the snake wrapped around the column. On the left, the uncorrected pose is shown with projection corrections in red arrows. On the right is the corrected pose.

Setting Up a Joint

Joints tend to be tricky to set up, due to numerous interacting physics along with a few assumptions that are less than obvious. Here are some suggestions when first attempting to make a joint:

1. When making a joint, create it in the absence of anything else and then import into your main scene or level when done. This is to ensure that offsets are to the local object and not to the world, which is desirable in most cases.
2. Align with the main axes when possible. Most limits are based on the main axis.

There is a catch to suggestion 2, however. Often, limits are aligned with the *forward* vector, which means that the limits are in local coordinates, whatever the definition of that may be. The door in Fig. 16.9 is a good example. There, the door is aligned with the main axis, but the length of the door extends along the *negative z*-axis. If the shown quarter circle angle limit (θ) is used, the angle limit of the dotted arrow (θ') would show instead. This is the reason why a T-pose of a joint is shown as the starting pose in most models. Align the axes and the forward direction to minimize any confusion on directions when possible.

Joint Categories

Joint categories vary by engine. Unreal has a single component, called a Physics Constraint, to handle most joints, plus a dedicated Spring component. Unity also has a generic joint, called a Configurable Joint, but has some helper component joints for

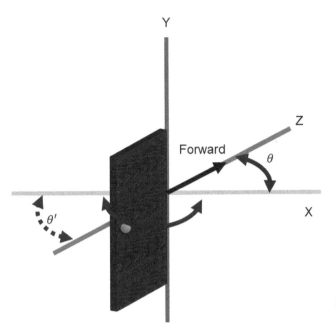

Fig. 16.9 An example of adding a hinge, 1-DOF joint to a door.

common movement. It is possible to make all the helper joints with a configurable joint and would be required in Unreal.

In addition, Unity uses anchors for joints, which comprise the position of the joint origin and the connection point, which moves around the origin. This can add layers of complexity to where the rotation occurs, as anchors can be offset from the rotation point when chained. Unreal has something similar but is performed with a joint transformation and is better visualized.

The remainder of this section focuses on some common types of joints and their applications, along with the basics for their settings in a generic joint.

Constant Joint

When items need to be glued together and no other motions are required, a constant or fixed joint can be used. Usually, this is done by specifying two bones and disallowing any movement, which results in 0 DOF. A common example of this is placing something into the users hand. The object is "glued" to the hand.

A parameter may arise regarding breaking strength. This is to allow the joint to break under certain conditions (Fig. 16.10).

A constant joint can be defined with a generic joint by setting all the linear and angular limits to "locked" or no movement. Projection should be turned on in a fixed joint.

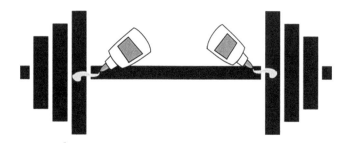

Fig. 16.10 Example of a constant joint, where the different parts of a dumbbell are glued together with fixed joints.

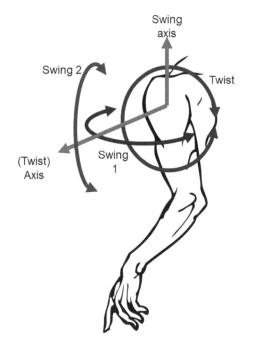

Fig. 16.11 Ball-and-socket joint for a shoulder with rotation axes.

Hinge

Hinges are joints with 1 rotational DOF about an axis perpendicular to the movement direction. This includes real-life objects, such as doors, flaps, and elbows.

Some of the common parameters that come with hinges are angle limits, breaking strength, motor, and spring.

When making a hinge joint, the main task is choosing a rotation axis and then having a free or limited 1-DOF rotation along that axis with every other rotation and linear DOF locked. The trouble spots concern the terms and which ones to lock. A generic joint names the rotation axes twist, swing 1, and swing 2 in both Unity and Unreal. The rotation relative to the "twist" and "swing" axes are shown in Fig. 16.11. Twist is the one to leave open and lock both swings. This means that the rotation axes must align with the twist axis to work properly.

If the joint tries to leave only a swing axis open, a new problem arises. Limits are usually symmetric except for the *twist* 1-DOF rotations. As an example, the (θ) in Fig. 16.12 is a 90° range if the Y-axis if the twist axis. If the Y-axis is the swing axis, however, the rotation range of (θ') is seen instead because the range must be symmetric.

A motor on a hinge can push or pull the object to a specific angle. The spring (Soft Constraint in Unreal) allows bounce back if pushed too far.

Ball and Socket

A ball-and-socket joint has 3 DOF rotation around one rotation point. Real-life examples include shoulders and hip joints. These joints can have some challenges in the setup since Euler rotations

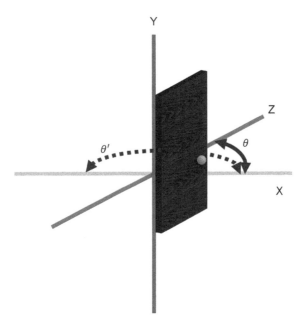

Fig. 16.12 Hinge example with corrected axes.

are often not listed in the component. Instead, this joint starts with a rotation axis of the user's choosing. Therefore, the original Euler axis tends not to make much sense.

The parameter to note for this joint is a twist parameter, which is the rotation about that axis. THE other two rotations are called Swing 1 and Swing 2 in both Unity and Unreal as shown in Fig. 16.11. Unity calls a ball-and-socket joint a Character Joint.

The twist axis will allow for different min and max angles, while the swing axes are symmetrical.

When setting up a ball-and-socket joint in a generic joint, start by picking the axis to twist around. Using the shoulder example above, this would be a vector from the clavicle to the shoulder. A min twist angle may be –90°, and a max twist angle may be 45°. Next is choosing the swing axes. Normally, this should be perpendicular to the twist axis, but others are allowed. The rotation about the swing axis is Swing 1. For the shoulder example, this is somewhere around ±50° to move the arm front and back. Swing 2 is the last remaining axis formed at a right angle to both the twist axis and swing axis. For the shoulder example, this is somewhere around ±90° to move the arm up and down.

Motors and springs on a ball and socket work the same way as they do in a hinge. But just like how a swing angle is symmetric but a twist is not, the motors are, too. Swing motors are symmetric.

Spring

Springs in VR are just translation movements with distance limits and rebounds. They are closer to rubber bands or bungee cords than the coil spring many expect. Neither Unity nor Unreal restricts the direction of the spring with the Spring Joint component.

Some of the common parameters that come with springs are stretch distances, spring strength, breaking strength, and damping.

Springs, or rubber bands, can still be made somewhat in a generic joint. All the limits are free or limited. However, the linear limit needs to be set to give the initial rubber band length. This is not set independently per translation DOF; there is only one distance setting. Then, the rubber band's stiffness is set with the linear spring and damper. The spring is the stiffness, and the damper settles the spring on a bounce.

Complex Joints

If any of the joints above are not sufficient, there is still a generic joint. As mentioned above, this is the Configurable Joint in Unity and the Physics Constraint in Unreal. Consider the shoulder example above. The original ball and socket joint is closer to a robot than a human. A human's shoulder still has some stretch to it. If that stretch is to be added, a generic joint is needed.

In essence, a generic joint supports everything in the prior joints all at once, but that is also why they are harder to start with. There is a tradeoff of flexibility and complexity.

As an example, consider making a bouncy board as opposed to a bungy cord that can wobble. None of the prior joints could support the bouncy board individually. But all the components needed are available in a prior joint, somewhere. Specifically, this bouncy board would need a stretchy linear limit, twists and swings, and a motor to get back to its original position.

To explain, let's apply these components one at a time in a generic joint. To start, a metal coil is attached to a board, as shown in yellow in Fig. 16.13.

If physics is applied when every DOF is free, the board would simply fall to the ground no matter how far it is to the ground. Instead, all translation DOF would be set to limited, and a distance limit would be applied, that is, the original distance between the joint ends. However, if physics is applied now, the board would still drop, and even swing (since rotation is unlocked), but only by the original distance rather than to the floor. This is taken from the spring joint settings but has no "give" (Fig. 16.14).

To keep this upright, a motor needs to push it back to its original position. The force would vary with the weight, but if physics were

Fig. 16.13 A springboard composed of a board, a spring, and a generic joint in yellow holding the object together.

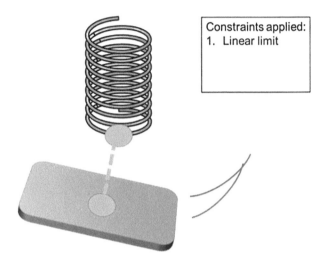

Fig. 16.14 Springboard with the generic joint. If only with the linear limit applied, the board can drop and swing down.

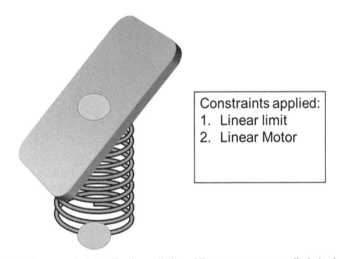

Fig. 16.15 Springboard with the generic joint. If a linear limit and linear motor are applied, the board can rotate all around, similar to a ball-and-socket joint.

applied, the board would stay above the coil, sort of. Since there is no rotation restriction, the board could rotate on a pivot at the top, like that shown in Fig. 16.15, as sort of a ball-and-socket joint with 360° × 360° freedom of movement.

This needs the rotation DOF to be set to limited so the board can only rotate a little. The twist axis can be set to point up, and the swing axis can be any right angle if the swing axis angle limits are

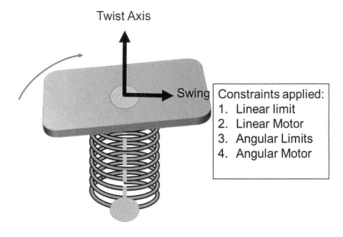

Fig. 16.16 Springboard with the generic joint. If all of the constraints are applied, the motion is similar to a worn springboard that does not return to its original position.

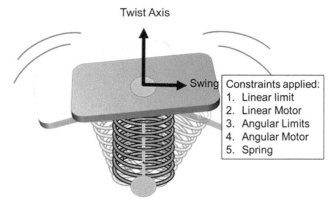

Fig. 16.17 The final spring board that bounces back into place after having been pressed.

symmetrical. That will stop the board from flopping over, but with any weight, it stays that way. So, angular motor is needed as well so that the board will return to its original rotation (Fig. 16.16).

One last issue. This doesn't really bounce. The reason is that the limits are too hard. To allow this to bounce, there needs to be a spring, or soft constraint, on all the DOF. Now, it will bounce and wobble if hit but then return to its starting location (Fig. 16.17).

This demonstrates how even complex joints can be made with a generic joint.

Acknowledgments

A thank you to Patrick McBride, who was a student working at the SD Mines VR lab the semester this text was written. His dedication to fully research and understand all the joints and their interactions with the physics engines gave many good case examples. In particular, his commitment to get a jump rope working (in the associated tutorial) went well past expectations.

## 17

Inverse Kinematics

This chapter introduces inverse kinematics (IK), their key elements, how the kinematics are used, and creating an IK chain. The IK chain is illustrated in both a highly conceptualized example of a snake reaching a target position and a more applied example of a character model placing a hat on its head with pseudocode. IK are commonly used to do minor corrections on animations. As IK are typically developed in code, this topic sits squarely on the developer's side. IK have applications in VR for avatars and hands.

From Forward Kinematics to IK

Thus far in this text, only forward kinematics have been used, which is when the kinematics and angles are determined and forwarded from the root bone to the child bone. As an example, consider Fig. 17.1. If the shoulder is rotated by 45° and then forwarded to the elbow, which is rotated by another 45°, the arm points up.

In IK, the situation is somewhat reversed. Let's say that model now has to put a hat on its head, as shown in Fig. 17.2. The head position could potentially change with nodding or turning, so setting the angles using constant values from the clavicle is insufficient. Instead, the final position of the hat is determined, and the kinematics and rotations are calculated in inverse order, hence *inverse kinematics* (IK for short).

IK are heavily used
- To touch up animations
- To keep all feet on the ground, even if the surface is uneven
- To correctly grip a surface
- To make dynamic animations
- To implement virtual reality (VR) avatars and hands

IK is implemented in code and thus is squarely the developer's responsibility.

Some additional terminology is worth mentioning here.

Items that a character may be holding are called *props*. In graphics, a prop can be moved by one bone in the skeleton. In Fig. 17.2, the model's left arm moves the top hat prop.

Another term worth mentioning is an *IK chain*. An IK chain is a linear list of bones from some starting bone to some ending bone,

A Practical Introduction to Virtual Reality. https://doi.org/10.1016/B978-0-443-14036-5.00017-0

Fig. 17.1 Example of forward kinematics, where one arm of the model is bent. The left is the initial model, and the right is with some forward kinematics applied.

Fig. 17.2 Example of where IK come into play. What are the angles needed for the model to place the hat on its head?

where there is a potential assumed DOF change for every bone except for the last bone. The last point on the end of the chain is the *end effector*. In the case of Fig. 17.3, the end effector is at the Hand and the translation is used for the Hand object.

Conceptual IK

The items required to perform the IK chain reaction are
1. The model being transformed in proper hierarchical form
2. The start and end bones of the IK chain plus the target position
3. The data structures to hold the transform states
4. The calculation that runs from the end effector back and attempts to map the node point directly to the target

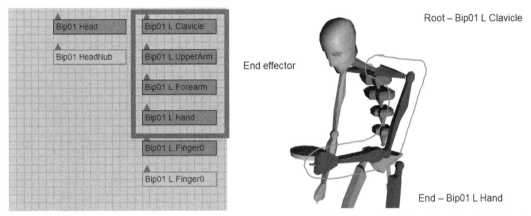

Fig. 17.3 Example of IK chain. The portion of the chain that can have a DOF change is outlined in red on the left and outlined in orange on the model on the right. (Courtesy of Charles Owen, used with permission.)

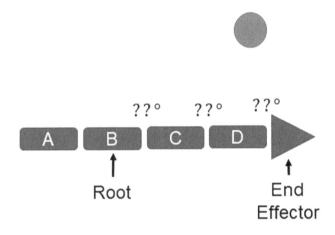

Fig. 17.4 Example for applying IK. The snake object is to turn to reach the orange target. The rotated angles of the joints need to be determined.

Before moving into the details of applying IK to a more complicated example, such as the model placing a hat on its head, let's outline how this works conceptually to better understand the overall goals when applying IK.

Let's take a highly conceptualized snake, similar to the snake in the previous Joints chapter, and an orange target, as shown in Fig. 17.4. Each joint can turn a maximum of 45° per vertebrae.

Applying IK means working backward, so let's adjust the angles from the end effector back, attempting to get the head of the snake as close to the target as possible at each step.

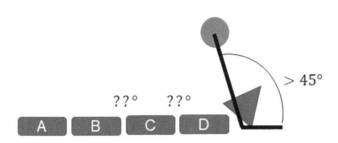

Fig. 17.5 The first step of the IK chain is to rotate the end effector toward the target as much as is allowed.

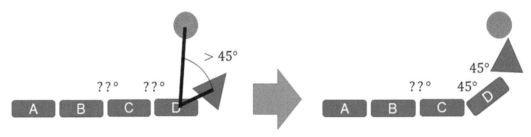

Fig. 17.6 The second step of the IK chain rotates bone D by the maximum allowed amount.

The head is first rotated as far as allowed. The angle from the head's starting position to the target is greater than 45°, so the head is rotated the maximum allowed 45° and the IK moves up the chain. This step is shown in Fig. 17.5.

The interesting parts of the IK occur after the first rotation. The angle difference between the target and the current position of the head is now determined from the rotation point of its parent bone D. This is still greater than 45°, so bone D is rotated by the maximum amount. The result is shown in Fig. 17.6.

Because the target has not quite been reached yet, one more step in the IK chain is applied. This time the angle between the head and the target from the rotation point at bone C is only about 20°. When bone C is rotated by that amount, the head lands in the center of the target, giving the final transform. The final positions are shown in Fig. 17.7.

With that, the concepts can now be applied to pseudocode in the hat example.

Applying IK

Let's illustrate how to apply IK to the example of the model placing a hat on its head. Given where the hand is to place the hat, the appropriate transform for each joint is to be determined using IK. The required items for applying IK are described in terms of steps for this section.

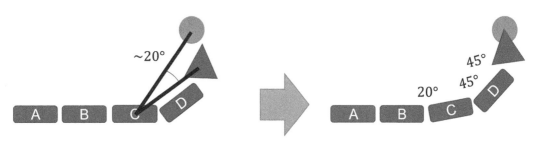

Fig. 17.7 The third and final step in the IK chain rotates bone C less than the maximum amount for the head to reach the target position.

Proper Hierarchical Form

Let's assume that item 1 for the IK requirements is met. The model is already in proper hierarchical form, as shown in Fig. 17.8. To better understand what makes a proper hierarchical form, it might help to recall the root motion from the chapter on Models and Animations. The root is the center of the animation and can also be the start of the hierarchy. Most human model skeletons will have the root bone as either the clavicle or the pelvis. While both structures are common, a human's center of mass is nearer to the pelvis and may help with some physics.

Fig. 17.8 Model for hat example with hierarchy scene tree relationships shown in orange arrows.

IK Chain Definition and Target Position

Item 2 requires defining the outline of the IK chain and any other needed parameters, such as the target position. To set up the IK chain, the model needs to be understood enough to determine the root and end bones required for the transformation. Other parameters are determined from defining where the end of the chain needs to reach. That gives the target position but also a matrix to convert a point relative from the model's root bone to its global coordinates for distance calculations.

```
class InverseKinematicsCCD
    // the model
    ModelObject model
    // what is the start of the chain
    ModelBone root
    // what is the end of the chain
    ModelBone end
    // where should the end be after running
    ModelBone position
    // model's root to its global transform
    Matrix rootLocalToWorld
```

ModelObject and ModelBone here are generic references to the model and one of its bones. This will change with the game engine.

IK Data Structures

The next challenge is to determine the bone placement parameters for the IK. At a high level, the IK needs to observe the angle limits and have enough data to calculate the distance between the bone and the target. To meet the first requirement of observing angle limits, the IK requires the

- Angle limits
- Starting orientation (θ)
- Current orientation (θ')

The second requirement of calculating distance requires a method for converting between local and world coordinates. This is because the IK is comprised of a chain of bones affecting the final position.

Let's take a closer look at the IK chain involved for placing a hat. Consider the IK chain for the model in Fig. 17.9. The end effector is at the hand and the IK chain works up the arm to the root. Then the final model to world placement is added. The model shown is the current position of the model in the world. This is before rotating any joints and uses a left-hand system. T_b in the figures here and below refer to the transform, where b refers to the bone position in the chain.

This can be used by starting with the original pose transform for a bone to its parent (*bind* for short) transform. Then, the rotation is added to the current bone. To make the limits more straightforward, let's use Euler angles for rotation, which is designated as R_n, where n is the axis of rotation. This gives the formula for a single joint transform, T_{joint} (Fig. 17.10).

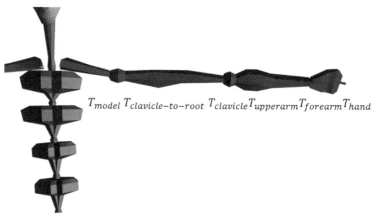

$$T_{model}\ T_{clavicle-to-root}\ T_{clavicle}T_{upperarm}T_{forearm}T_{hand}$$

Fig. 17.9 Model with IK chain for left arm. (Edited from model from Charles Owen.)

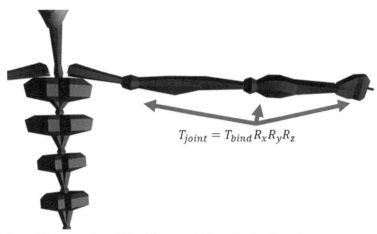

Fig. 17.10 The IK chain with the rotations. (Edited from model from Charles Owen.)

With this, the final position can be calculated by subbing in the original orientation and its rotation. Here, the original transform is

$$T_{chain} = T_{model}T_{clavicle-to-root}T_{clavicle}T_{upperarm}T_{forearm}T_{hand}.$$

The rotation for the hand only is

$$T_{hand} = T_{bind}R_xR_yR_z.$$

The transform for the IK chain then becomes

$$T_{chain} = T_{model}T_{clavicle-to-root}T_{clavicle}T_{upperarm}T_{forearm}T_{bind}R_xR_yR_z.$$

The full chain becomes a local to world transform. That allows for checking distances between the target and the model. To apply this in pseudocode, the data structures can be applied into matrices and vectors:

```
class IKBone
  // The bone in the model
  ModelBone bone
  // The original local transform (local to parent)
  Matrix bind
  // Computed local to world transform
  Matrix localToWorld
  // current working orientation
  Vector rotation
  // min\max allowable angles
  Vector limitsMin
  Vector limitsMax
```

This allows for matrix math later, so let's use 4×4 transformation matrices rather than a transform class to reduce clunkiness.

This is a simpler version of the constraints. Fuzzy limits, collisions considerations, and other elements can be added as needed.

Transformation Calculation

There are a few IK algorithms available. The Cyclic Coordinate Descent (CCD) is one of the mathematically simpler options. Since CCD is also quite stable and reliable, let's use this algorithm.

At a high level, CCD works with the following steps:

1. Find the bones in the chain.
2. Put the bones in proper order and pull associated limits.
3. For each bone from the end to the root and for each DOF within each bone, compute the DOF that puts the end effector closer to the target.
4. Repeat from step 3 until the end effector cannot become any closer to the target.

In the pseudocode below, this can be done by first getting the bones in the chain. The main code chunks are numbered in the comments. The *end.bone* (1) in this case is the bone variable of the hand's associated IKBone instance and also the end effector. Starting from the hand and working back, the chain is formed. The initial transform of the model in the world also needs to be pulled for reference (2).

Next, the algorithm walks up the chain and for each bone (3)

- The local transform is saved (4).
- The angle limits are pulled (also 4).
- The global rotation is pulled (5).

This is repeated until the root of the chain is reached. A final conditional statement is also added as a sanity check to make sure that the root given was the root found (6). This gives steps 1 and 2 of CCD.

```
IKBone[] ikChain
function InitializeChain()
  // 1) Find the target bone for an end effector
  endEffectorBone = end.bone

  // 2) What is the transform for the root of the chain?
  if root.Bone.parent!= null
    rootParentBone = root.Bone.parent
    rootLocalToWorld = rootParentBone.globalTransform
  else
    rootLocalToWorld = Matrix.identity

  ikChain.Clear()
  bone = endEffectorBone
```

```
// 3) travel up the chain until the root is found
while bone != null
  IKBone ikBone
  ikBone.bone = bone

  // 4) What is the transform and limits
  // for the bone in the bind position?
  ikBone.bind = bone.localTransform
  ObtainLimits( bone, ikBone.limitsMin, ikBone.limitsMax )

  // 5) Convert to Euler angles XYZ
  ikBone.rotation = bone.globalTransform.eulerAngles
  ikChain.Add( ikBone )
  if bone == rootBone
    break
  bone = bone.transform.parent

  if bone != rootBone
    // 6) Root found was not root given. IK will fail
    throw Exception()
```

Fig. 17.11 shows the active IK chain and order. One item to note from the pseudocode is that while the angle limits for CCD step 2 (pseudocode section 4) are pulled from the ObtainLimits function, finding the angle limit is not outlined in detail. This is because angle limits can come from different places, such as joints, models, classes, and more, which makes the function context sensitive.

CCD steps 3 and 4 are next. The challenges with these steps are the computation and the coordinate systems. The bones are in local coordinates, and the target is in global coordinates. Regardless, the

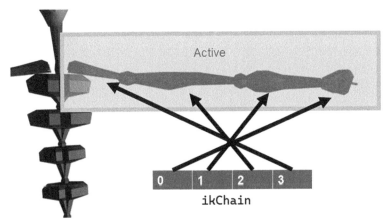

Fig. 17.11 The active area of the IK chain is highlighted in yellow, and the positions of the different bones in the list are shown by the arrows. (Courtesy of Charles Owen and heavily edited.)

computation requires the current positions of all the items in the same coordinate system.

To meet this requirement, a transform matrix is needed to convert a point on each local system back to the global coordinates:

```
function ComputeCurrentPlacement()
  // Compute the local to world transforms for the chain
  // We'll use localToWorld to keep a running
  // local to world transform
  localToWorld = rootLocalToWorld
  for i = ikChain.count - 1 to 0
    ikBone = ikChain[ i ]
    // add new parent offset to the running local to world
    localToWorld = localToWorld *
                   ikBone.bind *
                   ikBone.rotation.ToMatrix()
    ikBone.localToWorld = localToWorld
```

In this function, the transform matrix starts at the root's local coordinate system before applying the loop. On the first pass, the clavicle's local transform is added. The second pass assists in the adjustment of the upper arm and so on. This function essentially calculates the global transforms for each child from the scene tree.

With that, the transforms to reach the target can be computed. At a high level, the Compute() function refreshes the solver (1) and then repeatedly calculates the best angles until the distance between the end effector and the target is either 0 or at least stable (2). Once the solution is found, the resulting rotations are copied to the bones (3).

```
function Compute()

  // 1) reset rotations for a new pass
  for bone in ikChain
    bone.rotation = [ 0,0,0 ]

  epsilon = 0.001
  lastErr = ∞        // Big
  do // 2) the main IK calculation that continues
     // until the error is acceptable
    ComputeCurrentPlacement()
    err = StepCCD( position )
    if ( lastErr - err ) < epsilon
    break
    lastErr = err
  while err > epsilon
```

```
// 3) Write the computed results to the model
for ikBone in ikChain
  ikBone.bone.localTransform = ikBone.bind
                             * ikBone.rotation.ToMatrix()
```

The large item yet to be complete is the StepCCD() function used above. This will choose the new angles and give the distance error between the end effector and target. The angles are computed using a method similar to the conceptual snake example. To start, let's look at applying a rotation about the Z-axis at the elbow, such as the one shown in Fig. 17.12. The rotation angle, θ, can be found by finding the initial, relative angle, θ_i, and the target angle, θ_t:

$$\theta_i = \tan^{-1}\left(\frac{y_i}{x_i}\right),$$

$$\theta_t = \tan^{-1}\left(\frac{y_t}{x_t}\right),$$

where (x_i, y_i) is the initial, relative end position and (x_t, y_t) is the target position.

Then,

$$\theta = \theta_t - \theta_i.$$

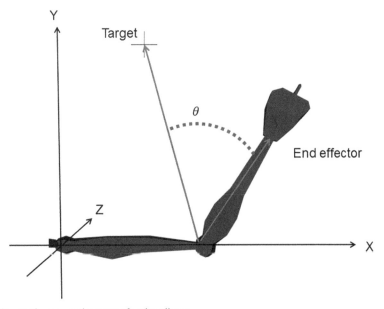

Fig. 17.12 Example rotation toward a target for the elbow.

There is a potential caveat to IK at this point. Namely, IK can very well compute impossible joint angles. Some limits will need to be applied to prevent this, which can be applied with a small helper function:

```
function EnforceLimitX( a )
  if a < limitsMin.x
    return limitsMin.x
  else if a > limitsMax.x
    return limitsMax.x
  return a
```

With this, the final function for CCD steps 3 and 4 can be outlined in StepCCD() below. First, the target position is converted into the bone's coordinates (1). Then the offset is pulled from the parent (2). Note that here, if the targetRelative variable uses index 1, the target is on the bone, while 0 aims for the tip of the bone. This can vary with preference.

Next, the DOF change can be computed for each bone in the chain (3). Recall the data structure defined earlier for a bone's transform:

$$T_{bone} = T_{bind}R_xR_yR_z.$$

To apply this in pseudocode, each axis is calculated separately. Let's start with the x rotation value (4). In the X rotation part of the loop, then, the target and relative angles are computed with just the X axis rotation applied (4), then the x angle is computed relative to the YZ plane (5), limits to the angle values are applied (6), and finally, the bone is rotated to its new position (7).

The y and z values are computed in the same way except for the starting plane (8):
- $X \rightarrow YZ$ plane
- $Y \rightarrow XZ$ plane
- $Z \rightarrow YX$ plane (left-handed)

The last item to do is to apply the binding. Doing so allows for putting the transform into the same coordinate system (9) and calculating the distance of the end effector to the target (10).

```
function StepCCD( targetPosition )
  // 1) convert global target to relative to bone
  targetRelative = position
                 * ikChain[ 0 ].localToWorld.inverse

  // 2) And where is the end effector relative
  // to its parent?
  endRelative = ikChain[ 0 ].bind.position
```

```
// 3) Step forwards through the bones
for ikBone in ikChain

  // 4) Do the X rotation,
  // and calculate new target and bone positions
  rotate = CreateRotationX( ikBone.rotation.x )
  targetRelative =  targetRelative * rotate
  endRelative = endRelative * rotate
  // 5) If not aligned in the YZ plane, rotate more around X
  if ( endRelative.z * endRelative.z )
     + ( endRelative.y * endRelative.y ) > 0.0001f

    // 6) What is the rotation angle to the end effector?
```

$$\text{toEndEffector} = \tan^{-1} \left(\frac{endRelative_z}{endRelative_y} \right)$$

```
    // What is the rotation angle to the target?
```

$$\text{toTarget} = \tan^{-1} \left(\frac{targetRelative_z}{targetRelative_y} \right)$$

```
    // Difference?
    deltaAngle = toTarget - toEndEffector

    // Make this in the range -π to π to help with limits
    if deltaAngle < -π
      deltaAngle += π * 2
    if deltaAngle > π
      deltaAngle -= π * 2

    // clamp new angle
    newAngle = ikBone.rotation.x + deltaAngle
    newAngle = ikBone.EnforceLimitX( newAngle )
    deltaAngle = newAngle - ikBone.rotation.x
    ikBone.rotation.x = newAngle

    // 7) Rotate the end effector to indicate this change
    rotate = CreateRotationX( deltaAngle )
    endRelative = endRelative * rotate

  // 8) Do the Y and Z rotations
  //...

// 9) add in original rotation to the IK rotation
rotate = ikBone.bind
targetRelative = targetRelative * rotate
endRelative = endRelative * rotate

// 10) done with the pass. How close are we?
diff = targetRelative - endRelative
return diff.magnitude
```

There is one last bit of pseudocode to the algorithm: how to use it in a larger program. After placing the required data into the solver, the algorithm largely just needs to initialize and run:

```
InverseKinematicsCCD ik
ik.Model = modelObject
ik.Root = rootObject
ik.End = endObject
// Update as needed
ik.position = someVector

// get starting positions
ik.InitializeIKChain()

// run the solver
ik.Compute()
```

Suggestions When Using IK

There are some advantages and disadvantages to using IK. The two big advantages are that
- The position of an end effector can be changed in an animation, allowing the end effector to touch a point or prop.
- The areas that could not normally be reached can be adjusted to do so.

There are some disadvantages as well:
- The default IK solution may not be a normal pose.
- Solutions can result in a self-collision.
- Some conditions can cause the IK to lock up.

Most systems restrict the number of number of times the StepCCD function can run to prevent locking up.

Regardless, there are a few tweaks that can be applied to further reduce the disadvantages. For one, instead of initially rotating to the maximum allowed angle, intermediate stages of the angle are tested first. This method spreads the angle to reduce the possibility of self-collisions but also increases the number of iterations. The second tweak is to put resistance to joint changes past a certain threshold. This will decrease the movement.

Unity has a built-in IK solver in the additional packages called Animation Rigging. The package is focused on humanoids, however, and has limited applications outside of that. Unreal has a built-in solver called IK Rig that also focuses on humanoids but aims to be effective for a wider range of skeletons when needed.

When using the built-ins, they largely follow the same steps as shown above, and simply hide the code. These require a skeleton in proper hierarchical order. The user gives the solver the root and end effectors, the user selects the target, and the solver is run.

Usability Design and Publishing

This chapter introduces usability design (UX) for virtual reality (VR) applications and publishing a finished application. On the publishing side, the content focuses on where to publish and common elements needed to publish. On the UX side, the content focuses on user interface heuristics, unit testing, and cybersickness prevention. UX is a large research field. This section gives an overview to get started.

Publishing

There are many options for publishing a VR application. Here is a short list:

- Oculus store
- Vive port
- Steam
- itch.io
- gamejolt.com
- Personal website

Different systems will have different publishing options and requirements. For example, Oculus will not publish an application that uses older Vive code. However, there are certain common requirements from publishing platforms. These include a publishing name, identity keys, and proper use contracts.

In general, there are three main steps to publishing an application:

1. Make an executable.
2. Register as a developer.
3. Post the application.

Let's walk through these steps with a focus on commonly required elements. Steam will be used as a case example where appropriate due to its breadth of service.

Make an Executable

There are slight differences when making an executable in either Unreal or Unity. In Unity, the File > Build Settings are set before making the executable with File > Build And Run. In Unreal, the supported platforms for making the executable are under File > Package Project.

A Practical Introduction to Virtual Reality. https://doi.org/10.1016/B978-0-443-14036-5.00018-2

Additional build settings are under File > Package Project > Packaging Settings… or Edit > Project Settings > Packaging. Either path leads to the same settings. Since a publishable executable must be self contained, expect to take a few tries when first starting to ensure the user specific executable runs properly while trying to minimize the published size.

Before making the executable, a number of settings need to be defined:

- The scenes (Unity) or maps (Unreal)
- The target platform

In Unity, the platform is chosen in the Build Settings before making the executable. In Unreal, the platform is chosen under Package Project to make the executable.

There are some additional settings to check as well. If the project requires some additional debugging, a development build can be made instead.

When choosing the settings, it is helpful to keep some publishing requirements in mind:

- Some platforms have size limitations for assets.
- iOS and Android may require additional build settings, such as Distribution mode (Unreal) or using Build App Bundle (Unity).

With the settings chosen, the executable can then be built. When first building, warning messages may appear due to some missing packages or modules required for compiling. What an engine needs to run is not necessarily the same as what it needs to make a consumer executable. Installing the missing packages in the Hub (Unity) or the Editor (Unreal) will fix this issue. For example, while the code for Unity is in C#, the program compiles in C++ for speed. As a result, C++ needs to be installed as well.

Once a clean build is made, it's important to test the executable without the VR development engine.

Register as a Developer and Royalty Notes

Before the application can be uploaded, the developer typically must register with the publishing system. The costs and waiting time can vary vastly depending on the system. For example, on Steam, this means filling out the registration paperwork, paying the registration fee, and finally waiting for final approval, which has a 30-day waiting period at the time of this writing.

The amount of information required, as well as other paperwork, usually follows a support information-required tradeoff. Steam has quite a bit of extra security and marketplace elements for an application and, as a result, has a much more thorough set of forms and information requirements. Itch.io does not offer that support and therefore is much faster to register.

Beyond the publishing registration, there are some additional notes regarding royalty fees for using a VR engine to produce an application. For both engines, fees are not incurred by the developer unless the application product meets a minimum revenue threshold. How the fees are applied varies, though. Unreal applies a 5% royalty on the lifetime gross revenue past $1 million. Unity does not apply a direct royalty, per se, but does require that the developer purchase the yearly license once the application project's yearly revenue exceeds $100,000.

Post the Application

What to do after registering depends on the publishing system. Most systems use a key system to uniquely identify the application. This is roughly a four-step process:

1. Make a key to uniquely identify the application.
2. Add data about the application.
3. Upload the executable.
4. Wait for approval.

Not all publishers require a key, but most of the larger ones, like Steam, require it. A *key* does more than make an ID that pairs to your application. This key is often used by publishers to monitor the use of your application for management purposes, marketing purposes, and to charge fees. As a result, this is one of the most critical elements when publishing your applications to keep safe.

After approval, the project has been published. Before moving on to UX suggestions, though, let's outline some suggestions for maintaining projects in the long term.

Maintaining Projects in the Long Term

The first organizational items needed for long-term maintenance are the source control and file structure. Source control, overly simplified, is marking changes to the code over time and keeping them synced across different computers and\or coders. It can be thought of as an advanced version of tracking changes in Word, only dedicated to code. The most used version at the time of this writing is Git. In general, the file structure should be determined early in the project development as it affects source control. Some base file structure is required for both engines, which includes some reserved folder names.

Beyond this basic structure, there are some common elements across presented formats online.

- Minimum of one folder per content\code group.
- Use subfolders when a folder becomes large.
- Apply a consistent folder structure to the hierarchy.

Another item is to add editor scripts. Editor scripts are additional code elements that show in the game engine during development

Code source control is not designed for large blobs of data like sound or model files, which is why not including it in version control is usually suggested. However, this disconnect can cause GIGANTIC issues syncing a project across computers. Those files still need to be downloaded and updated. Unity's meta files add additional difficulty in that they give an ID and other import settings. Just saving the files can lose the meta file, which causes all the connections will break and the scene to need to be completely remade! Unity is starting to introduce their own version of version control to cope.

rather than in the application. These can be efficient aids or support for noncoders in the application. Both engines offer support for creating and adding scripts.

While the set of required folders and reserved folder names differ across systems, developer defined folder structure past that is permitted. Unity permits a bit more flexibility in the location of code versus content (e.g., model and sounds), while Unreal wants noncode content in a Content folder and code in a Source folder. However, having the code and content separated is good practice in general. Content tends to be large and does not work well with coding source controllers. In fact, *excluding* content from code source control is recommended if not required in some development companies. More recently, there are forms of version control dedicated to content, but these are different software packages from the code versions. Therefore, it is usually good to have content ignored in source control, which is much easier to do if it is in a separate folder.

As an example, consider the two, very simplified, hierarchies in Table 18.1. Unity combines all content and code under Assets, but there is a dedicated folder for scripts. Unreal forces that separation, but the user can still have a dedicated folder per group for easy lookup.

Table 18.1 Simplified folder structure for Unity and Unreal with reserved folders removed.

Unity	Unreal
Assets	Source
├─ Scripts	└─ Character
│ └─ Character	└─ ...
│ └─ ...	└─ Environment
│ └─ Environment	└─ ...
│ └─ ...	└─ ...
│ └─ ...	Content
├─ Audio	├─ Audio
│ └─ ...	└─ ...
├─ Models	├─ Models
│ └─ ...	└─ ...
├─ Materials	├─ Materials
│ └─ ...	└─ ...

Unit Testing

Before publishing an application, it is important to test the application's accuracy and robustness. This is where unit testing comes in. Unit testing is checking for the output of functions against known values to ensure accuracy. The focus of the test is on model logic, not on the appearance or system specific user input. Integration testing, while often paired with unit testing, may consider the effects of input on the application. For example, let's take a function that returns the absolute value of a number:

```
function Absolute( value )
  ??? // pretend the implementation is unknown
```

To check if the function completes its task correctly, some form of test needs to be applied. Without a framework, a test could look like the following:

```
function Absolute( value )
  ???

function Test_Absolute()
  x = Absolute( 1 )
  if x != 1
    print "Error: 1 should become 1. Got " + x + " instead"
  x = Absolute( -1 )
  if x != 1
    print "Error: -1 should become 1. Got " + x + " instead"
```

The function is run with some hard coded input, and then the result is checked for accuracy. This is an example of a unit test. In general, unit tests tend to be true/false based.

One aspect that can seem odd about unit tests is that code is being written to test code. Bugs can occur in either the tested code or in the unit test. There are several reasons to perform unit tests despite the potential bugs:

- *Compiler errors are easier to track down than runtime errors.* Unit tests attempt to add more checks at a compiler level determined by the developer.
- *The expected result is determined and known.* Since unit tests largely focus on true/false cases, checking for correct results tends to be simple.
- *The method gives confirmation of working base logic.* When bugs do arise, unit tests can narrow the location of the possible bug. The method also provides a safety check to determine whether later edits will or will not break the base logic.

Unit tests are considered important enough that most systems have a built-in framework. In Unreal, the framework is called the Automation System. In Unity, it's the Unit Test Framework.

All this hinges on the unit tests being developed correctly. Regardless of purpose or logic, a bad test is still a bad test. At this point, it is common to have already experienced code breaking due to a missed test. Conversely, focusing too much on tests can lead to paralysis by analysis and prevents the application from being published at all. The remainder of the section goes through the steps of designing good unit tests and then applying unit tests to larger classes.

Writing a Good Unit Test

Before writing any unit test, let's pick a format to work with. Most frameworks use a general pattern of

- Including the framework.
- Marking a function as a test in some specific way.
- Using assertion calls, or assert for short, to check if the resulting value is correct. They *assert* something must be true. If the assert fails, the output usually will look similar to the framework-less test shown above.

Using the Absolute() function example, two example tests are shown below. TestA() is the pattern to check if the actual value (the value returned by a function) matches the expected value. TestB() is the pattern to check if a boolean value is correct:

```
[Test]
function TestA()
  actual = 1
  expected = 1
  assertEqual( expected, actual )

[Test]
function TestB()
  value = true
  assertTrue( value )
```

Here, the functions are marked as being tests with a [Test] notation, and the assertion calls use an assert<type>() format. Real frameworks use similar structures. The inclusion of the framework is skipped, since that tends to be system specific.

With the framework format defined, the focus can switch to writing good unit tests. First, let's describe what can be tested:

1. All code paths
2. Edge cases

3. Invalid data
4. Exceptions
5. Collections of elements

At a minimum, all the code paths plus the edge cases are highly suggested to be tested.

Using the Absolute() function as an example again, let's test the code paths and edge cases. The function has two paths, so two asserts are needed to test all code paths. The edge cases are a bit harder to outline. As an initial list, the numerical boundaries of the function can be determined. For an absolute function, that means the largest positive and negative values that the system can handle as well as the transition point between the paths at 0. If the values are floating point numbers, underflow type errors can occur, which may double as invalid data. That gives three more asserts. The last item to check is how the function handles invalid data. An example of this would be a string input. This can be tested with a try-catch block as the last assert. The function is one item, so a test for collections of elements does not apply here. With that, a reasonable list of unit tests can be applied to the function, as shown below:

```
function Absolute( value )
  if value < 0
    return -value
  else
    return value

//--------------------------
[Test]
function TestPositive()
  actual = Absolute( 1 )
  assertEqual( 1, actual )

[Test]
function TestNegative()
  actual = Absolute( -1 )
  assertEqual( 1, actual )

[Test]
function TestEdges()
  actual = Absolute( 0 )
  assertEqual( 0, actual )
  actual = Absolute( ∞ )
  assertEqual( ∞, actual )
  actual = Absolute( -∞ )
  assertEqual( ∞, actual )
```

```
[Test]
function TestError()
  try
    actual = Absolute( "abc" )
    assertNull( actual )
  catch valueTypeError
    // everything is good!
  catch
    assert( "wrong exceptions type" )
```

Testing collections of elements applies to objects, such as lists and arrays. To hit all paths, the collection generally needs to test the collection with sizes of 0 to 3 elements at a minimum. Linked lists are a good example. Tests for 0 to 3 elements can usually test all the linked lists code paths. An example of an object that requires testing more elements is a "sort" function.

Overall, the characteristics of a good test
- Hit all paths in a function
- Hit all reasonable edges cases
- Add more checks as applicable
- Test a targeted part of the function
- Have a meaningful name

The last two items are necessary because the test generally stops on the first failure.

Integration Testing with Classes

This situation changes when testing classes, since object creation steps and connections come into play. At this point, keeping the model separate from the view and system-specific user input code is important for properly checking the class. This means using the MVC pattern since only the model is being checked.

Let's illustrate this with a small class with two variables:

```
class Model
  x = 0
  y = 0

  function AddX()
    x++

  function AddY()
    y++
```

The different functions can be tested the same as any other functions. The main addition at this point is that the value changes with multiple calls to the same function, so that test is added . The following is an example to test that the Model.AddX() function properly affects *x*.

```
[Test]
function AddX_IsCorrect()
  m = Model()  // make the class
  assertEquals( 0, m.x )  // check starting value

  m.AddX()
  assertEquals( 1, m.x )  // check first call

  m.AddX()
  m.AddX()
  m.AddX()
  assertEquals( 4, m.x ) // check multiple calls
```

Checking the controller and view requires testing beyond the base logic. Since the required testing is more involved, this form of unit testing is sometimes called integration testing instead as it integrates outside sources that can affect the model.

Integration testing essentially either runs the application with the code faking the user input, or some of the components are made with the GUI context so that the code is then tested similarly to unit tests. Because of the increased complexity, setting up for integrated tests tends to be much more involved.

Usually, there is a special way to set up the run time and to call the commands. After that, the test largely involves adding extra getters to be able to check the results. Below is an example that checks whether the model is updated with the control scheme. This parallels the original unit test on *x*.

```
[Test]
function TestXUpdate()
  // special start up
  main = Launch( mainClass )

  // initial value correct
  assertEqual( 0, main.GetModel().x )

  // special way to perform a user action, in code
  main.GetButton( "addX" ).Click()
  assertEqual( 1, main.GetModel().x )

  // test a few more clicks
  main.GetButton( "addX" ).Click()
  main.GetButton( "addX" ).Click()
  main.GetButton( "addX" ).Click()
  assertEqual( 4, main.GetModel().x )
```

The next integration test focuses on the view. Here, a box is to be set as red if $x < 2$ and green otherwise. This requires testing all paths and edge cases as before. However, a full test file for color would include additional tests for y and x and y together.

```
[Test]
function TestXColor()

  // special start up
  main = Launch( mainClass )

  // additional getter to reach the color box
  // initial value correct
  assertEqual( Red, main.GetArea( "colorBox" ).GetColor() )

  // check right before threshold case
  main.GetButton( "AddX" ).Click()
  assertEqual( Red, main.GetArea( "colorBox" ).GetColor() )

  // check right after threshold case
  main.GetButton( "AddX" ).Click()
  assertEqual( Green, main.GetArea( "colorBox" ).GetColor() )

  // make sure color holds
  main.GetButton( "AddX" ).Click()
  assertEqual( Green, main.GetArea( "colorBox" ).GetColor() )
```

Integration tests tend to be much more critical in VR due to the more involved interaction methods. The tests can provide a means to place a controller at a particular location and orientation. The catch is figuring out the controller and position. In this case, running and outputting the position and orientation first and then using that to write the test is a reasonable method. This is a common part of testing: running and testing interaction.

One caveat to this is that many systems do not offer integrative testing at all. This is not the case with Unity and Unreal, fortunately. Other systems, however, do provide some additional support in the form of mocking. Mocking approximates some of the nonmodel part for integrative testing. If high levels of mocking are needed, then either true integration testing is not available or the model was not sufficiently separated. The available mocking can vary tremendously with the framework.

Cybersickness Prevention

Cybersickness was briefly mentioned before in Walking Chapter 10. This section goes into some overall design suggestions to mitigate that possibility.

To review for our purposes, an incomplete definition of *cybersickness* is the feeling of motion sickness due to visuals in a VR system. The VR system can raise the probability or severity of sickness as opposed to the real-life version. For example, if something like a roller-coaster makes people sick in real life, it will be worse in VR.

Symptoms of cybersickness are predominately visual based followed by nausea but can include fatigue, visual problems, and disorientation. Cybersickness can occur quickly (<20 to 30 min) in standard 3D console-like gameplay and 40% to 60% of the population is susceptible in more modern systems [1].

There are several techniques to reduce the problem [2].

- Use predictable motion whenever possible: One example of this is snap motion.
- Go "turtle slow" or "interstate" fast. The theory as to why these speed restrictions work is that cybersickness occurs because of a theory that mismatch between visuals and the inner ear induces cybersickness. Slowing the motion down reduces the mismatch. Speeding up enough can shut down the visual's comprehension and eliminate the mismatch.
- Use any and all horizons. Flight simulations tend to generate low levels of cybersickness when set in the air, but the level jumps substantially when landing or taking off horizon. The reason for this is assumed to be the amount of available, which is fairly static and has low jitter.
- Avoid Jitter. Jitter refers to frame rate stalls or anything that results in a similar effect. The effect can also be seen with motions, such as moving up and down ladders, short jumps, and some repeating textures that have a flicker-like effect when moving. Any jitter could cause cybersickness and may require an epilepsy warning. If an effect could require an epilepsy warning, the effect should be removed.
- Use dynamic field of view. This is often applied in the form of a vignette, where the outer part of the visual is darkened. Applying this takes some shaders but is one of the most effective means to drop cybersickness.
- Add a stabilizing visual. This is just something that is always present in the same part of the screen. Some examples include
  - Nose (this is a drawing of a nose on the screen...really!)
  - HUD
  - Reticle
  - Grid lines

Stabilizing visuals if correctly implemented do not detract from the sense of immersion and in some cases increases immersion. For example, a stabilizing visual is mapping a body or avatar to the player that increases immersion. Apparently being a ghost in VR is that disorienting.

Some publishers require a cybersickness comfort rating. The general levels are

- Low: No long-distance motion. This includes games like Beat Saber or visual stories.
- Mid: Some movement, but teleport focused or similar. Most systems fall into this category.
- High: Lots of user movement over large spaces. This includes rollercoasters, sports applications, and others.

As of the writing, Oculus requires a comfort rating and Steam offers options for a comfort setting.

User Interface Design

There are two items to keep in mind about VR user interface (UI) design, especially for games.

The first is

"Good graphics cannot save a game, but good graphics can make a good game, great."

—Unknown

What this means is that it's more important to take the time to make robust interaction and a good UI than to spend all development resources on graphics.

The second is

"A user interface is like a joke. If you have to explain it, it's not that good."

—Martin Leblanc

Despite its importance, there are many difficult-to-use UIs. A conflict that can arise when designing a UI is that there are a huge number of considerations needed to make a *great* UI. However, there are surprisingly few rules needed to make at least a *good* UI. For this reason, the focus here is on the few rules for making a *good* UI, not on the rabbit hole of making a *great* UI.

Good UI Design Steps

There are three steps that get halfway to a good UI (Fig. 18.1):

1. Pretend you did not code anything to stop the code structure from influencing the UI.
2. List the first action items for an application of the project's type.
3. Focus on reaching the application's purpose goals as efficiently as possible.

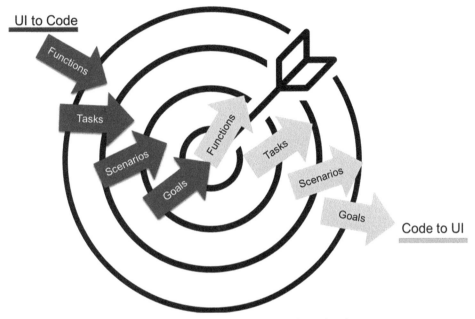

Fig. 18.1 Graphical representation of differing directions of developing UI and code.

The main challenge for these initial steps is applying them in an efficient manner. One of the habits that tends to develop when creating UIs is to start from the developer's point of view:

1. Get functions
2. Get tasks
3. Get scenarios
4. Get goals

However, that is the reverse of an efficient UI design process:

1. Get goals
2. Get scenarios
3. Get tasks
4. Get functions

There are additional considerations for finishing a good UI in the following section.

Additional UI Requirements

There are a few additional items worth mentioning to generate a good UI.

The first is to limit the number of navigation levels. If possible, it is best to auto change to the next element in an application or at least ensure the next element is clearly outlined. In terms of the overall navigation structure, there are several different methods for structure and many different preferences. Regardless, the multilevel navigation structure tends to be three levels or less for most applications. More levels than that tend to create harder-to-recall UIs. Exceptions to the 3-level max rule are previously well established taxonomies such as location data.

The second item is to maximize computer processing speed. Haptic sensitivity for humans can occur at rates faster than 1 kHz and visual sensitivity can occur at about 90 Hz, depending on lighting. However, the main issue with speed is the load time of the UI. Here are some of the reactions to different load times:

- Under 0.1s → instant to users.
- ~ 1s → acceptable.
- < 10s → generates comments akin to "Hey, this is slow."
- > 10s → generates rage quit.

In general, keeping the load time to under 1s is usually acceptable unless dealing with timing sensitive controls.

The third item is regarding how quickly users forget they are in VR. This is formally called *presence* or the feeling of being there. VR users forget the outside world shockingly fast even with poor visuals due to the immersive nature of VR. This does mean making the environment have a buffer to where the boundary system is in the environment as a safety recommendation.

Case example: During the first run of the VR course by one of the authors, the professor had to regularly dodge VR controllers and heard the clunks of controllers hitting the walls when the headsets had not been put on for more than 30 s. The students were all sitting.

The last item is in regard to privacy. In general, it is better not to force users to make extra changes or give extra information. While it is acceptable to request required changes and to specify the consequence of not accepting those changes, that is not the case for saving unnecessary information, such as credit card numbers. Ethics aside, there is an increasing number of privacy laws that require opt-out options for users, such as Maine, USA's default opt-out law. Any application may need to meet these requirements with ease for a wide range of applicability.

Optional Heuristics

There are many game specific heuristics available, but this text does not restrict to game applications only. Therefore, the optional heuristics mentioned here are an overview for general applications.

Jakob Nielsen gives 10 general heuristics for any application [3]:

1. Visibility of system status
2. Match between system and the real world
3. User control and freedom
4. Consistency and standards
5. Error prevention
6. Recognition rather than recall
7. Flexibility and efficiency of use
8. Aesthetic and minimalist design
9. Help users recognize, diagnose, and recover from errors
10. Help and documentation

Let's go over a few of these heuristics in more detail. Consider examples in a VR application that may use the heuristic and then how to design the applications that are outlined below.

Visibility of system status

- Indication selections → Attempt to make the UI work as similar to the real world as possible.
- HUDs → The environment moves relative to the head.

Match between system and the real world

- Hand visibility → As indicated, the hands should be as visible as in the real world. A lack of stabilizing visual feedback is a cause of cybersickness.
- Other expectations made visible → This requires making user expectations visible, whatever the expectations might be.

User control and freedom

- Support undo and redo → Allow safe exploration of commands.
- Allow partial completion or piece-by-piece completion → Allow tasks to be completed in the outlined method or in the method used in >90% of similar applications.
- Allow safe exploration → Make the application robust enough to prevent exploration errors.

Consistency and standards

- Easiest to reach button → Assign the most commonly used task.
- Pair commands that are used together → Exceptions are harder to learn.

One of the central ideas to this heuristic is to *not underestimate the power of familiarity.*

Error prevention

- Potential ridiculous errors do not cause a crash → This can be reduced by allowing only legal values and not allowing incorrect input.

Recognition rather than recall

- Consistency → This often refers to keeping the modes as consistent as possible. This can potentially conflict with flexibility.

The essential design here is to use gentle reminders over memorization.

Flexibility of efficiency of use

- Pointing, 2D axis, and voice all map to the same action → This allows for users to apply their preferences on a subset of tools, be it beginner mode or customization options.
- Reduce repetition → This requires a balance between oversimplifying (with, say, a one-button interface) and the design error of "form over function."

Games can intentionally violate this heuristic but with risks.

Aesthetic and minimalist design

- Preferences → This allows for users to adjust to their method of use.
- Beginner mode → This balances the mental load of too many objects while still allowing more advanced users to have access to the less used functions. In games, this is the tutorial.

Help users recognize, diagnose, and recover from errors

Essentially, this heuristic refers to alleviating Murphy's law of "if it can fail, it will."

- Add certain expected features, such as autosave → In general, being able to back up when an error occurs is helpful.
- Good error messages → If an error does occur, the message should contain what the error is, why the error occurred and suggestions to fix the error. The last item tends to be missed.

Help and documentation

- Training takes time and repetition. → If the training counteracts previous training or if the training does not repeat within one week, the training needs revision. This mitigates the effect.

- Immediate explanation of controls → What are the key buttons to start? This, oddly, is the most violated UI element in VR. The user is often left floundering to figure out which button to press to do *anything*. An easy way to look up controls is also invaluable. Consider how many console game have indicators of button control on screen!

There is one last heuristic worth mentioning: testing with users. When testing with users, it is very helpful to use the *think-aloud protocol*. This protocol has the testers say what they are thinking as they are using the test system. The protocol takes less time than often thought as the overlap on overall reports is high. So long as the testers are from a wide sample, and not from the coding team, about five testers are enough to catch the bulk of critical errors.

References

[1] Stanney K, Lawson BD, Rokers B, Dennison M, Fidopiastis C, Stoffregen T, Weech S, Fulvio JM. Identifying causes of and solutions for cybersickness in immersive technology: reformulation of a research and development agenda, *Int J Human-Computer Interact* 36(19):1783–1803, 2020. https://doi.org/10.1080/10447318.2020.1828535.

[2] Rebenitsch L, Owen C. Review on cybersickness in applications and visual displays, *Virtual Reality* 20:101–125, 2016. https://doi.org/10.1007/s10055-016-0285-9.

[3] Nielsen J. Updated *10 Usability Heuristics for User Interface Design*, 2020, Nielsen Norman Group. https://www.nngroup.com/articles/ten-usability-heuristics/.

Appendix 1

Object-Oriented Programming and Patterns Common to Virtual Reality

The purpose of Appendix 1 is to review the object-orientated programming (OOP) main techniques, SOLID principles for good coding with classes, and OOP patterns' place in virtual reality. This assumes knowledge of what classes, inheritance, and polymorphism are but does not assume much experience.

Some of the structures covered include

- OOP
- Encapsulation
  - Private/protected/public
  - Nesting classes/data design options
- Inheritance + polymorphism and related techniques

OOP Review

To understand OOP, it's important to first understand what comprises an "object" in programming in general. The absolute minimum requirement for a bundle of code to qualify as an object is that **the code bundles data and "legal" functions on the data together** (Fig. A1.1).

Specifically, the code bundles operate as an entity with a state and functionality, where state refers to the data and the functionality refers to the methods and functions.

OOP takes this fundamental object concept and adds three additional components to the relationships between objects.

- Encapsulation
  - Binds data with functions and stops outside direct control.
- Inheritance
  - Reuses past code and functions by "copying" past functions and data in a controlled manner

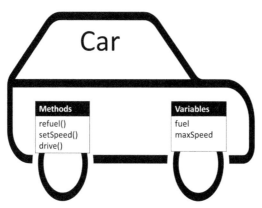

Fig. A1.1 Example of a car object with methods and variables.

- An object that derives/extends/refines another class and reuses some of its code.
- Dynamic method binding or polymorphism
  - Functions can be overridden.
  - Allows updates/changes/extensions to functions.
  - Side note: C++ uses static binding by default (cannot override) for speed and C# requires the keyword **virtual** on the function.

Any code that does not use these fundamental concepts in the design is not considered to be true OOP.

These elements are fundamental in most modern game engines. Objects are paired with how they respond to events (encapsulation), and objects are typically derived from standard classes to ensure certain functions exist (inheritance and polymorphism).

The following subsections review the three object interaction concepts in more detail.

Encapsulation

In OOP, there are three main available permission/access levels (Fig. A1.2):

- Public
- Protected
- Private

While all three access levels are usually available in different OOP languages, the meaning and options of the different levels can vary between languages. For example,

- Protected
  - In C++/C#, protected members are accessible in this class and derived classes.
  - In Java, protected members are accessible to the package and derived classes.

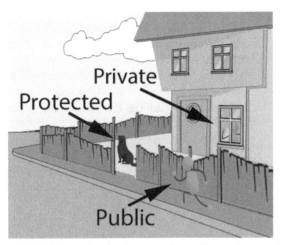

Fig. A1.2 A conceptual drawing of the different levels of access. (https://openclipart.org/detail/300393/outdoor-street-corner-scene-elements and https://openclipart.org/detail/203624/brown-dog.)

- Other variations of the three access levels may be present, such as package-private, friend, partial, etc.

Public and private access levels are fairly consistent, but protected is not. In this textbook and associated tutorials, we use the access levels according to the following coding conventions:

- Variables
  - Protected: only the base and derived classes should have access
  - Public: struct-like objects and constants
  - Private: everything else
- Functions
  - Protected: only the base and derived classes should have access.
  - Private: only with the needed class, such as a helper function to break up long functions
  - Public: everything else

When making variables and functions, they may work on either the class definition, which will affect all current object instances made of that type, or on only a single object. This book uses the terminology as follows:

- Instance
  - Affects one object
  - Changes with each object
  - "Normal" case scenario
- Class/static
  - Belongs to the class definition
  - If changes are present, all instances are updated
  - No instance needed for use

Class or static variables are rare in regular coding, and rarer yet in VR. While powerful, they are very tricky to use correctly. If you think you need one, you probably need a new class altogether instead.

Polymorphism

Polymorphism can go by different names, such as late binding or dynamic method binding. Regardless of the term used, the main concept here is the option to **override methods**. One of the key elements in OOP is that multiple child classes use the same code without the coder doing any copypasting. The reused code is placed in the parent class and access is controlled by the run time environment. Another key feature is ensuring a certain function will be available in child classes. As an example, consider having an array of Shapes, but each shape has its own area function. Suppose the following code is required to be able to run:

```
shapes = Shape[ 10 ]

// make random instances of triangles and squares
for s in shapes
  print p.Area()
```

The only way for this to work is to guarantee that there is an area function in each class in shapes. To do that, the parent class must have the function, and the children may define their own version:

```
class Shape
  function Area()
    return 0

class Triangle inherits Shape
  width = 0
  height = 0

  constructor( w, h )
    width = w
    height = h

  function Area()
    return 0.5 * width * height

class Square inherits Shape
  sideLength = 0

  constructor ( side )
    sideLength = side

  function Area()
    return sideLength * sideLength
```

Guaranteeing an instance will have a function is one of the key tenants of OOP programming. Interfaces and pure abstract classes are a good example of this. There has also been recent push to decrease the number of levels of polymorphism and instead use more interfaces.

Polymorphism allows for some useful coding technique paradigms in OOP: extend, override/redefine, and chaining.

Common Polymorphism Techniques

Polymorphic coding gains power through a few common *techniques* that will be used extensively in the book. To emphasize, these are techniques, not coding syntax, though languages may use some of theses names as keywords. All have the same goals: reuse as much code as possible, and make it so an update to the class occurs in one place.

Extend

Extend starts with the inherited function from the parent class and then adds to the original function.

```
class Parent
  function Foo()
  // do parent's Foo()'s work

class Child inherits Parent
  function Foo()
    Parent.Foo()
    // Add more code that does more
```

The key element here is that the original function is still used. It is simply *extended*.

Override

Override/redefine swaps the inherited function with a new function.

```
class Parent
  function Foo()
    // do parent's Foo()'s work

class Child inherits Parent
  function Foo()
    // New code (completely erases parent's option)
```

While it seems like past code was lost, often only *some* of the children classes may need to adjust a particular function in the parent. *Default* behavior is not a bad thing, as long as the user can adjust if needed later. This technique is very common in VR.

Chaining

Chaining takes one function and forwards the function's work to another function within the same class. This "chains" the functions so that the same function can be used with different input parameters.

Please note, while override is a coding technique here, the term can also refer to overriding a dynamically bound method. This is often denoted with the override annotation or keyword in code. Redefine can have a similar terminology challenge. The term can also mean completely overwriting a method that uses static binding and Is often denoted with the new annotation or keyword in code.

Chaining is very common in constructors. This paradigm is also sometimes mixed with the extend technique.

```
function Foo()
  Foo( someVar )

function Foo( var )
  Foo( someVar, someVar2 )

function Foo( var, var2 )
  // do what Foo() needs to do... fully specified!
```

While the jumping around may seem odd at first, this technique gives us something very important: a *single* place to update/fix the code.

Initialization

Initialization normally means the constructor, but it also can be delayed initialization. Delayed initialization in game engines is *really* common. There are two common methods.

First, there is an initialization function. In pseudocode, initialization typically looks like this:

```
class MyClass
  constructor()
    // do some but not all of the setup

  function Init()
    // finish setup
```

The other common option is a "first-time" flag. In game engines, it is usually the first frame or update after everything is loaded. Essentially, a boolean is used to denote if the initialization has finished. For example,

```
class MyClass
  firstDone = false

  function SomeUpdateFunction()
    if !firstDone
      // finish setup
      firstDone = true
```

In Unity's case, this is usually in the Update() function. In Unreal, this is often a Tick() function.

One-way reference

OOP requires multiple classes to be connected. In raw code, this is simply a member variable to the second class like in a linked list.

```
class MyClass
  other = OtherClass()

  function SomeUpdateFunction()
    other.DoSomething()
```

This works in some cases in entity-component structures, but if the desired object is a different GameObject, the object is already made elsewhere. Moreover, there is no "hub" class to send this object to a constructor. There isn't even a guarantee on creation order! However, the most similar method to the above is to mark a member variable in an engine specific way (or public, if using bad form) of the wanted type and then set it in the editor.

Two-way reference

Two-way references are similar to double-linked lists. The objects can reference each other. In code, that could look like this with the call order as noted:

```
class ClassA
  ClassB otherB

  constructor()                      // 2
    ...

  function SetClassB( ClassB obj )   // 7
    otherB = obj                     // 8

class ClassB
  ClassA otherA

  constructor( ClassA obj )          // 4
    otherA = obj                     // 5
    obj.SetClassB( this )            // 6

// setup then looks like this
a = ClassA()                         // 1 start the call path here
b = ClassB( a )                      // 3
```

Using the public access modifier to allow access to the editor is common, but it is bad practice. It breaks encapsulation as well as SOLID principles discussed later in this appendix. Instead, both Unity and Unreal have ways to mark a variable as accessible to the editor, but not other code files.

Full UML becomes far more complex very quickly and is not in wide use anymore. However, high level white boarding as presented here is extremely common and is still often seen in official documentation. Unity's documentation on how to extend their XR interaction toolkit uses something similar. Just because UML is made fun of, doesn't mean a high level "connection" diagram is bad.

If coming from a C++ background, this double reference may be initially disconcerting. However, it is a common and important feature in game engines and with careful memory management will not cause a memory leak.

Diagramming

When only the structure and connections between classes are needed, pseudocode can add unneeded complexity. This text uses some basic whiteboarding techniques with the basics taken from UML (unified modeling language). The diagrams are meant to be a high-level overview, not a documentation tool. A class is diagrammed as the boxes shown in Figs. A1.3 and A1.4.

The top line is the class or interface name; member variables and functions\job are in the following two lines, in that order, as needed. Variables are in **name [: dataType]** format when a datatype is needed for clarity. For example, a Dog class with an age and name is shown in Fig. A1.5.

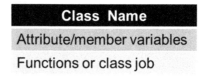

Fig. A1.3 Examples of diagramming a class.

Fig. A1.4 Examples of diagramming an interface.

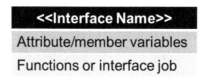

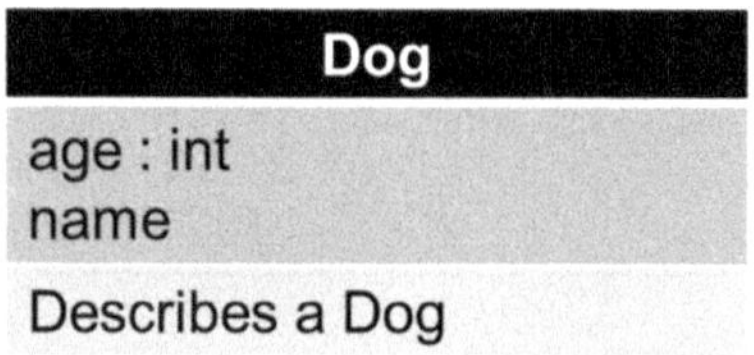

Fig. A1.5 Example of class diagram with variables.

Inheritance is shown with an arrow pointing to the parent (Fig. A1.6):

Fig. A1.6 Example of diagramming inheritance: the Dog class inherits from the Animal class.

Connections between classes are plain lines with the count and/or role on the *far* side of the line. An asterisk (*) stands for 0+ connections. For example, the following states a Line Segment has two points as member variables (Fig. A1.7):

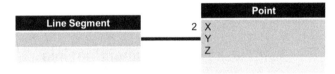

Fig. A1.7 Example of connections between classes: both classes have two points as member variables.

SOLID Review

OOP organization can be summarized into the following principles:
- S—single responsibility
- O—open/closed principle
- L —Liskov substitution principle
- I—interface segregation principle
- D—dependency inversion

Not following these principles usually results in code that was "welded" together with little to no flexibility or options for code reuse, which also results in more difficult maintenance and debugging. SOLID principles also make references to "interfaces" regularly. For those coming form a multiple inheritance language background, think of interfaces as close to a pure abstract class.

S for Single Responsibility

S in OOP usually just means that one class has one and only one responsibility. Another way of viewing S is that there should be only ONE reason for a class to change. If there are two reasons for a class to change, then there should be two classes.

For example, a Dog class should only change if there is a new function that works on the dog data or if additional information is needed to describe a dog. In both cases, there was some fundamental change to Dog. If this class needs to be changed because a doghouse was somehow added to the class, this would mean two things can change the class.

O for Open/Closed Principle

This principle is short for "open for extension but closed for modification." If a module is used, it should no longer be modified. Instead, the module needs to be extended if new methods/data are needed.

This usually just means that inheritance should be used instead of potentially breaking previously tested code.

The general rule here is that the instant the class is used, the class can no longer be open for editing. Why risk breaking a working class!?

L for Liskov Substitution Principle

The Liskov substitution principle comes from Barbara Liskov and Jeanette Wing who defined the principle as follows:

Let $\Phi(x)$ be a property provable about objects x of type T. Then $\Phi(y)$ should be true for objects y of type S where S is a subtype of T.

This principle is usually applied in SOLID to mean how a subclass can be substituted for its parent and used in the same way as the parent. To put more simply, this is polymorphism.

There are caveats to this, namely, on what gets overridden. It's acceptable to override a function and the returned values change. It's not acceptable if the override changes the meaning. Consider the Area() function from earlier. A Square and a circle will have different areas despite the one member variable. That is a good use of the Liskov principle. If the circle's Area() function suddenly returns the perimeter instead, that violates the principle because the meaning changed.

A good check is to ask this question: can the summary of the parent's function still be used "as-is." If it cannot, the Liskov principle is likely broken.

I for Interface Segregation Principle

I can be summarized as "No callee should be forced to depend on methods the callee does not use." While this might seem obvious, multiple versions or developments in code can result in this design problem popping up. For example, an interface is added with multiple functions, but after some revisions, only 1 of 5 functions are used. As another example, if heavy special casing is showing in the program, I is probably being broken.

Interface segregation is easier to identify than to implement. To achieve this aspect, careful planning of how an interface is used is required.

D for Dependency Inversion

Both high- and low-level modules should depend on abstractions, not detail. In D, the implementation can change without affecting the caller if the function format and return value remain the same.

An example of this can be a call to sort an array. Does the caller care if the sort uses merge or quick sort? Normally the answer is no! The Sort() is still Sort() and the returned values are the same.

This principle is often broken because it is tempting to design classes based on the current state of the class components.

This component is not stating that defaults are bad. It is a common misunderstanding of this principle to think that all classes must start as a pure abstract class or interface. Instead, the default uses the abstraction but allows for customization if later needed. For example, consider a color class. There are numerous different ways to define colors, but red, green, and blue in the ranges 0-255 are extremely common. The Color class itself may implement the color as RGB but allow Children classes to define their own set of values. If the default is the correct choice 90%+ of the time, why complicate the code with another polymorphic level before the color range rather than just marking it as available to override if needed?

OOP Patterns

This section discusses the origin and purpose of patterns in general. It also includes a brief description of patterns common in VR along with more detail of some foundational patterns in GUIs, such as the Composite patterns. Knowing these patterns can greatly reduce the time and length of a project. Design patterns can be put into three groups depending on the purpose of the pattern. These patterns were codified in *Design Patterns: Elements of Reusable Object-Oriented Software*, by Erich Gamma, Richard Helm, Ralph Johnson, and John Vlissides, the authors of which are sometimes referred to as Gang of Four (GoF) on other texts.

Patterns arise due to common problems in coding. After enough coding iterations over time, there evolved a pattern of the classes that solve the common problem. The patterns can also be derived by trying to make a flexible and maintainable solution by applying the SOLID principles iteratively.

The main purpose of patterns is to improve efficiency in coding. If readily able to identify certain problems and their associated patterns, the pattern can be applied swiftly to solve the problem and future edits take less time to integrate.

One caveat is that patterns are only that, patterns. While the exact format may have changed over the years, the ideas and purposes of these patterns are still very pertinent today. Patterns must adapt to the problem and the language's support, or they may fail. This is particularly true in the entity-component structure of Unity and Unreal where blind application of a pattern may fail spectacularly. Patterns with class/static variables, in particular, must be applied with great care.

Patterns are often grouped into three categories.

Creation—how a set of classes are made.

> The *Factory* is common in VR. The purpose of the pattern is to make complex objects quickly. This is common enough that both Unreal and Unity have dedicated systems for this pattern.

Structural—how a set of classes are organized.

> *Composite* and *Adapter* are common in VR. The purpose of the composite pattern is handling a bidirectional IS-A relationship. For example, a family tree has children and parents, and all are people. The entity-component structure is a specific of Unity and Unreal and a kind of composite pattern.
>
> The *Adapter*'s job is to convert from one class's API to another. This is like the adapter cord seen for computers to convert from USB-A to USB-C.

Behavioral—how a task is completed across multiple classes.

> *Observer* and *Template* are common in VR. The *Visitor* pattern is extremely common in game and simulation applications. The *Observer*'s purpose is to notify specified classes when something they care about changed. It is very useful in keeping things synced. This is like a notification system on a phone.
>
> The *Template*'s purpose is to give default behaviors to a multistage process. This is often how game loops are implemented.
>
> The *Visitor*'s purpose is to easily allow operations that require multiple objects with different data types in a type specific way. Consider modeling chemical reactions. Each reaction needs multiple molecules, atoms, and/or conditions. Standard

collection structures like arrays or lists will be very unwieldy to implement these reactions.

Source Making (https://sourcemaking.com/) has an excellent introduction with examples in code of many of the patterns. It also provides a list of names of problems when SOLID principles are violated.

Several patterns are included in the main text when they are heavily used by that topic.

- The Template pattern is described in Chapter 0 (Object-Oriented Programming in Virtual Reality).
- The Factory pattern is described in Chapter 0 (Object-Oriented Programming in Virtual Reality).
- Game engine specifics of the Composite pattern, or the entity-composition structure, is described in Chapter 0 (Object-Oriented Programming in Virtual Reality). The standard version is below.
- The Observer pattern is in Chapter 4 (Multiple System Interaction Frameworks), but more details and the event version of the pattern are presented here for a review.
- The Mediator pattern is in Chapter 4 (Multiple System Interaction Frameworks).
- The Strategy pattern is in Chapter 5 (Virtual Reality Interactions).
- A simplified version of Visitor is in Chapter 5 (Virtual Reality Interactions). The standard version is used below as a case example of how patterns are derived.
- The Model-View-Controller pattern is first introduced in Chapter 0 (Object-Oriented Programming in Virtual Reality) but is revisited in Chapter 6 (Menus and Heads-Up Devices) and Chapter 18 (Usability Design and Publishing).

Full Visitor

The full visitor is one of the larger patterns and requires a bit more initial code than most other patterns. Rather than describing the final version and then explaining why and how to use it, this pattern will first be derived using SOLID principles using a case example. This is to show why patterns arose and to better explain the multiple moving parts of this pattern.

Suppose we have a farm. There are many different animals including chickens, pigs, and cattle. Suppose the farmer wants to know how many chickens they have, total milk production per day, how many animals have not been vaccinated, and how many females/males of each type?

A naive solution without this pattern would probably look like this:

```
class Farmer
  Animals[] animals
  // other farmer code

class Animal
  function IsChicken()
    ...
  function GetMilk()
    ...
  function IsMale()
    ...
  function GetEggs()
    ...

class Chicken inherits Animal
  // override all the above

class Pig inherits Animal
  // override all the above

class Cattle inherits Animal
  // override all the above
```

This is not only a lot of work, but why on Earth are we asking cows how many eggs they laid?! To make matters worse, now assume the farmer wants to know how many animals are ready to be sold. All the classes would have to be modified to answer that!

This is bad for flexibility and extendibility with the answers for the questions in a lot of places. This implementation severely violates the Open-Closed principle of SOLID.

Here's the key part of the problem, though. The farmer (class) only knows there are animals, not what type of animal they are. The crazy question to the cow on how many eggs it laid comes from that. The first thought may be to make a giant switch class where case is animal type. But, where should this switch go? The derived class (like chicken) doesn't work, because a chicken doesn't have all the information to answer these questions. The parent, Animal class, also doesn't work because it doesn't know what the derived animal classes are. That leaves the farmer. Let's try adding a Farmer. GetMilk() function that will check if an animal is of type "Cattle" and then ask for Cattle.GetMilk(), which only exists in Cattle instances.

```
class Farmer
  function GetMilk( Animal animal )
    if animal.GetType() == Chicken
      // skipped
    else if animal.GetType() == Pig
      // skipped
    else if animal.GetType() == Cattle
      return ( (Cattle)animal ).GetMilk()
```

Now, the farmer just has to loop through each animal to ask it for the milk amount, and then tally the milk when the amount is requested.

```
class Farmer
  Animal[] animals

  function GetMilk( Animal animal )
    // code from above

  function GetTotalMilk() // NEW tallying function
    milk = 0
    for animal in animals
      milk = GetMilk( animal )

    return milk
```

But wait, this breaks open-closed in SOLID. Every time a new operation is needed (like say, those eggs from earlier), the farmer class needs to be reopened. That can be solved by making Farmer. GetMilk() its own class. Except, since this is a separate class, the milk total must be a member variable so that it can be requested after the calculation is done.

```
class GetMilkClass
  milk = 0

  function RunOp( Animal animal )
    if animal.GetType() == Chicken
      // skipped
    else if animal.GetType() == Pig
      // skipped
    else if animal.GetType() == Cattle
      milk != ( (Cattle)animal ).getMilk()
```

Now, all the farmer needs to do is run this and ask for the result.

```
class Farmer
  Animal[] animals

  function GetMilk
    tallyMilk = GetMilkClass ()

    for animal in animals
      tallyMilk.RunOp( animal )

    return tallyMilk.milk
```

There is a problem here, however. This breaks the Interface Dependency Inversion in SOLID. This should rely on interfaces (abstractions). Right now, the Farmer.GetMilk() operation is "duct taped" to the class that has our giant switch block. This isn't too obvious yet, but think about what would happen if a new animal with milk was added, say a special breed of cattle? GetMilkClass is "duct taped" to Cattle. Moreover, as more of the operations are added, many will look almost identical other than the class name. That's a waste of code!

Let's make the operation its own class from which other classes can derive. Let's call it a visitor because it will "visit" all the items sent to it.

```
class Visitor
  abstract function RunOp( Animal animal )
```

Then the Farmer.GetMilk(Animal) function is pulled from the farmer class and placed in a child of Visitor.

```
class GetMilkClass inherits Visitor
  // identical to prior GetMilkClass
```

Now, all the farmer needs to do is run a given Visitor thanks to polymorphism. Then the caller can ask for the result:

```
class Farmer
  animals = Animal[]

  function RunVisitor( Visitor visitor )
    for animal in animals
      visitor.RunOp( animal )

// Some caller uses this. Notice, it is NOT inside Farmer
function GetMilk()

  // user wants total milk
  getMilkOp = GetMilkClass ()
  farmer.RunVisitor( getMilkOp )
```

```
// get the amount saved in the GetMilk class
// after all animals have been sent in
print getMilkOp.milk
```

The main advantage from that shift to making the GetMilk() function generic is that any visitor can be sent the Farmer.RunVisitor() instead. Consider a new task to count the number of males. To add that operation, derive a new GetMaleCount from Visitor, and then use is identical to the GetMilk() code shown in the above code. There is no change to the animal or farmer classes!

There are two remaining problems. One, GetType() is considered bad form as it is a sign of poor hierarchical structure and can quickly lead to violating Interface Segregation in SOLID. The other item is that good coding practice will have the code inside the else-if statement be its own function call if past a few lines, like so:

```
if obj.GetType() == "A"
  DoAFunc( (A)obj )
else if ( obj.GetType() == "B" )
  DoBFunc( (B)obj )
else if obj.GetType() == "C"
  DoCFunc( (C)obj )
…
```

Both problems can be solved by adding one more layer. Animals know what they are, so they could jump straight to the RunTypeOperation(). This means the Animal class needs an abstract function to accept a visitor, and the child class will call the correct function. This yields the Visitor pattern version for this case example:

```
class Animal
  abstract function RunVisitor( Visitor visitor )

class Chicken inherits Animal
  function RunVisitor( Visitor visitor )
    visitor.RunChickenOp( this )

class Pig inherits Animal
  function RunVisitor( Visitor visitor )
    visitor.RunPigOp( this )

class Cattle inherits Animal
  function RunVisitor( Visitor visitor )
    visitor.RunCattleOp( this )

class Visitor
  abstract function RunChickenOp( Chicken animal )
  abstract function RunPigOp( Pig animal )
  abstract function RunCattleOp( Cattle animal )
```

Now we are done! And yes, the implementation of the RunVisitor() function in the derived classes is that tiny. Visually, we have the generic structure in Fig. A1.8:

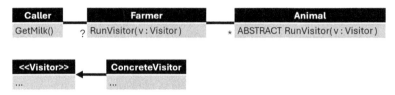

Fig. A1.8 Example of a diagrammed visitor pattern.

The caller makes the visitor instance and forwards it to the class that has the collection (the farmer in this example). The collection class then calls RunVisitor() on each element in the collection. Then when done, the caller uses the result stored in the visitor.

The advantage of this structure is that you can add new capabilities without changing the way the data are stored. Plus, all of the code for the task ends up in one place instead of being spread all over.

The down sides are the extra code to support the pattern, which is hard to add later if missed. Also, every time a new derived type is added, you have to add a new accept/visit function for that type. There are some techniques, like default functions to mitigate that, however the visitor does best when the operations change regularly, but the data types do not.

Composite

The composite pattern is defined as an object composed of 1+ objects of the same type. An example of this is a binary tree. It is a subset of "has a" relationships in that this only applies to objects that are incomplete without their subparts, and the subparts disappear if the "root" object is deleted. The key difference between composite and good decompositions is that a composite supports a walkthrough of a generic tree. Composite adds a task beyond "print"!

As an example, consider a dish set. Let's say that the dish set has a hierarchy of classes that looks like this:

- PlateSet
  - LargePlate
  - SmallPlate
  - TeaCup
  - Teapot
    - Pot
    - Lid

A plate set has a LargePlate, SmallPlate, TeaCup, and Teapot objects as member variables. A Teapot has a Pot and Lid objects as member variables. However, they are all dishes, which means that all of those classes can be derived from a Dish class. Visually, we have the format shown in Fig. A1.9:

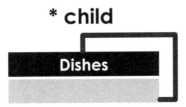

Fig. A1.9 Diagramming for showing parenting.

Dishes then can have a function that all children have, and that function can be recursive. Consider cleaning the dish set with this possible call order:

Task: Clean all dishes

1. Check LargePlate (clean, move on)
2. Check SmallPlate (clean, move on)
3. Check TeaCup (clean, move on)
4. Check TeaPot (clean, **forward call to subcomponents**)
    1. Check Pot (clean, move on)
    2. Check Lid (clean, no more dishes…stop)

Transformation in scene trees used in graphical systems uses this to its advantage to guarantee some functions in all the game objects.

Observer

An observer's main goal to is announce to different "viewers" that the model's data have changed. This helps keep the views synced. Consider the game engines. There is the central window and then the component. If the component changes, the object in the window updates instantly. If the object in the main window is updated, the component is updated!

In this case of the pattern, the "**Viewer**" means ANY item that needs to be notified as an observer. The viewer could be an online database!

There are a few levels of observers. The "toy" version just has an "UpdateAll()" function to ensure everything updates. Every button push, every radio button, every menu, etc, calls the **UpdateAll()** at the end, and then EVERYTHING is checked and then **redrawn/refreshed**. This works great for smaller projects but does not work with the entity-component structure of modern game engines. What happens when the "view/game object" disappears and reappears? That would require some nasty levels of special casing.

Visually, the observer pattern has the basic format shown in Fig. A1.10:

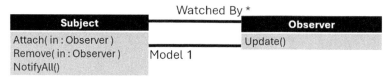

Fig. A1.10 Example diagramming of the observer.

The way it works is that there are subjects. The subject is something that needs to be watched.

There are observers that need to be told when something changed, so they can do their job.

When the subject changes, it lets its observers know **directly**.

Consider a street intersection, where the item being watched is the streetlight. The observers are the pedestrian and car. The photon notifies the observers (Fig. A1.11).

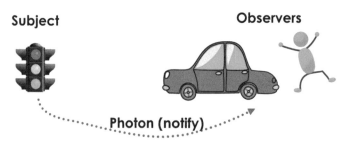

Fig. A1.11 Graphical example of the observer pattern in real life.

In code, this is typically implemented in this order:
1. Create the subject.
2. Create the observer.
3. The observer gets the subject and registers itself with Attach().
4. Later in the run, the subject has its data change.
5. The subject calls Update() on all attached observers.
6. If an observer is destroyed, it deregisters from the subject with Remove().

In game code, this is considered so important that an **event** datatype is usually implemented, which does the above in fairly short syntax. In pseudocode, this would look like this:

```
// create event-----------------
event EventName

// add\remove callbacks----------
EventName += callback
EventName -= callback

// trigger event-----------------
EventName()
```

Events also allow for repeat calls to be added to the callback list. Because searching the event list is not permitted, the standard technique to ensure that a callback is only added once is to attempt removal first (which does nothing if the item is not in the list), then add as follows:

```
// ensure callback occurs at most once
eventName -= callback
eventName += callback
```

As a concrete example using the intersection, the event parts may look like this:

```
class StreetLight // 1) The subject

    // 2) create event-----------------
    event lightChange

    whichLight = 0
    timeUntilNext = [ 20, 10, 20 ]
    currentTime = 0

    // 3a) Update that can cause an event
    function TimeTick()
      currentTime++

      if currentTime > timeUntilNext[ whichLight ]
          whichLight = ( whichLight + 1 ) % 3
          currentTime = 0

          // 3b) notify all registered observers
          lightChange( this )
```

```
// 4a) An Observer
class Pedestrian

  // 5a) Register as an observer
  constructor( StreetLight light )
    light.lightChange += this.watch

  // 6b) What to do when notified
  function Watch( StreetLight light )
    if light.whichLight == 2
      Walk()
      // past intersection,
      // stop watching and remove callback
      light.lightChange -= this.watch
    else
      Stop()

// 4b) An Observer
class Car

  // 5b) Register as an observer
  constructor( StreetLight light )
    light.lightChange += this.watch

  // 6b) What to do when notified
  function Watch( StreetLight light )
    if light.whichLight == 0
      Drive()

      // past intersection,
      // stop watching and remove callback
      light.lightChange -= this.watch

    else if light.whichLight == 1
      Slow()

    else
      Stop()
// 7) How to use
light = StreetLight()
pedestrian = Pedestrian ( light )
car = Car( light )
while running every second
  light.TimeTick()
```

That's a lot of code! Let's walk through the important bits. The class marked with (1) is the the subject. The StreetLight is what is watched. (2) is the event data type which is just a fancy list that can be notified. (3a) is a function that can cause an event. More specifically, (3b) is what starts a look at the list and notifies each object. (4a) and (4b) are the observers. They need to know when the light changes, and they register themselves for notification at (5a) and (5b). This registration says to call (6a) or (6b) on the event. To use this code, the pedestrian and car register themselves at construction time at (7).

A caveat to the event type is that the above is about all that is supported directly. If only some events or a certain order is desired, the event data are too restrictive.

To gain extra control, if *not* using the built-in support, the psuedo-code code looks a bit more like this:

```
// create event------------------
class EventName

  list = CallbackFormat[]

  function Add( CallbackFormat callback )
    list.Append( callback )

  function Remove( CallbackFormat callback )
    list.Remove( callback );

  function Trigger()
    for CallbackFormat x in list
      x.Callback();

interface CallbackFormat
  function Callback()

// add\remove callbacks----------
// callback must be an instance derived from CallbackFormat
event = EventName()
myEvent.Add( callback )
myEvent.Remove( callback )

//trigger event------------------
eventName.Trigger()
```

This does basically the same things as the event data type, but it is clearer where the loop over the callbacks occur (in Trigger()). The event data type is normally faster, so it is suggested when feasible. However, there are also many instances where the callbacks need to be filtered, so implementing this yourself is also likely.

Appendix 2

Programming Languages Guide

This textbook assumes prior programming skills but attempts to avoid assuming a deep understanding of a particular language. However, since Unreal uses C++ , Unity uses C#, and Godot uses C# or a python inspired language, this book uses a pseudocode structure with bias toward the C-family of languages. The primary purpose of Appendix 2 is to demonstrate the pseudocode format used in the textbook by comparing it to C++, C#/Java, and Python. C# and Java are largely combined due to high overlap in syntax, but the section will note when they are different. The secondary purpose is to be a quick look-up guide, with some additional explanation for constructs used in the book but may be new if coming from other languages. This is not meant to teach a new language, and as such, the standard file formats and common libraries are skipped. This chapter is arranged in the 10 near universal structure of programming languages in comparison tables, a standard code file structure, and then focuses on some more specialty items common to C++ and C#.

Function capitalization standards vary with the language. In this text, functions and classes typically use the C# standard where the first letter capitalized to better indicate what they are. Functions will have a () at the end while classes will not to indicate the difference. Variables are lower case. However, conventions for C++, Java, and Python typically have the first letter in lower case for functions. These conventions are applied in the example code.

The 10 structures are
1. Commenting
2. Assignment
3. Output
4. Input
5. Selection
6. Repetition
7. Functions
8. Exceptions
9. File I/O
10. Classes

Some specialty elements that also tend to come up in VR work include:
- Enums
- Resizable arrays
- Hashes

Commenting

Pseudocode	C++
`// single line`	`// single line`

`/*`
`Multi`
 	
`Line`
`*/`
	`/*`
	`Multi`
	
	`Line`
	`*/`

C#/Java	Python
`// single line`	`# single line`

`/*`
`Multi`
`Line`
`*/`
	`'''`
	`Multi`
	`Line`
	`'''`
	
	`"""`
	
	`Multi`
	`Line`
	`"""`

Commenting can also include some specialty formats for class and function commenting. These are usually for autogeneration of documentation.

Assignment

Pseudocode	C++
`// primitive assignment----------` `x = 0`	`// primitive assignment----------` `int x = 0;`

`// uninitialized type assignment`
`// as needed for clarity`
`ClassName x`
	`// uninitialized type assignment`
	`ClassName x;`

Pseudocode	C++

```
// general math----------
x = 2 + 3
x += 3
x++
x = √4
```

```
// general math----------
x = 2 + 3;
x += 3;
x++;
x = sqrt(4);
```

```
// class assignment\access----------
y = SomeClass()
y.w = 0
```

```
// class assignment\access----------
// stack allocation
SomeClass y = SomeClass();
y.w = 0;

// dynamic allocation
SomeClass y = new SomeClass();
y->w = 0;
delete y; //release memory
```

```
// 1D arrays--------------------
z = [4]
z[0] = 2
```

```
// 1D arrays------------------
// stack allocation
double z[2];
double z[2] = {0, 0};
double z[] = {0, 0};
z[0] = 2;

// dynamic allocation
double* z = new double[2];
delete z; // release memory
```

```
// 2D arrays--------------------
a = [2][4]
a[0][0] = 2
```

```
// 2D arrays------------------
// stack allocation
double a[2][4];
double a[2][4] =
        {{0, 0, 0, 0},
         {0, 0,0, 0}};
double a[][] =
        {{0, 0, 0, 0},
         {0, 0,0, 0}};

// dynamic allocation
double** a = new double*[2];
a[0] = new double[4];
a[1] = new double[4];
delete a[0];  // release memory
delete a[1];  // release memory
delete a;     // release memory

a[0][0] = 2;
```

C#/Java	Python
``// primitive assignment----------
int x = 0;```	```# primitive assignment-----------
x = 0```
``// uninitialized type assignment
ClassName x;```	```# uninitialized type assignment
x = None```
``// general math----------
x = 2 + 3;
x += 3;
x++;
x = Math.Sqrt(4);```	```# general math-----------
x = 2 + 3
x += 3
x = x + 1 # no increment op
x = sqrt(4)
x = 4 ** (0.5) # alternate power operator```
``// class assignment\access---------
SomeClass y = new SomeClass();
y.w = 0;```	```# class assignment\access----------
y = SomeClass()
y.w = 0```
``// 1D arrays--- ---------------
double[] z = new double[2];
z[0] = 2;```	```# 1D arrays----------------------
# technically lists, not arrays
z = [] * 4
z[0] = 2```
``// 2D arrays---------------------
// rectangular
double[,] a = new double[2,4];
a[0,0] = 2;```	```# 2D arrays (lists of lists)-----
a = [[0]*2 for i in range(4)]
a[0][0] = 2```
``// jagged
double[][] a = new double[2][4];
double[][] a = new double[2][];
a[0] = new double[4];
a[1] = new double[4];

a[0][0] = 2;``` | ```# or numpy arrays ---------------
a = np.zeros((2,4))

b = np.array([[2,3],[4,5]])``` |

If coming from a dynamically typed language like Python or JavaScript, the static typing in C++ and C# may feel odd at first. The C family and Java are statically typed, meaning the data type is set at creation and cannot change. That may feel restrictive at first, but there are major benefits to pushing the data type check onto the compiler rather than at runtime. There is a reason both Python and JavaScript now have syntax to help with datatype checks at compiler/coding time. This is be noticeable in the assignment section.

C++ allows for both stack allocation and dynamic (or heap) allocation of memory based on the syntax used. This means the C++ syntax is more involved, and the programmer has to remember to delete the variable if not using smart pointers. However, it has the benefit of better spread and more control over garbage collection. The charts note what is being used.

Output

Pseudocode	C++

print "Hello World"	```// must include a special package```
	```#include <iostream>```
	
	```// cout is the function to print```
	```// << separates components```
	```// endl stands for end line or \n```
	```// std:: is only needed if```
	```// "using namespace std:"```
	```// is not used```
	```std::cout << "Hello World" << endl;```

C#/Java*	Python
```Console.WriteLine("Hello World ");```	```print("Hello World!")```

*Java is just different in the source library here. Java code is

```
System.out.println("Hello World!");
```

VR generally will not use console output for the user. Debug information may be sent to console-like areas, but calls are usually specialized to the framework.

In Unity, a basic call is this:

```
Debug.Log("Hello World");
```

In Unreal, a basic call is this:

```
UE_LOG(LogTemp, Warning, TEXT("Hello World"));
```

Input

Pseudocode	C++

x = GetInput()	// must include a special package
	#include <iostream>
	
	// cout is the function to print
	// << separates components
	// endl stands for end line or \n
	// std:: is only needed if
	// using namespace std;
	// is not used
	string name;
	double x;
	std::cin >> name;
	std::cin >> x;

C#/Java*	Python

string name = Console.ReadLine();
 	
// casting is required for
// anything but text.
double x = Convert.ToDouble (
        Console.ReadLine());
	name = input()
	
	# casting is required for
	# anything but text.
	x = double(input())

*Java input is more involved as there is no static class for console input. A Scanner calls is commonly used. Here is an example:

```
Scanner cin = new Scanner(System.in);
String name = cin.nextLine();
double x = cin.nextDouble();
```

In general, VR code will not be using console input.

Selection

Pseudocode	C++

```
// example conditionals-----------
&&
||
==
<
!


// if-else ----------------------

// (optional else if, and else)
if x == 2 && !z
    // code to run if true
else if x == 2
    // code to run if true,
    // and above is not
else
    // code to run if all else
    // is false


// switch------------------------
switch val
    case v1
        // if val == v1, code to run
    case v2
        // if val == v2, code to run
```

```
// example conditionals---------
&&
||
==
<
!


// if-else ------------------

// (optional else if, and else)
if (x == 2 && !z)
{
    // code to run if true
}
else if (x == 2)
{
    // code to run if true,
    // and above is not
}
else
{
    // code to run if all else
    // is false
}


// switch ------------------

// all primitive data types
// supported
switch (val)
{
    case 1:
        // val == 1, code to run
        break;
    case 2:
        // if val == 2, code to run
        break;
}
```

C#/Java	Python
```// example conditionals--------```	```# example conditionals---------```

```
// example conditionals--------
&&
||
==
<
!


// if-else ------------------

// (optional else if, and else)
if x == 2 && !z
{
    // code to run if true
}
else if x == 2
{
    // code to run if true,
    // and above is not
}
else
{
    // code to run if all else
    // is false
}


// switch -----------------

// all primitive data types
// supported
switch (val)
{
    case 1:
        // val == 1, code to run
        break;
    case 2:
        // if val == 2, code to run
        break;
}
```

```
# example conditionals---------
and
or
==
<
not


# if-else --------------------

# (optional else if, and else)
if x == 2 && !z:
    # code to run if true

else if (x == 2):
    # code to run if true,
    # and above is not

else:
    # code to run if all else
    # is false

// switch -------------------

'''
Technically, does not exist.

Newer versions of python support
    "matching" which can mimic a basic
    switch in many cases but does not
    have the speed of a switch.
'''
```

Syntactically, C++, C#, and Java are the same here, but convention places the opening { on the if-else line in Java, and after in C-family.

If coming from Python or a non–C-family language, the "break" keyword in a switch may be new. Without the "break", the switch will continue running the code in later case blocks until a "break" is hit. This is extremely easy to forget when coding.

Repetition

Pseudocode	C++
``// while -------------------
while !flag
  // run this code

// do-while -----------------
do
  // run this code
while !flag

// for loop -----------------
for x = 0 to 10
  // run this code

// for each\range\enumeration -----
for x in collection
  // run this code``` | ```// while -----------------
while(!flag)
{
    // run this code
}

// do-while -----------------
do
{
  // run this code
} while(!flag);

// for loop -----------------
for(int x = 0; i < 10; i++)
{
  // run this code
}
// for each\range\enumeration -----
for(int x: collection)
{
    // run this code
}``` |

C#/Java*	Python
``// while -----------------
while(!flag)
{
   // run this code
}

// do-while -----------------
do
{
   // run this code
} while(!flag);``` | ```# while ----------------------
while not flag:
    # this is an indented block
    # run this code

# do while - no direct implementation
# but equivalent...
while True:
    # indented block
    # run this code
    if not flag:
    break``` |

C#/Java*	Python
```// for loop```	```# for loop```

```
// for loop
for( int x = 0; i < 10; i++)
{
   // run this code
}
```

```
# for loop
# range params are ( start, stop, step )
for n in range(0,10,1):
    # indented block
    # run this code
```

```
// for each\range\enumeration
foreach( int x in collection)
{
    // run this code
}
```

```
//for each\range\enumeration
for item in list:
    # indented block
    # run this code
```

Syntactically, C++, C#, and Java are the same here, but convention places the opening { on the if-else line in Java, and after in C-family.

*Java uses the following for each:

```
for( int x : collection)
{
   // run this code
}
```

Functions

Pseudocode	C++

```
// void function
function Foo()
   // run this code

Foo()
```

```
// void function
void foo()
{
   // run this code
}

foo();
```

```
// static function
function static Foo()
   // run this code

Foo()
```

```
// static function
static void foo()
{
   // run this code
}
foo()
```

Pseudocode	C++
| ```
// return value function----------
// only used if the data type
// is unclear
function dataType Foo()
  // run this code
  return val

x = Foo()

// input parameters-------------
function Foo( x )
  // run this code with x

Foo( y )
``` | ```
// return value function-----------
int foo()
{
    // run this code
    return 0;
}

x = foo();

// input parameters ------------
void foo(int x )
{
    // run this code with x
}
foo(y);

// pass by reference parameters--------
// if x is updated, y is too
void foo( int &x )
{
    // run this code with x
}

foo( y );
``` |

C#/Java	Python
| ```
// void function-------------------
void Foo()
{
  // run this code
}

obj.Foo();// * see note

// static function----------------
static void Foo()
{
  // run this code
}
Class.Foo() // * see note
``` | ```
# function w/ no return value-----
def foo():
    // run this code

foo()

# static function --------------
class bar():
    @staticmethod
    def foo():
        # run this code
bar.foo()
``` |

C#/Java	Python
| ```
// return value function
int Foo()
{
    // run this code
    return 0;
}

x = obj.Foo(); // * see note

// input parameters **
void Foo( int x )
{
    // run this code with x
}
``` | ```
# return value function
def foo():
    # run this code
    return 0

x = foo()

# input parameters
def foo( x ):
    # run this code

foo( y )
``` |

```
obj.Foo( y ); // * see note
```

*All functions must be in classes in C# and Java. The functions can be called without the **obj** or **Class** if inside the class.
** C# and Java have a different set of parameter options. Primitives like int, are pass-by-value, and cannot be changed by default in both. A class variable can have its *contents* (not memory address) changed in all languages listed, by default. However, C# has the option of **in**, **out**, and **ref** keywords that Java and Python do not. C++ does have a reference option, but not **in** or **out**. **in** means the value is read-only. **out** means the value is write-only, and **ref** is read-write.

As an example, the following is legal in C#:

```
static void AddRef(ref int x, int y)
{
    x = x + y;
}

int m = 1;
int n = 2;
AddRef(ref m, n); // in\out\ref needed on both the call and parameter

// m is now 3
```

Exceptions

Pseudocode	C++

```
//try-catch----------------
try
  // some code that could
  // cause a crash
catch exception1
  // do something with the error 1
catch exception2
  // do something with the error 2
catch
  // do something with
  // any other error

// throw an exception-----------
throw exception()
```

```
// try-catch----------------
try
{
  // some code that could
  // cause a crash
}
catch (const std::format_error e)
{
  // do something with the error 1 }
catch (const std::out_of_range& e)
{
  // do something with the error 2 }
catch (…)
{
  // do something with
  // any other error
}

// throw an exception-----------
throw exception("message");
```

C#/Java	Python

```
// try-catch----------------
try
{
  // some code that could
  // cause a crash
}
catch( FormatException e )
{
  // do something with the error 1
}
catch( ArgumentOutOfRangeException e )
{
  // do something with the error 2
}
catch( Exception e )
{
  // do something with
  // any other error
}

// throw an exception-----------
throw new Exception("message");
```

```
# try-except ----------------
try:
    # some code that could cause
    # a crash
except TypeError:
    # do something with the
    # error 1
except IndexError:
    # code to respond to a
    # particular error
except:
    # do something with the
    # error 2

# raise (throw) an exception -----
raise Exception("message")
```

File I/O

Pseudocode	C++
<pre>// open to read
fin = Open(name)
x = fin.ReadLine()

// open to write
fout = Open(name2)
file.Write("stuff")

// close
fin.Close()
fout.Close()</pre> | <pre>// must include a special package
#include <fstream>

// open to read
ifstream fin;
fin.open(name);
fin >> x;

// open to write
ofstream fout;
fout.open(name2)
fout << "stuff";

// close
fin.close()
fout.close()</pre> |

C#/Java*	Python
<pre>// open to read
StreamReader fin =
        File.OpenText(name);
line = fin.ReadLine();

// open to write
StreamWriter fout =
        new StreamWriter(name2);
fout.WriteLine(line);

// close
fin.Close();
fout.Close();</pre> | <pre># open to read
file = open(name,'r')
file.readline()

# open to write
file = open(name,'w')
file.write(line)

close
file.close()</pre> |

*Java is very similar. Largely, the differences are just the classes and parameter datatypes.

Classes

Pseudocode	C++*

```
// basic class------------
Class XX

  // instance member variable
  y = 0

  // static\class member variable
  static z = 2

  // constructor
  constructor()
    // setup instance

  // instance function
  function Foo()
    // run code
```

```
// basic class------------
class XX
{

    // instance member variable
    int y = 0;

    // static\class member variable
    static const int z = 2;

    // constructor
    XX()
    {
        // setup instance
    }

    // instance function
    void foo()
    {
      // run code
    }
};
```

```
// inherit from class XX----------
Class YY inherits XX
  class code

// make a class-----------------
x = XX()

// call an instance function-------
x.Foo()

// call a static\class member-----
XX.z = 2
```

```
// inherit from class XX----------
class YY : XX
{
  // XX() is optional if there
  // is only one parent
  // constructor
  YY(): XX()
  {
      // setup instance
      // must name parent, if used
      XX::foo();

  }

      // remaining code
};
```

Pseudocode	C++*
| | ```
// make a class--------------------
// static allocation
XX x = XX();
// dynamic allocation
YY *y = new YY();

//call an instance function-------
x.foo();
y.foo();

// call a static\class member-----
XX.z = 2;
``` |

C#/Java	Python
| ```
// basic class--------------
class XX
{

    // instance member variable
    int y = 0;

    // static\class member variable
    static int z = 2;

    // constructor
    XX()
    {
        // setup instance
    }

    // instance function
    void Foo()
    {
        // run code
    }
``` | ```
# basic class --------------------
class XX:

    # class variable
    z = 0

    # constructor and instance
    # variables
    def __init__( self, y ):
        self.y = y

    # instance function
    def foo( self ):
        # run code

# inherit from class
class XX( yy ):

    # instance function
    def foo( self ):
        # run code
``` |
```

C#/ Java	Python
| ```
// inherit from class XX
class YY: XX
{
    // base() is optional if there
    // is only one parent
    // constructor i
    YY(): base()
    {
        // setup instance
    }

    // remaining code
}

// make a class
XX x = new XX();

// call an instance function
x.Foo();

// call a static\class member
XX.z = 2;
``` | ```
# instantiate an object of a class
x = XX()

# call an instance function
x.foo()

# access a class member
// python allows unedited instance
// access to class variables
print(XX.z)
print(self x.z self)

# change a class member
XX.z = 2
x.z = 2 # for x instance only
``` |

*The shown code does not use separate compilation which is the de facto standard in C++ to keep the size small.

The above ignores access levels like public, protected, and private as those are context specific. However, the default access level does differ between languages. C# defaults to private, Python to public, and so on.

C#/java use the format of

```
access member;
```

As an example:

```
private int x;
protected double y;
public void foo(){}
```

C++ uses the format of

```
access:
    member;
```

where everything has that access level until it changes. As an example:

```
private:
  int x;
  int x2;
protected:
  double y;
public:
  void foo(){}
```

Python uses varying numbers of _ before the name to indicate access, although protected is by convention only. There is no compiler protection. As an example:

```
self.__x    # private
self._y     # protected
self.z      # public
```

There is also variation in single versus multiple inheritance. C++ and Python are multiple inheritance, while C# and Java are single and use interfaces as a controlled workaround. If coming from C++ and Python, think of interfaces as very restrictive classes. They are meant to hold a list of functions that must be implemented later. They often work similarly to C++ pure abstract classes.

Specialty

Enums

Pseudocode	C++

`enum EnumType = X, Y, Z`	`enum Coordinate`
	`{`
	`    X, Y, Z`
	`};`

C#/Java	Python

`enum Coordinate`
`{`
`    X, Y, Z`
`}`
	`Coordinate = enum(X, Y, Z)`

Resizable Arrays

Pseudocode	C++

`X = []`
`x.append( y )`
`length = x.length`
	`std::vector<int> x;`
	`x.push_back( y )`
	`length = x.size;`

C#/Java*	Python
```ArrayList< Object ArrayList<> x = new ArrayList<>(); x.Add(y); int length = x.Count;```	```x = [] x.append(y) length = len(x)```

*The only difference here is that Java uses lowercase function names.

Hashes/Dictionaries/Maps

Pseudocode	C++
```x = {} x[key] = value y = x[key]```	```std::unordered_map < int, std::string > x; x[1] = "one"; std::string y = x[1];```

C#/Java*	Python
```Dictionary< int, string > x = new Dictionary< int, string >(); x.Add(1, "one"); string y = x[1];```	```x = { key_0:value_0, key_1:value_1 } x[key_2] = value_2 y = x[key_0]```

*Java calls this a hash table.

Some Advice When Shifting Languages

It is very tempting to jump and simply start coding in a new framework. However, it is often more efficient to get the basics down first and then go to the framework. Also, the concepts are often less understood while learning the new syntax as the code is difficult to read.

One of the quickest methods to learning a new language, if already comfortable with another, is to write a smaller program. A good program to write when learning a new language is any basic, linked list collection (linked list, link queue, etc.), using inherited objects (e.g., derive square/circle from shape), with user input and output with error checking, and saving and loading the list state.

This hits all 10 common structures and usually will only take a few hours.

Appendix 3

Mathematical Foundations

The purpose of this section is to explain the mathematical notation used in the book. Some reviews of mathematical foundations are also included. These include trigonometry/geometry, imaginary numbers, vector calculus, quaternions, and basic linear algebra, which are used throughout the book, although in specific ways. Geometry and matrices will assume a left-handed system unless otherwise noted.

Notation

Points use tuple notation:

$$(x, y, z)$$
$$P = (x, y, z)$$

Vectors may use angle notation, with bolded variables:

$$\boldsymbol{V} = \langle x, y, z \rangle$$

Matrix notation uses

$$M = \begin{bmatrix} a & b & c \\ d & e & f \\ g & h & i \end{bmatrix} = M_{\text{row} \times \text{col}}$$

Noting an element is in row-column order, 1 indexed:

$$M_{1,2} = b$$

Vectors can also be noted in matrix notation, with bolded variables:

$$\boldsymbol{V} = \begin{bmatrix} x & y & z \end{bmatrix} = \begin{bmatrix} x \\ y \\ z \end{bmatrix}^{T}$$

Rays use arrow notation with point-vector format (Fig. A3.1):

$$\overrightarrow{PV}$$

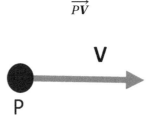

Fig. A3.1 An example ray. P is the point and **V** is the vector.

Magnitude is noted with bars:

$$|V| = \sqrt{\sum a_i^2}$$

The difference between two points is a **vector** (Fig. A3.2):

$$V = P - Q$$

Fig. A3.2 An example vector. P and Q are both points and **V** is the resulting difference vector.

The sum of a vector and a point is a **point** (Fig. A3.3):

$$P = V + Q$$

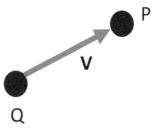

Fig. A3.3 Example result of adding the point, Q, and the vector, **V**. The summation leads to point P.

The sum of two vectors is a **vector** (Fig. A3.4):

$$\boldsymbol{W} = \boldsymbol{U} + \boldsymbol{V} = (Q - R) + (P - Q) = (P - R)$$

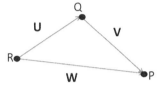

Fig. A3.4 Two vectors, **U** and **V** are summed and result in vector **W**, tracing out a triangle of points P, Q and R.

Trigonometry and Geometry

Assuming a right triangle, here are some useful trigonometric identities (Fig. A3.5):

$$\cos(\theta) = \frac{a}{c}$$

$$\sin(\theta) = \frac{b}{c}$$

$$\tan(\theta) = \frac{b}{a}$$

$$\cos^{-1}\left(\frac{a}{c}\right) = \theta$$

$$\sin^{-1}\left(\frac{b}{c}\right) = \theta$$

$$\tan^{-1}\left(\frac{b}{a}\right) = \theta$$

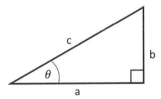

Fig. A3.5 Example right triangle for trigonometric identities.

Line Equations

Slope Intercept form: $y = mx + b$

Point − slope form: $(y - y_1) = m(x - x_1)$

Normal form: $Ax + By + C = 0$

Plane Equation

***Vector equation* (*where p and p_0 are on the plane*):**

$$a(x - x_0) + b(y - y_0) + c(z - z_0) = 0$$

***Scalar equation*:** $ax + by + cz = d$

Common Geometric formulas

Projection of a point, p, onto a Ray, $\overrightarrow{p_0 v}$, uses this formula

$$Q = p_0 + \frac{v(p - p_0)^T}{vv^T} v$$

Worked example: Projection of a Point onto a Ray (Fig. A3.6)

Let

$p = (3, 5)$

$p_0 = (1, 1)$

$\mathbf{v} = \langle 2, 1 \rangle$

Visually:

$Q = (1, 1) + \dfrac{[2\ \ 1]((3, 5) - (1, 1))^T}{[2\ \ 1][2\ \ 1]^T}[2\ \ 1]$ *sub in values*

$Q = (1, 1) + \dfrac{[2\ \ 1][2\ \ 4]^T}{[2\ \ 1][2\ \ 1]^T}[2\ \ 1]$ *subtract point*

$Q = (1, 1) + \dfrac{[2\ \ 1]\begin{bmatrix}2\\4\end{bmatrix}}{[2\ \ 1]\begin{bmatrix}2\\1\end{bmatrix}}[2\ \ 1]$ *transpose*

$Q = (1, 1) + \dfrac{8}{5}[2\ \ 1]$ *multiply vectors*

$Q = (1, 1) + \begin{bmatrix}\dfrac{16}{5} & \dfrac{8}{5}\end{bmatrix}$ *multiply scalar*

$Q = \left(\dfrac{21}{5}, \dfrac{13}{5}\right)$ *add point plus vector*

$Q = (4.2, 2.6)$

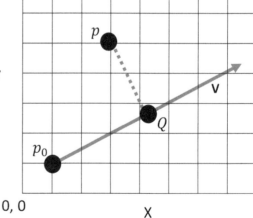

Fig. A3.6 Example projection. Point p is projected onto the ray $\overrightarrow{p_0 v}$. The position of the projected result is Q.

Imaginary Numbers

An imaginary number is defined as

$$i = j = \sqrt{-1}$$

$$i^2 = -1$$

Complex numbers are represented as

$$x + iy,$$

where x is real and y is imaginary.

Addition and subtraction of imaginary numbers is as follows:

$$(x + iy) \pm (v + iw) = (x \pm v) + i(y \pm w)$$

Worked example: Complex Number Addition

Let
a = 2 + 3*i*
b = 1 − 5*i*
Calculate
a + b
(2 + 3*i*) + (1 − 5*i*) *sub in values*
(2 + 1) + (3*i* − 5*i*) *pair real and imaginary*
3 − 2*i* *simplify*

Multiplication operates as follows (standard polynomial multiplication):

$$(x + jy)(v + jw) = (xv - yw) + j(xw + yv)$$

Worked example: Complex Number Multiplication

Let
a = 2 + 3*i*
b = 1 − 5*i*
Calculate
a × b
(2 + 3*i*) × (1 − 5*i*)   *sub in values*
(2 × 1) + (3*i* × 1) + (2 × −5*i*) + (3*i* × −5*i*)   *distribute like a polynomial*
(2) | (3*i*)   (10*i*)   (15*i*²)   *multiply individual terms*
2 + 3*i* −10*i* +15   *i² becomes −1*
(2 + 15) + (3*i* − 10*i*)   *pair real and imaginary*
17 − 7*i*   *simplify*

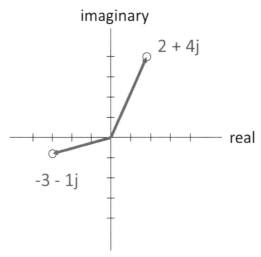

Fig. A3.7 Example points on a complex number plane. Imaginary numbers are along the vertical axis and real numbers are along the horizontal axis.

Division of complex numbers is not used in the text.

Complex numbers can be visualized on a plane where the y axis is imaginary, and the x axis is real (Fig. A3.7).

Vector Calculus

Derivatives with respect to time are common in graphics. Starting with a general equation that takes time as its parameter:

$$x = f(t)$$

The derivative is notated with

$$x' = \frac{dx}{dt}$$

This is defined as the change in x with respect to time.

Derivatives are not used directly but are discretized in graphics and physics engines. When this

$$\frac{dx}{dt}$$

is seen, d becomes delta, or Δ. Therefore, the above becomes

$$\frac{\Delta x}{\Delta t} = \frac{x_{i+1} - x_i}{t_{i+1} - t_i}$$

The above is one dimension. Given VR is usually in three dimensions, each dimension is calculated individually. For example, if p is a point, each dimension becomes its one element in a matrix:

$$\frac{dp}{dt} = \begin{bmatrix} \dfrac{dp_x}{dt} & \dfrac{dp_y}{dt} & \dfrac{dp_z}{dt} \end{bmatrix}$$

Worked problem: Position with Delta Time	
Generic	**Concrete**
$\dfrac{dp}{dt}$ Convert to vector notation $= \begin{bmatrix} \dfrac{dp_x}{dt} & \dfrac{dp_y}{dt} & \dfrac{dp_z}{dt} \end{bmatrix}$ Discretize it $= \begin{bmatrix} \dfrac{\Delta p_x}{\Delta t} & \dfrac{\Delta p_y}{\Delta t} & \dfrac{\Delta p_z}{\Delta t} \end{bmatrix}$ Substitute in the Δ formula $= \begin{bmatrix} \dfrac{p_{x_{i+1}} - p_{x_i}}{t_{i+1} - t_i} & \dfrac{p_{y_{i+1}} - p_{y_i}}{t_{i+1} - t_i} & \dfrac{p_{z_{i+1}} - p_{z_i}}{t_{i+1} - t_i} \end{bmatrix}$	Assume $t_i = 0.1$ $t_{i+1} = 0.2$ $p = (1, 2, 3)$ $p_{i+1} = (1, 4, 4)$ Then to do the derivative $\dfrac{dp}{dt}$ Convert to vector notation $= \begin{bmatrix} \dfrac{dp_x}{dt} & \dfrac{dp_y}{dt} & \dfrac{dp_z}{dt} \end{bmatrix}$ Discretize it $= \begin{bmatrix} \dfrac{\Delta p_x}{\Delta t} & \dfrac{\Delta p_y}{\Delta t} & \dfrac{\Delta p_z}{\Delta t} \end{bmatrix}$ Substitute values for the Δ formula $= \begin{bmatrix} \dfrac{1 - 1}{0.2 - 0.1} & \dfrac{4 - 2}{0.2 - 0.1} & \dfrac{4 - 3}{0.2 - 0.1} \end{bmatrix}$ $= [0 \quad 20 \quad 10]$

Linear Kinematic Equations for Trajectories

Where v is velocity, d is displacement, a is acceleration, and t is delta time.

$$v_f = v_i + at$$
$$d = v_i t + \frac{1}{2} a t^2$$
$$v_f^2 = v_i^2 + 2ad$$
$$d = \frac{1}{2}(v_f + v_i)t$$

Quaternions

Quaternions are a method to indicate a rotation around a specified axis using imaginary numbers. It is defined by

$$q = ix + jy + kz + w$$

where

$$i^2 = j^2 = k^2 = -1$$

$$i \neq j$$

$$i \neq k$$

$$j \neq k$$

$$ijk = -1$$

$$x^2 + y^2 + z^2 + w^2 = 1$$

Short-hand for a quaternion using a scalar and quaternion unit vector as an axis is

$$q = (q, \boldsymbol{q_v}) = q + iq_x + jq_y + kq_z$$

When used for rotations in graphics, the quaternion is normalized by $\sin(\theta/2)$ and the scalar normalized by $\cos(\theta/2)$. Therefore, the formula used in graphical contexts follows this form

$$q = (\theta, \boldsymbol{q_v}) = \sin(\theta/2)(iq_x + jq_y + kq_z) + \cos(\theta/2)$$

Worked problem: Creating a Quaternion

Make a quaternion that rotates 45° around the (1, 1, 1) axis

$\sin(45°/2)(i + j + k) + \cos(45°/2)$ *sub in values*

$0.383(i + j + k) + 0.924$ *calculate trig functions*

$i0.383 + j0.383 + k0.383 + 0.924$ *distribute*

This means a quaternion is defined in code as the amount of rotation (θ) around a specified axis ($\boldsymbol{q_v}$).

Properties of quaternions

- Multiplying quaternions adds the rotations.
- $\boldsymbol{q_1} * \boldsymbol{q_2}$ represents rotation $\boldsymbol{q_2}$ followed by rotation $\boldsymbol{q_1}$.

- q and $-q$ are the same rotation.
- Inverting the quaternion negates the vector components of the quaternion. If $q = (q, \, q_v)$, then $q^{-1} = (q, \, -q_v)$ or

$$q^{-1} = (ai + bj + ck + d)^{-1} = -ai - bj - ck + d$$

Multiplication of a quaternion

$$q_1 q_2 = (q_1, \, q_{1v})(q_2, \, q_{2v}) = (q_1 q_2 - q_{1v} \cdot q_{2v},$$
$$q_2 q_{1v} + q_1 q_{2v} + q_{1v} \times q_{2v})$$

Converting between quaternions and rotation matrices

Because projects may use both quaternions and rotation matrices, it is important to also outline the conversion between the different methods. In the interest of maintaining succinctness, the derivations of the conversions between quaternions and rotation matrices use vector calculus identities. For simplicity, all items are assumed to be normalized to length one.

For converting quaternions to rotation matrices, it is helpful to recall how both quaternions and rotation matrices affect vectors. For a vector, V, rotated to vector V', either a rotation matrix or a quaternion can achieve the same rotation,

$$V' = qVq^{-1}$$
$$V' = RV$$

where q and q^{-1} are the regular and inverse quaternion and R is the rotation matrix operating on the vector. Rotating with a quaternion means changing the alignment of the axis, which is the same as a change of basis in 3D space, so both the regular and inverse quaternions are used for the rotation. Since both formulas result in the same rotation, then

$$qVq^{-1} = RV$$

If the quaternion and vectors are represented in quaternion notation with scalar and vector parts, the rotation matrix can be found from the above relation. To demonstrate this, take the quaternion, $q = (q, \, q_v)$, where q_v is the vector with the imaginary axes and q is the real scalar component. The inverse is then $q^{-1} = (q, \, -q_v)$. Since the vector has no scalar component, the vector is represented in quaternion form as $V = (0, \, V_v)$, where V_v is the vector with imaginary axes and the 0 is used for the scalar component. The relation then becomes

$$(q, \boldsymbol{q_v})(0, \boldsymbol{V_v})(q, -\boldsymbol{q_v}) = R(0, \boldsymbol{V_v})$$

If the vector is a unit vector, then $VV^{-1} = (0, V_v)(0, -V_v) = 1$. This can be used to find the matrix formulation for the rotation:

$$RV = (q, \boldsymbol{q_v})(0, \boldsymbol{V_v})(q, -\boldsymbol{q_v})$$

$$RVV^{-1} = (q, \boldsymbol{q_v})(0, \boldsymbol{V_v})(q, -\boldsymbol{q_v})V^{-1}$$

$$R = (q, \boldsymbol{q_v})(0, \boldsymbol{V_v})(q, -\boldsymbol{q_v})(0, -V_v)$$

From here, the multiplication rule can be applied. In general, the resulting rotation matrix takes the form

$$R = \begin{vmatrix} 1 - 2\left(q_y^2 + q_z^2\right) & 2(q_x q_y - q_z q) & 2(q_x q_z + q_y q) \\ 2(q_x q_y + q_z q) & 1 - 2\left(q_x^2 + q_z^2\right) & 2(q_y q_z - q_x q) \\ 2(q_x q_z - q_y q) & 2(q_y q_z + q_x q) & 1 - 2\left(q_x^2 + q_y^2\right) \end{vmatrix}$$

Converting the rotation matrix to the quaternion takes two steps. Looking at the resulting rotation matrix above, different components of the diagonal can be used to find the magnitude of the quaternion components. For example, summing the diagonal or tracing the matrix gives

$$1 - 2\left(q_y^2 + q_z^2\right) + 1 - 2\left(q_x^2 + q_z^2\right) + 1 - 2\left(q_x^2 + q_y^2\right)$$
$$= 3 - 4\left(q_x^2 + q_y^2 + q_z^2\right)$$

This is very close to the unit quaternion squared and times 4. This means that taking the trace plus 1 and dividing by 4 gives

$$q^2 = \frac{1}{4}\left[1 + \left(3 - 4\left(q_x^2 + q_y^2 + q_z^2\right)\right)\right]$$

If unfamiliar with the term, trace here refers to taking the trace of a matrix, tr(R), which means summing the diagonal components.

Using a similar method, the other quaternion components can also be found. Setting the components of the rotation matrix to

$$R = \begin{bmatrix} 1 - 2\left(q_y^2 + q_z^2\right) & 2(q_x q_y - q_z q) & 2(q_x q_z + q_y q) \\ 2(q_x q_y + q_z q) & 1 - 2\left(q_x^2 + q_z^2\right) & 2(q_y q_z - q_x q) \\ 2(q_x q_z - q_y q) & 2(q_y q_z + q_x q) & 1 - 2\left(q_x^2 + q_y^2\right) \end{bmatrix}$$

$$= \begin{bmatrix} r_{11} & r_{12} & r_{13} \\ r_{21} & r_{22} & r_{23} \\ r_{31} & r_{32} & r_{33} \end{bmatrix},$$

then means that the magnitude of the quaternion components can be found with the following formulas:

$$q^2 = \frac{1}{4}(1 + r_{11} + r_{22} + r_{33})$$

$$q_x^2 = \frac{1}{4}(1 + r_{11} - r_{22} - r_{33})$$

$$q_y^2 = \frac{1}{4}(1 - r_{11} + r_{22} - r_{33})$$

$$q_z^2 = \frac{1}{4}(1 - r_{11} - r_{22} + r_{33})$$

The sign of the quaternion components is determined in the next step. First, set the largest component as positive. Remember that q and $-q$ are the same rotation, so setting the largest component as positive is arbitrary to avoid potentially dividing by small numbers. Looking at the rotation matrix again, the sign and magnitude can now be determined using the same method as the first step but on the nondiagonal matrix components. Let's say that q is the largest component and thus set as positive. The remaining components, including sign, can be found with

$$q_x = \frac{1}{4}\frac{(r_{32} - r_{23})}{q}$$

$$q_y = \frac{1}{4}\frac{(r_{13} - r_{31})}{q}$$

$$q_x = \frac{1}{4}\frac{(r_{21} - r_{31})}{q}$$

One more common quaternion conversion is aligning one vector onto another. In this case we have the initial vector, V_i, and the target vector, V_t. To solve this, the axis perpendicular to both vectors needs to be found, and then the initial vector needs to be rotated about that axis to the target vector by the angle between those vectors. Assuming these vectors are normalized, the angle between them can be found by

$$\theta = \cos^{-1}(V_i \cdot V_t)$$

The challenge here is the case where the vectors are parallel to each other, which will result in $\cos^{-1}(V_i \cdot V_t)$ being undefined. Therefore, there are three cases. When the vectors are flipped, $V_i \cdot V_t$ will be –1. When the vectors are aligned, $V_i \cdot V_t$ will be 1. All other cases of $V_i \cdot V_t$ will be between –1 and 1. These cases can be handled separately. In the normal case, the axis can be calculated with a cross product of the initial and target vector and then given to the quaternion:

$$q_v = V_i \times V_t$$

$$q = (\theta, q_v)$$

In the flipped case, any vector perpendicular to the line formed by the V_i and V_t will be sufficient as it is a 180-degree rotation. Typically, this is done using the "up" vector, but if the target is "up" then the "right" vector is used:

$$q_v = V_i \times V_{up}, \quad \text{if } \hat{V}_i \cdot \hat{V}_t \neq 1$$

$$q_v = V_i \times V_{right}, \quad \text{otherwise}$$

The last case is no rotation since the vectors are already aligned.

Linear Algebra

Matrix math uses left-handed notation in the book as both Unity and Unreal use left-handed notation. However, most math textbooks use right-handed notation (Fig. A3.8). The hand is determine by setting the index finger to Y, the thumb to X, and using which hand will make the middle finger the postive Z.

A vector in left-hand notation is

$$\begin{bmatrix} x & y & z \end{bmatrix}$$

A vector in right-hand notation is

$$\begin{bmatrix} x \\ y \\ z \end{bmatrix}$$

To convert from left-hand to conventional right-hand notation, transpose the matrices:

$$M = AB \quad \text{left hand}$$

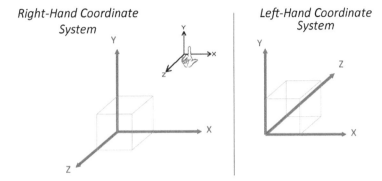

Fig. A3.8 Example right-hand and left-hand coordinate systems.

$$M^T = B^T A^T \quad \text{right hand}$$

That's a lot of terms that might not be mentioned in a typical math textbook. Let's outline some of these.

In conventional 3D math, the axes are oriented to align with the fingers and shape of the right hand, hence the term, right-hand notation. This usually orients one axis going in towards the observer rather than out. Having one axis pointing out away from the observer, however, is more useful in graphics. Doing so results in the axes being oriented to the fingers and shape of the left hand. This gives the left-hand notation or coordinate system (see Fig. A3.8).

Most of the matrix operations work the same way in either notation. The challenge is to convert the matrices from one hand to the other and reversing the order of operations.

Let's look at how to change the handedness (this is a real term) by finding the transpose.

A **transposed matrix** is noted with a superscript T such as M^T. Transposing flips j and i in $M_{i,j}$. Examples:

$$\begin{bmatrix} a & b & c \\ d & e & f \\ g & h & i \end{bmatrix}^T = \begin{bmatrix} a & d & g \\ b & e & h \\ c & g & i \end{bmatrix}$$

$$\begin{bmatrix} x & y & z \end{bmatrix}^T = \begin{bmatrix} x \\ y \\ z \end{bmatrix}$$

Worked problem: Left-hand to right-hand notation	
Generic	**Concrete**

$$[x' \quad y' \quad z'] = [x \quad y \quad z]\begin{bmatrix} a & b & c \\ d & e & f \\ g & h & i \end{bmatrix}$$

$$[x' \quad y' \quad z'] = [1 \quad 2 \quad 3]\begin{bmatrix} 4 & 1 & 0 \\ 2 & 5 & 2 \\ 0 & 0 & 1 \end{bmatrix} = [8 \quad 11 \quad 7]$$

$$[x' \quad y' \quad z']^T = \begin{bmatrix} a & b & c \\ d & e & f \\ g & h & i \end{bmatrix}^T [x \quad y \quad z]^T$$

$$[x' \quad y' \quad z']^T = \begin{bmatrix} 4 & 1 & 0 \\ 2 & 5 & 2 \\ 0 & 0 & 1 \end{bmatrix}^T [1 \quad 2 \quad 3]^T$$

$$\begin{bmatrix} x' \\ y' \\ z' \end{bmatrix} = \begin{bmatrix} a & d & g \\ b & e & h \\ c & g & i \end{bmatrix}\begin{bmatrix} x \\ y \\ z \end{bmatrix}$$

$$\begin{bmatrix} x' \\ y' \\ z' \end{bmatrix} = \begin{bmatrix} 4 & 2 & 0 \\ 1 & 5 & 0 \\ 0 & 2 & 1 \end{bmatrix}\begin{bmatrix} 1 \\ 2 \\ 3 \end{bmatrix} = \begin{bmatrix} 8 \\ 11 \\ 7 \end{bmatrix}$$

If transposing a formula, the order of the matrices is reversed, and each individual matrix is transposed:

$$(AB)^T = B^T A^T$$

This gives the basics for converting between notations. If the axes are further swapped around, as different systems assume different axis orientations, such as Unity setting the y axis as up and Unreal setting the z axis as up, column and row swapping may also be needed for a full coordinate system conversion.

Let's go through some other matrix operations and topics in left-handed notation. Many of these topics are identical to right-hand notation.

An **identity matrix** is noted as I. It is a square matrix with 1 where j = i and 0 otherwise. This is an example $M_{3\times3}$ identity matrix:

$$I = \begin{bmatrix} 1 & 0 & 0 \\ 0 & 1 & 0 \\ 0 & 0 & 1 \end{bmatrix}$$

An **inverse matrix** is a matrix when multiplied by the original will yield an identity matrix. In a graphics context, this is to reverse an affine transformation. Here's an example

$$M = \begin{bmatrix} 2 & 0 & 0 \\ 0 & 3 & 0 \\ 0 & 0 & 1 \end{bmatrix}$$

$$M^{-1} = \begin{bmatrix} \dfrac{1}{2} & 0 & 0 \\ 0 & \dfrac{1}{3} & 0 \\ 0 & 0 & 1 \end{bmatrix}$$

$$MM^{-1} = \begin{bmatrix} 2 & 0 & 0 \\ 0 & 3 & 0 \\ 0 & 0 & 1 \end{bmatrix} \begin{bmatrix} \frac{1}{2} & 0 & 0 \\ 0 & \frac{1}{3} & 0 \\ 0 & 0 & 1 \end{bmatrix} = \begin{bmatrix} 1 & 0 & 0 \\ 0 & 1 & 0 \\ 0 & 0 & 1 \end{bmatrix} = I$$

Adding and Subtracting matrices is $M_{i,j} = A_{i,j} + B_{i,j}$ for each element.

Worked problem: Adding Matrices	
Generic	**Concrete**
$\begin{bmatrix} a & b & c \\ d & e & f \\ g & h & i \end{bmatrix} \pm \begin{bmatrix} a' & b' & c' \\ d' & e' & f' \\ g' & h' & i' \end{bmatrix}$	$\begin{bmatrix} 1 & 2 & 3 \\ 0 & 1 & 0 \\ 3 & 4 & 2 \end{bmatrix} + \begin{bmatrix} 0 & 1 & 2 \\ 4 & 1 & 5 \\ 2 & 0 & 6 \end{bmatrix}$
$= \begin{bmatrix} a \pm a' & b \pm b' & c \pm c' \\ d \pm d' & e \pm e' & f \pm f' \\ g \pm g' & h \pm h' & i \pm i' \end{bmatrix}$	$= \begin{bmatrix} 1 & 3 & 5 \\ 4 & 2 & 5 \\ 5 & 4 & 8 \end{bmatrix}$

Multiplying matrices, including vectors in matrix notation, is $M_{i,j} = \sum_{n=0}^{i=row} A_{i,n} B_{n,j}$ for each element.

Worked problem: Multiplying Matrices	
Generic	**Concrete**
$\begin{bmatrix} a & b & c \\ d & e & f \end{bmatrix} \begin{bmatrix} a' & b' \\ c' & d' \\ e' & f' \end{bmatrix}$	$\begin{bmatrix} 1 & 2 & 3 \\ 4 & 5 & 6 \end{bmatrix} \begin{bmatrix} 7 & 8 \\ 9 & 10 \\ 11 & 12 \end{bmatrix}$
$= \begin{bmatrix} aa' + bc' + ce' & ab' + bd' + cf' \\ da' + ec' + fe' & db' + ed' + ff' \end{bmatrix}$	$= \begin{bmatrix} 1 \times 7 + 2 \times 9 + 3 \times 11 & 1 \times 8 + 2 \times 10 + 3 \times 12 \\ 4 \times 7 + 5 \times 9 + 6 \times 11 & 4 \times 8 + 5 \times 10 + 6 \times 12 \end{bmatrix}$
	$= \begin{bmatrix} 7 + 18 + 33 & 8 + 20 + 36 \\ 28 + 45 + 66 & 32 + 50 + 72 \end{bmatrix}$
	$= \begin{bmatrix} 58 & 64 \\ 139 & 154 \end{bmatrix}$

Subject Index

Note: Page numbers followed by *f* indicate figures.

Associated Tutorial Index

Chapter(s)	Associated Tutorial(s)*
Preface	(Installation)
0	0 (OOP)
1	1A and 1B (VR Objects)
2	2 (Scene Trees)
3	3 (Basic Physics)
4	4 (Interaction Framework)
5	5A and 5B (Interactions)
6	6A, 6B, 6 Supplemental (HUDs, Menus, and Scenes)
7, 9, 10	7, 9, 10 and Supplemental (Creating and Navigating Large Spaces)
8, 11, 12	8, 11, 12 (Lights and Sounds)
13	13 (Particle Systems)
16	16 (Joints)
17	17 (IK)

*Online only